Determinants of Pro-Poor Growth

Determinants of Pro-Poor Growth

Analytical Issues and Findings from Country Cases

Edited by

Michael Grimm

Stephan Klasen

and

Andrew McKay

First published 2007 by
PALGRAVE MACMILLAN
Houndmills, Basingstoke, Hampshire RG21 6XS and
175 Fifth Avenue, New York, N.Y. 10010
Companies and representatives throughout the world

PALGRAVE MACMILLAN is the global academic imprint of the Palgrave Macmillan division of St. Martin's Press, LLC and of Palgrave Macmillan Ltd. Macmillan® is a registered trademark in the United States, United Kingdom and other countries. Palgrave is a registered trademark in the European Union and other countries.

ISBN-13: 978–1–4039–8762–4
ISBN-10: 1–4039–8762–9

This book is printed on paper suitable for recycling and made from fully managed and sustained forest sources.

A catalogue record for this book is available from the British Library.

Library of Congress Cataloging-in-Publication Data
Determinants of pro-poor growth:analytical issues and findings from country cases/edited by Michael Grimm, Stephan Klasen and Andrew McKay.
    p. cm.
Includes bibliographical references and index.
ISBN-13: 978–1–4039–8762–4
ISBN-10: 1–4039–8762–9
1. Economic development—Case studies. 2. Poverty—Case studies.
3. Poor—Case studies. I. Grimm, Michael. II. Klasen, Stephan.
III. McKay, Andrew D., 1964–
HD82.D3834 2007
339.4′6—dc22   2006049330

10 9 8 7 6 5 4 3 2 1
16 15 14 13 12 11 10 09 08 07

Printed and bound in Great Britain by
Antony Rowe Ltd, Chippenham and Eastbourne

Contents

v

List of Figures

List of Tables

ix

Preface

While the importance of poverty reduction as the key objective of development policy is now widely accepted, there remain substantial challenges in trying to achieve this. This is evident in the difficulty the world faces in trying to meet the Millennium Development Goals. Some countries have achieved impressive progress in poverty reduction, but the majority have had much less success. Many factors are responsible for this, but it is increasingly accepted that economic growth is one important means of achieving sustained poverty reduction, as long as the poor are also able to participate in this growth – in other words, growth is pro-poor.

There is much less agreement and understanding among governments, development agencies and researchers about how pro-poor growth can be achieved. Faced with this concern, a consortium of donors launched a major international study, *Operationalizing Pro-Poor Growth*, seeking to specifically address this question. A key component of this was a series of country studies, applying a common set of analytic tools to try to understand the factors underlying the pattern of growth in each.

This book is focused around these country studies and the analytic tools they used. It looks both at these methods and at the specific conclusions from the country case studies about the factors that were important for pro-poor growth (or its absence). Many of the messages are country-specific, but there are also some important common themes. The studies in the book also help identify some important unresolved questions about how pro-poor growth can be achieved in practice.

MICHAEL GRIMM
STEPHAN KLASEN
ANDREW MCKAY

Acknowledgements

This book builds on country case studies conducted as part of the Operationalizing Pro-Poor Growth project, a programme of work conducted in 2003–05 and supported by a consortium of donors comprising the Agence française de Développement (AfD), the Bundesministerium für wirtschaftliche Zusammenarbeit und Entwicklung (BMZ) and its executing agencies (Deutsche Gesellschaft für Technische Zusammenarbeit (GTZ) GmbH and KfW Development Bank), the UK Department for International Development (DFID) and the World Bank. We are first and foremost very grateful to these supporting agencies and their staff with whom we have worked, for having the vision to launch this programme of work and for their willingness to see its findings disseminated through this book. In particular, we would like to thank Louise Cord and Ignacio Fiestas from the World Bank, Adrian Wood, Christian Rogg, Manu Manthri and Mandy Chatha from DFID, Christian Flamant, Jacky Amprou, Jean-Marc Chataigner and François Paquement from AfD, Ulrike Männer, Helmut Asche, Hartmut Janus and Julius Spatz from GTZ, Annette Langhammer from KfW, Birgit Pickel and Daniel Alker from the German Ministry of Economic Cooperation and Development. At the same time though, the sponsoring agencies are in no way responsible for the contents of the chapters, and any opinions expressed are those of the authors alone.

We wish to thank all the authors for contributing their papers to this volume, as well as for their efforts in revising, on a timely basis, their original country reports to the length of a book chapter. We are also grateful for their quick responsiveness to comments and suggestions on their draft chapters from us as editors. All authors gratefully acknowledge the very helpful and insightful comments from participants and discussants at various project workshops in Frankfurt, London, Washington and Tunis where this work was presented and discussed, as well as the invaluable comments we received from presentations of the work in the particular case-study countries.

We would like to thank Katie Button, Matthew Clacher, Alec Dubber and Amanda Hamilton of Palgrave Macmillan and Keith Povey of Keith Povey Editorial Services for all their help, flexibility and support throughout the process of producing this volume; Elke Büsing for her support in producing the index; and Yvonne Treichel for all her very hard work in editing the individual chapters. Finally, and importantly, we would like to thank our families for their patience and forbearance for the extra hours that editing this book inevitably involved.

MICHAEL GRIMM
STEPHAN KLASEN
ANDREW MCKAY

Notes on the Contributors

Ernest Aryeetey is a Professor of Economics at the University of Ghana and Director of the Institute of Statistical, Social and Economic Research (ISSER) in Ghana. His research work focuses on the economics of development with an interest in institutions and their role in development, regional integration, economic reforms, financial systems in support of development and small enterprise development. He is also a Resource Person of the African Economic Research Consortium, Nairobi, and a Managing Editor of the *Journal of African Economies*.

Jean-Paul Azam is a Professor of Economics at the University of Toulouse and at the Institut Universitaire de France. He is also Director of ARQADE (Research in Quantitative Applied Development Economics) and a member of IDEI. His research interest is concerned with African economies and in the economics of conflicts. Recent relevant publications have appeared in *Defence and Peace Economics*, *Economics and Politics*, the *Journal of African Economies*, the *Journal of Conflict Resolution*, the *Journal of Development Economics*, the *Journal of Peace Research*, *Public Choice*, and others.

Thomas Bonschab is project manager at the German Technical Cooperation (GTZ) within the scope of the project Economic Reform and Building up of Market Economy (WIRAM) and also researcher at the University of Frankfurt. His main research interest is pro-poor growth, poverty reduction, inequality and sustainable economic development with a regional focus on East Asia.

Michael Grimm is Professor of Development Economics at the University of Göttingen. He is also associated with the research institutes DIAL in Paris and DIW in Berlin. He works on problems related to income distribution and poverty in developing countries. Methodologically, his research is concerned with the development of instruments for the evaluation of distributional effects of macroeconomic shocks and policy reforms. He has consulted and managed various research projects commissioned by international and national organizations such as the World Bank, UNDP and the German Development Agencies.

Melanie Grosse is research and teaching associate in the Department of Economics at the University of Göttingen, Germany. She holds a Masters from the University of Göttingen and a Certificate of the Advanced Studies Program in International Economic Policy Research of the Kiel Institute for

World Economics, Germany. Her research focuses on poverty, inequality, and development in Latin American countries.

Isabel Günther is a research and teaching associate in the Department of Economics, University of Göttingen, Germany. She also works for the GTZ, the World Bank and the AfDB on a temporary basis. Her major research interests are dynamic poverty and inequality measurement, pro-poor growth analysis and international development cooperation with a regional focus on Sub-Saharan Africa.

Stephan Klasen is Professor of Economics at the University of Göttingen. He holds a PhD from Harvard University, and has since held positions at the World Bank, the University of Cambridge, UK, and the University of Munich. His research focuses on issues of poverty and inequality in developing countries. He has consulted for the World Bank, OECD, German Development Cooperation and DFID on issues of poverty, gender inequality and pro-poor growth.

Rainer Klump is Professor of Economics at the Johann Wolfgang Goethe-University Frankfurt, Germany. After studying economics at the Universities of Mainz, Paris I and Erlangen-Nuremberg, he first held academic positions at the Universities of Erlangen-Nuremberg, Würzburg and Ulm. His main areas of research are economic growth and development, economic policy and history of economic thought. He has published in the *American Economic Review*, the *Review of Economics and Statistics* and the *Scandinavian Journal of Economics*. Since 1996 he has investigated the effects of economic reforms in Vietnam in a series of research projects which included a country study for GTZ.

Jann Lay is Research Associate at the Kiel Institute for the World Economy and is currently completing a PhD in economics at the University of Göttingen, Germany. He has worked as a consultant to different development agencies. His research interests include pro-poor growth, poverty impact analysis (for example the possible poverty impact of the Doha round in Brazil and the poverty impact of coffee price fluctuations in Uganda), and the resource curse (for example work on transmission channels of different types of resources in the Sub-Saharan context).

Andrew McKay is Professor of Economics at the University of Sussex. He holds a PhD from the University of Cambridge and has previously held positions at the Universities of Bath and Nottingham, and also worked until recently as a part-time Research Fellow at the Overseas Development Institute (ODI), London. His research is focused on issues of poverty (including chronic poverty) and inequality in developing countries especially sub-Saharah Africa, and on how these are affected by policy factors such as growth and trade.

Wojciech Paczyński has been an economist at CASE – Center for Social and Economic Research – since 2000. His research interests include applied macroeconomics, economics of education, international relations and game theory. He has published on monetary policy, currency crises, EU integration and EU relations with neighbouring countries. He co-authored the OECD *Economic Survey of Poland 2006* and worked as a consultant for the World Bank. He holds an MA in economics from the University of Sussex and Warsaw University and an MSc in mathematics from Warsaw University.

Artur Radziwiłł is Vice-President of CASE – Center for Social and Economic Research. He has managed numerous research and analytical projects including evaluations of Armenia, Azerbaijan, Romania, Kazakhstan and the Ukraine. As a consultant to the World Bank, the United Nations Development Programme, the ILO, GTZ and the Global Development Network, he has contributed to dozens of additional research studies and policy advisory missions. His fields of expertise span European monetary integration, transition and development processes, public finance, and labour market dynamics.

Agnieszka Sowa is a Researcher at CASE, holds an MA in the field of public policy from Warsaw University, Department of Sociology, and an MSc in the field of social protection financing from Maastricht University, Department of Economics. Her experience includes involvement in the reform of the healthcare system in Poland, analysis of the intergenerational poverty dynamics in Poland, research on social assistance in Poland and Latvia and analysis of the impact of ageing on healthcare systems.

Julius Spatz is Economic Advisor and Head of the Pro-Poor Growth Team at German Technical Cooperation (GTZ). Prior to joining GTZ in 2005, he was Research Fellow at the Kiel Institute for World Economics and Visiting Fellow at the Instituto de Investigaciones Socio-Económicas (La Paz, Bolivia). He has published extensively on foreign direct investment as well as on growth and poverty diagnostics. He holds a PhD in economics from the University of Kiel.

Rainer Thiele is Head of the research area Poverty Reduction, Equity and Development at the Kiel Institute for the World Economy. His current research deals with the interactions between growth, inequality and poverty in developing countries, with a particular emphasis on rural income-generation and resource-based development. Methodologically, he focuses on the development and application of computable general equilibrium (CGE) models.

James Thurlow is a post-doctoral Research Fellow at the International Food Policy Research Institute in Washington, DC. His work focuses on understanding the role of rural/urban and macro/micro linkages in the development process, and more specifically on identifying strategies for growth and poverty reduction in Sub-Saharan Africa.

C. Peter Timmer is Senior Fellow at the Center for Global Development in Washington, DC. Before that he was a faculty member at Stanford, Cornell, Harvard and the University of California, San Diego. His research interests have focused on the role of agriculture in economic development, food security and food price stabilization, and the nature of pro-poor growth.

Irena Topińska holds a PhD in economics from the University of Warsaw (1980) and has been Associate Professor at the Department of Economics of the University of Warsaw since 1981. Her major fields of interest include social policy (poverty alleviation, social assistance, distributional effects of social policy measures), statistics (household budget surveys, income inequality and poverty measurement) and microeconomics (family economics, intergenerational and inter-vivos transfers). Her professional experience involves work on social assistance in various countries in many international advisory projects (sponsored by UNDP and World Bank, inter alia).

Mateusz Walewski graduated from the Department of Economics at the University of Sussex (1997) and Warsaw University (MA in 1998). He has been working as a researcher at the CASE Foundation since 1997. His research and publications primarily deal with labour markets, and he is also an author of numerous publications and unpublished reports on poverty, inflation, restructuring of the economy and taxation policy. He is responsible for labour market issues in the team working on the *Polish Economic Outlook Quarterly* (PEO). He has worked also as an adviser or a researcher in Georgia, Kosovo, Armenia and Belarus.

Manfred Wiebelt is a Research Fellow at the Kiel Institute for the World Economy, Germany, having previously worked at the University of Heidelberg, with special interests in development economics. His research activity focuses on pro-poor growth, resource-based development, stabilization and structural adjustment as well as on developing and applying computable general equilibrium (CGE) models, mainly for use in distributional and poverty analysis.

Peter Wobst is a Scientific Officer at the Sustainability in Agriculture, Food and Health Unit of the Institute for Prospective Technological Studies in Seville, Spain, which is part of the DG Joint Research Center of the European Commission. At the time of this study he was a Research Fellow at the Development Strategy and Governance Division of the International Food Policy Research Institute in Washington, DC. His main research interests include agriculture, rural development and international trade related to African and European economies.

1
Findings and Challenges in the Measurement and Analysis of Pro-Poor Growth

Michael Grimm and Stephan Klasen

Introduction

Recent years have seen a renewed emphasis on poverty reduction as the central goal of development policy and development cooperation. This is partly a consequence of the generally disappointing performance of structural adjustment programmes of the 1980s and 1990s in delivering high growth with associated rapid poverty reduction, particularly in Sub-Saharan Africa, Latin America and parts of Asia. As a result of this, the move towards debt reduction for highly indebted developing countries under the Highly Indebted Poor Country (HIPC) initiatives was explicitly linked to poverty reduction via the required production and implementation of Poverty Reduction Strategy Papers by recipient countries. In line with this change, the most important international development agencies, including the World Bank and most bilateral donors have increased their emphasis on poverty reduction in both their analytical as well as their policy and operational work (e.g. World Bank, 2000). Lastly, the Millennium Development Goals, agreed by world leaders in 2000, have put poverty reduction at the centre of the development agenda. The first goal is directly concerned with halving absolute income poverty, but also many of the other goals are essentially about poverty reduction in a wider sense.[1]

While sustained high growth is sure to lead to significant absolute income poverty reduction (e.g. World Bank, 2000; Dollar and Kraay, 2002), only a few countries (particularly in East, Southeast and more recently South Asia) have enjoyed such sustained high growth. In many others, growth has been slow, highly volatile, or even negative for sustained periods of time leading to little progress in poverty reduction. And even in many of the high-growth countries, high growth has been associated with rising inequality so that the poverty impact of growth has been slower than it could have

1

been. As a consequence, the impact of inequality on poverty reduction has received renewed attention given that poverty reduction will be slower in countries with rising inequality as well as in countries with high initial inequality. Conversely, reducing inequality would directly reduce poverty, increase the poverty impact of growth, and might even increase growth itself (and thus further accelerate poverty reduction, see World Bank, 2000, 2005a, Klasen, 2004).

To accelerate poverty reduction, it is thus crucial to devise strategies of 'pro-poor growth', that is growth that leads to particularly high increases in incomes of the poor. While there is a substantial amount of debate about what exactly constitutes 'pro-poor growth' (particularly its relation to inequality change) and how it can be measured (e.g. Ravallion and Chen, 2003; Kakwani and Pernia, 2000; Klasen, 2004, 2005a), it is clear from a policy point of view that the operational aim of 'pro-poor growth' must be to accelerate income growth among the poor. This can be achieved by high overall growth with the poor benefiting greatly from such growth, or by growth that is accompanied by declining inequality thus leading to disproportionate income growth among the poor.[2]

How to generate such pro-poor growth is therefore the critical challenge for policy-makers concerned with sustainable poverty reduction in developing countries. Previous work has tried to address this issue either using cross-country econometrics (e.g. Kraay, 2006; Dollar and Kraay, 2002; White and Anderson, 2000) or by household survey data to determine trends and determinants of poverty. While both approaches are useful and have generated many insights, the former approach suffers from insufficient attention to country heterogeneity in the growth-inequality–poverty relationship and was empirically not able to generate robust determinants of pro-poor growth that are valid across the developing world. The latter approach often was largely descriptive, was not directly connected to analyses of economic growth, and was typically not able to clearly link specific policies to identifiable inequality and poverty outcomes.

The Operationalizing Pro-Poor Growth research programme (OPPG)

Given the urgency of the issue and the problems with existing methods, a partnership of donors comprising the French, German and British development agencies and the World Bank, decided in 2003 to undertake a work programme entitled 'Operationalizing Pro-Poor Growth'. Parts of this work programme were concerned with measurement issues and extensions of the cross-country work. But the main focus soon turned to analysing country cases to better understand how initial conditions, institutions and policies interacted in generating (or failing to generate) pro-poor growth in the 1990s. Fourteen countries were chosen for study and an international team of researchers was assembled to study the determinants of pro-poor growth using common methods, approaches and common terms of reference. For operational purposes, all studies were asked to use the Ravallion–Chen (2003) framework for measuring pro-poor growth which uses the growth incidence curve and derived pro-poor growth measures as the key measurement tool. The growth incidence curve plots the income growth of percentiles of the income distribution (sorted in ascending order of incomes) between two time periods, and the resulting rate of pro-poor growth averages the income growth rates of all percentiles of the income distribution up to the poverty line in the first period (see Chapter 2 for further details).[3]

The countries were chosen to achieve broad regional coverage, countries with high and low growth performance and countries where there was household survey data available for at least two points in time covering most of the 1990s.

The studies aimed to explore the channels for the poor to participate in growth, including considering how the country context and initial conditions affect the efficiency of growth in reducing poverty. The studies looked at four broad policy areas and how each affected the ability of the poor to participate in growth: the macro framework and the composition of growth, agriculture and non-farm income, labour markets and employment, and public expenditure policies. The role of institutions, gender issues and initial conditions were meant to be examined as cross-cutting issues throughout.

Table 1.1 shows basic data on incomes, growth, poverty and inequality for the 14 case-study countries. As shown in the table, the sample includes some of the world's poorest countries as well as some middle-income countries, countries that achieved high growth and countries that contracted during the 1990s, and countries with both high inequality and relatively low inequality. As far as poverty is concerned, some countries achieved rapid poverty reduction in the 1990s (e.g. El Salvador, India, Vietnam), in some poverty fell quite slowly (e.g. Bolivia, Brazil, Burkina Faso) and in three it actually increased (Indonesia, Romania, and Zambia).[4]

Apart from the individual country case studies[5] and a range of academic papers that have emanated from this process (e.g. Grimm and Günther, 2006a, 2006b; Lopez, 2004; Klasen, 2005, 2006a), a synthesis study was produced in 2005 by the World Bank (World Bank, 2005b) trying to distil some of the critical findings from this work programme. A shorter version of that synthesis alongside shorter versions of eight of the country case studies were published in Besley and Cord (2006). In its analytical section the synthesis first emphasized that in the 14 country cases there appears to have been a trade-off between growth and equity in the 1990s. Most of the rapidly growing countries experienced rising inequality; but most of those were still able to achieve faster poverty reduction than the countries with low or negative growth where inequality did not change or improved.[6] Much of this rising inequality was driven by the performance of the non-agricultural sector which was also the main driver of growth. Conversely,

4

Table 1.1 Basic poverty, growth and inequality trends in the 14 country cases

	Survey year 1	Survey year 2	Initial GDP per capita (1995 $PPP)	Annual GDP growth rate	Initial poverty rate	Annual change in poverty rate	Initial gini coefficient	Annual change in gini
Bangladesh[+]	1992	2000	1128	3.09%	58.1	−2.8%	0.34	1.5%
Bolivia*	1989	2002	1949	1.17%	76.9	−1.0%	0.56	−0.1%
Brazil[+]	1993	2001	5999	1.47%	55.7	−2.3%	0.36	−0.2%
Burkina Faso*	1994	2003	838	2.25%	55.5	−1.8%	0.47	−0.5%
El Salvador	1991	2000	3392	2.54%	64.4	−5.4%	0.51	0.3%
Ghana*[+]	1992	1999	1559	1.63%	51.7	−3.9%	0.37	0.6%
India[+]	1994	2000	1736	4.18%	36.0	−3.8%	0.28	0.6%
Indonesia*[+]	1996	2002	2934	−0.81%	6.7	0.7%	0.40	0.9%
Romania*	1996	2002	5860	0.20%	20.1	6.1%	0.31	−1.2%
Senegal*	1994	2001	1198	2.47%	67.8	−2.5%	0.33	0.7%
Tunisia[+]	1990	2000	4181	3.03%	49.7	−3.8%	0.28	0.2%
Uganda[+]	1992	2002	830	3.34%	55.7	−3.9%	0.36	1.8%
Vietnam*[+]	1993	2002	1271	5.70%	58.1	−7.8%	0.34	0.9%
Zambia*	1991	1998	885	−2.26%	68.9	1.3%	0.59	−2.7%

Note: The poverty lines used here are national poverty lines. The countries marked with an * are included in this book. The countries marked with a + are included in Besley and Cord (2006).

Sources: Assembled from country case studies, Besley and Cord (2006) and *World Development Indicators* (2004).

agriculture, the sector where the poor predominate in most countries, was generally not able to generate high growth, thus leaving the poor behind. As far as policy recommendations are concerned, the synthesis emphasized the centrality of sustained growth to achieve significant poverty reduction as well as the need to explicitly design policies that link the poor to this growth process. Of particular importance for most countries are policies, for the reasons given above, which increase agricultural productivity and improve the ability of the poor to get access to non-agricultural employment opportunities. However, the range of policies needed will differ greatly between countries and depend on many factors including fertility and population density, initial asset and income inequality, the importance of agriculture, and the specific institutional environment. Country-specific research should focus on identifying the critical constraint that prevents the poor being able to participate in growth.

While these are interesting findings and recommendations, some of the particularly important messages emerging from the wealth of information and analysis contained in the country case studies were only insufficiently reflected in this work. Among them are the role of inequality in generating and preventing growth and poverty reduction (see also World Bank, 2005a, UNDP, 2005), the role of pro-active policies to either affect inequality or to improve the ability of the poor to participate in growth, the crucial role of transmission mechanisms (e.g. prices) between growth and the incomes of the poor, and the role of political economy and institutional issues. But equally importantly, the OPPG work programme was, in our view, particularly successful in designing and applying innovative analytical tools and methods in analysing pro-poor growth. Many of the case studies used innovative ways to study pro-poor growth in the 1990s using *ex post* analytical tools (such as growth incidence, decomposition, or regression analyses) as well as *ex ante* simulation and modelling methods to assess the potential for pro-poor growth policies. Thus the analytical and methodological tool box for assessing and modelling pro-poor growth might in fact be one of the most important and relevant outcomes from an analytical and policy point of view and hence merits to be presented in more detail.

Aims and scope of the book

The recognition of the importance of analytical tools and methods to analyse pro-poor growth led to this book, where we decided to compile insights, from selected country case studies focusing on the analytical and methodological issues that emanated from this work programme, and which we hope will provide new insights and guidance to analysts and policy-makers interested in studying the determinants of pro-poor growth.

The aim of this book is therefore to highlight key analytical and methodological issues and findings that have a critical bearing on an assessment of pro-poor growth from an *ex post* or an *ex ante* perspective. The book begins with a methodological chapter which presents and evaluates the many methods and analytical tools that were used in the work programme, and then includes eight country case studies. Apart from providing an assessment of the determinants of pro-poor growth in that country, a central aim is to focus on the critical analytical and methodological issues and findings that were particularly relevant in each country. These analytical issues cover a wide range of areas including the role of initial conditions and the political economy environment, measurement issues regarding poverty trends and determinants, the importance of inequality (including spatial disparities), the key role of price policies in affecting pro poor growth, and modelling approaches used for *ex ante* and *ex post* assessments of pro-poor growth.

Overview of the book

After a presentation on methods and analytical tools for pro-poor growth research, the book is divided into three sections where we sort the country cases by the analytical issues that were of particular importance. The first section deals with cases where regional inequality was of central importance for the determinants of pro-poor growth and includes the Ghana and Vietnam case studies. The second sections focuses on cases where price shocks, policy reforms (often generating such price shocks), and political economy issues are the central analytical issues studied. This section includes the case studies Senegal, Burkina Faso and Indonesia. The last section includes cases where the modelling and simulations of pro-poor growth policies, both from an *ex post* as well as an *ex ante* perspective, are critical ingredients of the analysis, and includes case studies of Bolivia, Zambia and Romania. Apart from these analytical foci, all case studies used as far as possible a similar set of core analytic techniques to assess the distributional pattern of growth and the links to poverty reduction. In Chapter 2, Andrew McKay provides an introduction to these core methods. We will discuss these chapters now in some more detail.

Methods for analysing the distributional pattern of growth

McKay begins with different types of basic disaggregation of growth such as by sector or region. Afterwards he provides a detailed presentation of standard measures of pro-poor growth such as the growth incidence curve, the rate of pro-poor growth and the growth elasticity of poverty. He also discusses some decompositions which can be used to describe the sources of poverty changes over time. Lastly, he presents techniques and modelling approaches able to link specific shocks and policy reforms to poverty. Each method is illustrated using examples, predominantly from the case studies included in this volume. The chapter seeks to provide an intuitive explanation as to why these tools can be useful in practice, highlight their limitations, and provide basic technical detail and follow-up references. The subsequent case studies take this introduction to these core methods for granted and then focus only on the results and on those techniques which are novel and unique to each study.

Pro-poor growth and regional inequality

The case study on Ghana by Ernest Aryeetey and Andrew McKay in Chapter 3 starts from the finding that despite quite good growth performance and falling income poverty and improvements in many other dimensions of well-being during the 1990s, spatial disparities, in particular between the north and the south, increased. Whereas some locations experienced reasonable growth and poverty reduction, significant areas of the country showed hardly any improvements. The analysis of the driving forces behind this (highly politically sensitive) phenomenon is the focus of this chapter. To investigate this issue the authors provide various pro-poor growth measures and poverty decompositions disaggregated by location and sectors of activity. They found that the highly spatially differentiated pattern of growth is first of all the result of an uneven sectoral growth, a pattern influenced by key policy choices (trade policy actions) and patterns of public spending. But they also emphasize that the slow growth and poverty reduction in the lagging, generally poorer, regions reflect several other factors, including infrastructure bottlenecks, import competition and limited scope for non-agricultural activities. The authors conclude that in order to realize the full growth potential the country has, improved key infrastructure, notably road connections, will be required, as well as investment in effective irrigation schemes. Moreover, they argue that a second important pillar of regionally balanced growth and poverty reduction will be the creation of secure employment opportunities outside of agriculture.

These kinds of factors are indeed identified as the main drivers of the remarkable poverty reduction experienced by Vietnam discussed in Chapter 4. However, they did not prevent spatial inequality from rising in this country too. Thomas Bonschab and Rainer Klump show that in Vietnam the average annual rate of per capita growth of 5.7 per cent led to an annual reduction of the poverty headcount by 7.8 per cent between 1993 and 2002. With this performance Vietnam outpaced not only the other countries examined in this volume, but almost all countries of the developing world as well. The authors highlight that this success was first of all related to an adequate mix of economic, sectoral and regional policies. They cluster these policies into three broad blocks: policies related to the quality and quantity of jobs created, policies related to the institutional and macro policies, and policies related to public expenditures. Regarding job creation, Bonschab and Klump identify as particularly important drivers trade liberalization, the world market price of coffee, structural transformation, land reform and institutional reforms which facilitated the movement of employment from the informal to the formal sector. To analyse the spatial structure of growth, poverty and inequality the authors use various decomposition techniques and perform an original regional convergence analysis. They find that income growth and poverty reduction occurred in both urban and rural areas, as the latter became increasingly linked to the growth dynamics of urban centres. Despite the outstanding growth performance inequality between the North and the South, between urban and rural areas and between some particular growth poles and the rest of the country was also rising. Bonschab and Klump warn that these widening gaps could, in the long run, generate political obstacles to further growth and poverty reduction.

Rising regional inequality is thus a defining feature of both these countries and has also been found to be a critical driver of inequality increase in other developing countries, notably China and Brazil. The two case studies highlight the inability of policy-makers to combat successfully this phenomenon. Hence, this remains as a major challenge for further policy research to define the scope and potential for successful policies to dampen regional disparities which threaten to undermine further progress in pro-poor growth. Some of the recommendations made by the authors regarding possible policy options therefore merit closer investigation in future work.

Price shocks, policy reforms and political economy

The following three case studies focus on the impact of climate-induced and policy-induced price shocks, policy reforms and political economy dynamics on pro-poor growth. The first two issues are analysed for the West African countries Senegal and Burkina Faso in Chapters 5 and 6, respectively. The third is analysed in Indonesia in Chapter 7. While all three are very complementary regarding their findings, the methodological approaches used are very different. Whereas Jean-Paul Azam uses mainly data on wages, prices and sectoral growth to link growth and poverty in Senegal, Michael Grimm and Isabel Günther rely on the analysis of three household surveys covering in total a period of ten years. Finally, Peter Timmer uses a historical political economy approach.

Azam concentrates his case study on Senegal on the sustained growth episode from 1994 to 2002 that followed the devaluation of the CFA Franc (Franc de la Communauté Financière d'Afrique) franc in 1994. This period was marked by a significant reduction in poverty. Azam shows that poverty reduction was possible thanks to severe cuts in real wages in the public and in the formal private sector. The former freed, he argues, scarce fiscal resources that the government used for boosting public investment. The latter led to an increase in profits that boosted investment in the private sector. These two effects combined to boost growth, particularly in the non-agricultural sector, combined with a significant fall in the share of agriculture in GDP. Hence, according to Azam, poverty was reduced not by redistribution from the rich to the poor, but from wages to profits, which boosted growth. Therefore Senegal constitutes a nice example of how a devaluation and structural adjustment can be turned into pro-poor growth. However, as Azam points out, the government was not rewarded for the fall in poverty induced by its investment policy, and it was ousted in elections in 2000.

The case study on Burkina Faso by Grimm and Günther is very complementary to the study on Senegal. Like Senegal, Burkina Faso also experienced the devaluation in 1994. The observation period is almost identical to that considered by Azam. However, an important difference is that in the case of Burkina Faso detailed household survey data for urban and rural areas is available not only for the beginning and the end of the period but also for a year in between allowing the authors to separate the short and medium-term effects of the devaluation. Two other important differences are that Burkina Faso undertook a policy of price liberalization alongside the devaluation and experienced severe droughts during the observation period, both of which constituted further price and earnings shocks. As shown by the authors, this led to quite a contrasting relationship between growth and poverty reduction. Over the whole period 1994 to 2003 growth led, as in Senegal, to poverty reduction and was thus pro-poor. However, in the mid-1990s rising food prices following the first drought and declining real earnings for workers in the urban formal private and public sector following the devaluation prevented growth from being translated into poverty reduction. Given the high cereal share in consumption among the poor, they were particularly hurt by rising food prices. As this differential shift in prices hurting poor people is not well-reflected in the standard pro-poor growth analysis and poverty decompositions, the paper focuses methodologically on how such shifts in relative prices can adequately be accounted for in the measurement of pro-poor growth. The authors show that despite falling over the whole observation period, the poverty impact of growth remained largely below its potential. One explanation put forward by the authors is that the price liberalization and price shocks were not accompanied by attempts to boost technical progress (particularly in agriculture), safety nets and improvements in the functioning of markets. Hence, these price changes did little to increase the household income of subsistence farmers. Unlike in Senegal, the freed resources resulting from the fall in the real value of the government wage bill were not productively invested in favour of the poor. Similar to the Ghana case, Grimm and Günther see investment in rural infrastructure to increase agricultural productivity, to integrate markets and to enhance non-farm activities in rural areas as one of the most important pillars to achieve poverty reduction in the time frame set by the Millennium Development Goals.

The case study on Indonesia by Timmer uses a historical political economy approach to studying pro-poor growth. While he also comments on developments in the 1990s, his chapter takes a much longer historical view, which he finds critical for understanding the determinants of pro-poor growth. In a first step he uses long-term time series on macro-economic growth and estimated calorie intake to establish the long-term relationship between growth and poverty. In a second step he explains the relationship period by period by referring to the long-run processes of structural transformation and how politics and policies influenced those processes. Timmer states that the Indonesian experience with 'pro-poor growth' has been highly varied since the late nineteenth century. Poverty was especially reduced during the Suharto regime. This was, according to Timmer, the result of a major shift in priorities towards rural development and a push towards increasing domestic rice production. Behind this push was the stabilization objective as well as the equity objective: To lose control of the rice economy was to lose control of what mattered to Indonesian society, according to his argument. Despite the remarkable involvement of the poor in the growth process, Timmer ends his chapter by concluding that the actual level of growth is not high enough to reduce the structural unemployment and heavy reliance on jobs in the informal sector that make the poor so vulnerable. Hence, according to Timmer, to raise the quality of employment and reduce the vulnerability of the poor to economic shocks is the next 'pro-poor' task for the government.

These chapters demonstrate the critical importance of price policies for pro-poor growth outcomes. In a favourable political economy environment, such price policies combined with policies to alleviate structural bottlenecks in rural areas can make a large contribution towards higher rates of pro-poor growth (this is also relevant to the above discussion about tackling spatial inequality). But the chapters also demonstrate the pitfalls and limitations of such price reforms in situations where the poor are unable to benefit from these reforms or are indeed adversely affected by them, at least in the short run. Moreover, the chapters show that dedication of the political leadership to pro-poor growth is more effective than simple reliance on a democratic constituency for pro-poor policies. Lastly, the chapters show that mechanical application of the pro-poor growth toolbox is unable to adequately take account of these price issues or to place them in the required historical context. Here adaptations to this toolbox as well as innovative new methods will yield better results for an understanding of the determinants of pro-poor growth.

Modelling and simulating pro-poor growth policies

In the third and last part of book we present case studies which make use of quantitative tools to compare various policy options *ex ante* and *ex post*. Two studies, Bolivia and Zambia, use a dynamic recursive Computable General

Equilibrium Model (CGEM) to compute the policy induced changes in macro-aggregates such as prices, wages and employment. The third study uses a simpler static macro-economic consistency framework. However, all three models are connected with household survey data to assess also the distributional impact of the policies under consideration. The principle is that the households in the household survey are classified in exactly the same groups that are defined in the macro model. The incomes of each group in the household survey are then simply expanded using the group specific growth rates in wages and profits calculated in the macro-model.[7] Such an approach provides a more complete assessment of the distributional impact than a simple CGEM, which usually uses only a few representative households and ignores how incomes are distributed within those groups. This type of model is also described in more detail in Chapter 2.

Besides the *ex ante* and *ex post* simulation of policies, the Bolivian case study written by Stephan Klasen, Melanie Grosse, Jann Lay, Julius Spatz, Rainer Thiele and Manfred Wiebelt focuses on an additional interesting methodological issue. Due to lack of household income surveys in rural areas in Bolivia, the authors describe and apply methods of cross-survey simulation, which combine urban-based income surveys with nationally representative demographic and health surveys to construct a consistent time series on poverty, inequality and pro-poor growth in rural and urban Bolivia. The backward looking part of the analysis shows that growth in the 1990s has been pro-poor overall, but anti-poor in capital cities due to the recent economic crisis, showing some similarities with the short-term impact of structural adjustment in the West African case studies of Senegal and Burkina Faso included in this volume. Hence, overall poverty reduction was only weak, due to only moderate economic growth and to the high initial income inequality. In particular, rural poverty was only little affected, as a result of large initial rural-urban inequality and the highly dualistic nature of Bolivia's economy where most growth has been generated by developments benefiting the urban economy. Using the dynamic CGEM, they also show that the growth-slowdown and poverty increase in the late 1990s were related to a series of external shocks that hit this small open economy which is highly exposed to trade shocks and highly dependent on capital inflows. In the forward looking part, the results of the simulations then show that the traditional policy-levers available to the government, such as structural reforms and the promotion of resource-based exports, will do little to promote pro-poor growth, in particular in rural areas, and that more attention needs to be placed on policy packages that address the high levels of inequality existing in Bolivia.

The case study on Zambia by James Thurlow and Peter Wobst aims to contribute in particular to the debate whether agriculture should be favoured relative to industry when pro-poor growth is the declared objective. Hence, the authors analyse the ability of the food and export crop sectors to generate pro-poor growth. Similar trade-offs arose in the case studies on Burkina Faso, Ghana and Indonesia. The Zambian case is, however, particularly interesting, first because it has more potential for agricultural growth than many other countries, although that potential is not evenly distributed within the country and has been periodically undermined by fluctuations in weather patterns and world commodity prices. Secondly, Zambia has substantial mineral resources, which offer also a potential for growth outside agriculture. Thirdly, Zambia has low agricultural productivity but a large rural population and agricultural sector, although the sector is smaller than the Sub-Saharan African average. Fourthly, Zambia has a liberalized trading regime but is landlocked within central Southern Africa. Fifth, it is among the Sub-Saharan African countries with particularly high inequality (see Table 1.1). Finally, like many Sub-Saharan African countries, Zambia is politically stable but suffers from corruption and generally poor governance. Zambia's initial conditions are therefore not biased in favour of either agriculture or industry, and reflect many of the opportunities and constraints facing many other African countries. When looking at the past the authors find that Zambia underwent significant changes in the structure of economic growth, with agriculture and industry playing important roles at different stages. The resulting shifts in the income distribution have had important implications for the effectiveness of growth in reducing poverty. Similar to the Bolivian case study, the authors then use a general equilibrium model combined with household survey data to assess how accelerating growth in alternative sectors could influence the rate of poverty reduction in the future. The authors show that industrial growth in Zambia is not strongly pro-poor, implying that recent growth may not generate broad-based poverty reduction. Rather, it is agricultural growth, especially in staple crops, that would contribute most effectively to poverty reduction.

The last study looks at the experience and prospects of pro-poor growth in Romania, which is the only transition country, and also the only European country within the sample selected for the OPPG project. The first interesting issue in that study written by Wojciech Paczyński, Artur Radziwiłł, Agnieszka Sowa, Irena Topińska and Mateusz Walewski is that it covers a period of recession (1996–99) followed by a period of economic expansion (1999–2002), which has continued to the present day. Hence the authors ask the important question of whether recession and recovery in Romania had a symmetric impact on poverty. They find that the poor suffered less than proportionately during recession but also benefited less than proportionately from economic recovery. In the second part of their study the authors look, as in the two previous studies, to the future. However, they do not use a CGEM but rather a macro-economic accounting framework developed at the World Bank. But similar to the Bolivian and Zambian models, the macro model they use is linked to household survey data in a simple top-down fashion such that the distributional impact of policies can be assessed. Their simulations reveal that the creation of productive jobs for the unskilled, the emergence of non-agricultural sectors in rural areas, and improvements in the education system are essential elements of any poverty reduction strategy.

The three studies demonstrate the potential and limitations of advanced modelling techniques combining macro and micro approaches. In particular, the macro modelling parts can identify the key drivers of growth, and the link to household surveys can be used to assess the distributional impact of policies at a significant amount of detail. This can, in principle, be used to assess the impact of pro-poor growth policies *ex post* but is probably most useful to study policy options *ex ante*. At the same time, one should always be aware of the rather mechanistic nature of the exercise. In particular, model parameters might change endogenously as a result of a changed policy environment. Moreover, in these models there is no feedback from the micro level to the macro level, an omission which might distort results. In an ideal case household behaviour and changes in macro-aggregates should be modelled and simulated simultaneously so as to achieve full consistency on both levels.[8] Substantively, the three chapters demonstrate the critical importance of agricultural and non-farm rural growth for overall pro-poor growth outcomes. Despite the fact that agriculture is likely to constitute a falling share in GDP, promoting agricultural productivity and non-farm rural growth remains central for pro-poor growth.

Analytical and substantive lessons

What are some of the lessons from taking this analytical approach to the study of pro-poor growth? A range of messages appear particularly relevant. We will first discuss some analytical and methodological issues and then some policy messages.

Turning to analytical issues, five messages appear particularly pertinent. First, while the toolbox of pro-poor growth measurement proposed by Ravallion and Chen is a powerful way to study the distributional impact of growth, the chapters in this book also reveal many shortcomings that become apparent only in their implementation. For example, the growth-incidence curves and the associated pro-poor growth measures make very high demands on the available micro data. Often data quality at the two ends of the income distribution is very poor and both the growth incidence curves as well as the pro-poor growth measures can be distorted as a result. They are also distorted when the surveys come from different time periods in the year or use different methods. Particular problems arise when household income surveys (rather than expenditure/consumption surveys) are used where the problem of zero or negative incomes among some of the poor, as well as irregular incomes, pose particular problems. This is also one among many reasons why the comparability of growth incidence curves and associated pro-poor growth measures across countries is still a major challenge.[9] Due to the problem of differential price movements between poor and non-poor groups, the link between growth incidence curves and poverty reduction cannot easily be made and poverty decompositions are similarly misleading if this is not allowed for. Lastly, this approach is treating percentiles of the distribution as anonymous entities disregarding whether different households find themselves in different percentiles at two points in time, thus disregarding the question of mobility of the poor over time, an issue which is critical in understanding households' links to the growth process.[10] Thus much analytical and empirical work lies ahead to determine the scope and limits of this set of interesting new tools, including the trade-offs between detail and robustness.

Second, focusing on the most relevant way to divide the analysis in sub-periods or in geographic or other entities remains a critical issue. As shown in the chapters below, the consideration of sub-periods leads to very different insights than considering the entire analysis period. Moreover, the choice of sub-periods is largely driven by available data rather than divisions that would make sense from an analytical or policy point of view. Extreme care is needed in drawing conclusions about long-term trends from comparisons of surveys at only two or three points in time. Similarly, the chapters below show that in many countries it is critical to take a sub-national perspective, as changes in regional inequality have often been a major driver of overall poverty and inequality change. But even here, it is not always clear what sub-national disaggregation is most suitable and to what extent one should explicitly consider the spatial dimension of poverty and inequality change (e.g. by explicitly considering neighbourhood effects using spatial econometric techniques in addition to simply using regional dummy variables or undertaking regional disaggregations).

Third, several of the chapters in this volume demonstrate nicely the scope and new insights brought about by explicitly linking macro and micro data and tools to analyse pro-poor growth. In this way it is finally possible to meaningfully link aggregate policy analysis tools (such as CGE modelling) with household survey information on income and expenditures and thus study the impact of policy on poverty at the household level. For analysts and policy-makers, this is critical and can help to finally overcome the disconnect between the largely descriptive poverty profiles using micro data and policy analyses using aggregate data and tools.

Fourth, the chapters in this volume demonstrate that methodological pluralism can have great advantages. Sometimes a historical narrative focusing on political economy considerations can bring as many insights as some quantitative assessment tool. In other cases, it is quite critical to test one's intuition with formal modelling approaches before jumping to conclusions.

Fifth, much of the work could have been further enriched if poverty had not been uniquely defined in the income dimension. In fact, the linkages between income and non-income dimensions of poverty are particularly important and thus further work should try to extend these tools and methods to broader conceptions of poverty that also explicitly allow an analysis of the linkages between income and non-income dimensions of poverty.[11]

Regarding the more substantive policy implications the case studies included in this volume show the following. First, in poor countries where still a large part of the poor population lives in rural areas, pro-poor growth strategies must include agriculture. This is for instance convincingly shown for the cases of Burkina Faso, Ghana and Zambia. The studies also show that while a focus on agricultural export crops can help, sustainable poverty reduction must include the food crop sector. Growth in agriculture has the advantage of reaching directly the incomes of the poor. The agricultural sector also has strong local spillover effects; in contrast, spillover effects from the secondary and tertiary sector through forward and backward linkages with the agricultural sector are usually very weak and hence growth in these sectors is not particularly pro-poor (see also Delgado *et al.* 1998). To foster agricultural growth the findings of the case studies suggest the need to invest in infrastructure and education to better link poor farmers to markets, to increase productivity through fertilizers, irrigation systems and agricultural research and to reduce the risk of farmers through better storage facilities, higher product diversification, processing of agricultural products and investment in non-farm activities. Finally access to the capital market through micro credit programmes seems very important. The case studies on Indonesia and Vietnam can serve as examples in this respect.

Second, almost all studies show that the state has to play an active role in the fight against poverty. Many policies which were strongly discouraged in the 1980s and 1990s, such as explicit redistributive policies, price regulation for the goods the poor households produce and consume, regional integration and, as mentioned just above, agricultural policies, should be reconsidered. Obviously such interventions bear always the risk of creating their own distortions, but clearly progress in pro-poor growth, particularly in rural and backward regions will critically depend on successful state intervention to improve the asset and income-earning potential of the poor, and reduce the vulnerability they face.

Third, the country's political economy plays an important role in turning growth into pro-poor growth. In countries where the government showed a clear commitment to reduce poverty as for instance in Indonesia or Senegal, resources for investment were used much more efficiently for the alleviation of poverty than in countries where growth in general was the primordial objective as in Burkina Faso or Bolivia. As the case studies of Indonesia and Senegal demonstrate, as well as political events in Bolivia over the past years, reliance on the ballot box alone will not generate pro-poor policies even if the poor are in the majority; in contrast, dedication of the political leadership to growth with equity will generally lead to more successful and more stable pro-poor policies.

Fourth, regional inequalities have been shown to be an obstacle to pro-poor growth in many countries covered by the OPPG project. In particular the studies on Bolivia, Burkina Faso, Ghana and Vietnam illustrated how such inequalities slow down poverty reduction. Regions which have geographical disadvantages, low endowments in terms of infrastructure and human capital and are far away from growth poles, prevent not only the population living in these regions from participating in growth, but also prevent a country's full potential being realized, so leading to slower growth. But these disadvantages are often partly endogenous in that they can sometimes be reduced by policy interventions such as effective infrastructure provision – if the political will exists. Here, there is a need for innovative policy solutions that can combine regionally-targeted investment and infrastructure policies, support for migration, fiscal equalization and special safety nets for poorer areas, among other interventions.

Lastly and fifth, some of the findings of these case studies as well as Besley and Cord (2006), might be read as suggesting that the rise in inequality in growing economies is an inevitable outcome of that growth, particularly since such dynamic growth tends to favour specific sectors and regions. While it is empirically true that such a positive relationship between growth and inequality increase existed for the case study countries as a whole, the inevitability of this link is open to question for several reasons. First, this positive link is unique to the 1990s and did not exist in prior periods, so that a critical question is what caused the change in the past decade. Second, as also discussed by Besley and Cord (2006), the link is much weaker in a larger sample of countries than the ones included here (see also Ravallion, 2005). Third, the example of Indonesia in this book (and a number of other East Asian countries including Taiwan, South Korea and Malaysia) demonstrate the ability to achieve high growth with equity over long periods of time, given the political will. Finally, as the discussion in many of the case studies presented here show, there is quite a lot more scope for policy reforms to tackle this rising inequality. Before such reforms have been tried and tested, it is far too early to pronounce the end of the ability to combine high growth with stable or falling inequality.[12]

Some issues for further research

We want to end with a few words on the need for further research in this area. As we hope to have shown, there is now a broad set of analytical and methodological tools for pro-poor growth research which each provide important new insights and findings. It is now time for a consolidation of this toolbox to determine which ones lead to particularly robust results and are particularly useful from an analytical and policy point of view. Secondly, future work should be directed towards improving the comparability of findings across countries where even seemingly small differences in data, methods and analytical approaches can yield significantly different outcomes. Third, extending and linking the pro-poor growth toolbox to non-income dimensions of poverty should be pursued as a matter of priority. Substantively, it appears that the five key items on the pro-poor growth research agenda should be the potential and limits to improve productivity and incomes in agriculture, the gender dimension of pro-poor growth (see Klasen, 2006b), the role of institutions and political economy on pro-poor growth outcomes, how to successfully stem rising regional inequality, and how to use pro-active policies to ensure that high growth does not lead to rising inequality.

Notes

1. This book is focusing entirely on the income dimension of poverty when analysing pro-poor growth. As shown by Klasen (2005) and Grosse, Harttgen and Klasen (2005, 2006), one can also extend the discussion of pro-poor growth to non-income dimensions of well-being such as education or health poverty. See also Chapter 2 in this volume.
2. Static redistributions could also lead to declining inequality and thus have a one-off effect on income growth of the poor.
3. The advantage of this approach is that it can be used to assess whether growth had been pro-poor in an absolute sense (i.e. income growth of the poor was greater than zero) as well as in a relative sense (whether growth was accompanied by declining inequality, leading to higher growth rates among the poor than the non-poor). See Klasen (2005) and Chapter 2 for further details.
4. Indonesia is a special case as the poverty increase is entirely due to the impact of the Asian financial crisis which hit Indonesia in 1998 and 1999. Before and afterwards, Indonesia achieved significant poverty reduction. See chapter by Timmer in this volume.
5. All country studies as well as seven thematic papers based on them are available on web-sites of the participating bilateral donors and the World Bank, as well as on http://www.oppg.de.
6. Whether this finding is generalizable beyond the 14 country cases is unclear. Ravallion (2005) finds that there is no poverty–inequality trade-off in the 1990s. See also Besley and Cord (2006) for a discussion.
7. Such a linkage does not take any behavior of households into account because the employment structure in the household survey is kept constant and thus such simulations can only represent the direct impact of policies.
8. Such an integrated model has recently been used to study poverty alleviation strategies in Madagascar (Cogneau and Robilliard, 2004) For a review of the various techniques available to link macro models with household survey data, see Cogneau, Grimm and Robilliard (2003).
9. As a result of these methodological differences, also the comparability of findings regarding poverty and inequality in Table 1.1 should be treated with some caution.
10. See Grimm (2006) for some alternative measures and analyses of pro-poor growth which incorporate mobility of the poor and thus remove the anonymity assumption.

11. See Klasen (2005) and Grosse, Harttgen and Klasen (2005, 2006) for first attempts in this direction.
12. See also Ravallion and Chen (2004) for further evidence against a growth–equity trade-off in China.

References

Besley, T. and Cord, L. (2006) *Delivering on the Promise of Pro-Poor Growth: Insights and Lessons from Country Experiences*. London: Palgrave Macmillan.
Cogneau, D. and Robilliard, A.-S. (2004) 'Poverty Alleviation Policies in Madagascar: A Micro–Macro Simulation Model', DIAL Working paper DT/11. Paris: DIAL.
Cogneau, D., Grimm, M. and Robilliard, A.-S. (2003) 'Evaluating Poverty Reduction Policies – The Contribution of Micro-Simulation Techniques', in J.-P. Cling, M. Razafindrakato and F. Roubaud (eds), *New International Poverty Reduction Strategies*. London: Routledge Books, pp. 340–70.
Delgado, C.L., Hopkins, J. and Kelly, V.A. with Hazell, P., McKenna, A.A., Gruhn, P., Hojjati, B., Sil, J. and Courbois, C. (1998) 'Agricultural Growth Linkages in Sub-Saharan Africa', Research Report 107. Washington, DC: International Food Policy Research Institute.
Dollar, D. and Kraay, A. (2002) 'Growth is Good for the Poor', *Journal of Economic Growth*, 7:195–225.
Grimm, M. (2006) 'Removing the Anonymity Axiom in Assessing Pro-Poor Growth', *Journal of Economic Inquality*, in press.
Grimm, M. and Günther, I. (2006a) 'Measuring Pro-Poor Growth when Relative Prices Shift', *Journal of Development Economics*, forthcoming.
Grimm, M. and Günther, I. (2006b) 'Growth and Poverty in Burkina Faso. A Reassessment of the Paradox', *Journal of African Economies*, forthcoming.
Grosse, M., Harttgen, K. and Klasen, S. (2005) 'Measuring Pro-Poor Growth with Non-Income Indicators', Ibero-America Institute Discussion Paper no. 132. Göttingen Ibero-America Institute of Economic Research.
Grosse, M., Harttgen, K. and Klasen, S. (2006) 'Measuring Pro-Poor Progress towards the Non-Income Millennium Development Goals', WIDER Discussion Paper 2006-38. Helsinki: WIDER.
Lopez, J.H. (2004) 'Pro-Poor Growth: A Review of What We Know (and of What We Don't)', mimeo, Washington, DC: World Bank.
Kakwani, N. and Pernia, E. (2000) 'What is Pro-Poor Growth?', *Asian Development Review*, 18: 1–16.
Klasen, S. (2004) 'In Search of the Holy Grail: How to Achieve Pro Poor Growth?', in B. Tungodden, N. Stern and I. Kolstad (eds), *Towards Pro Poor Policies. Aid, Institutions, and Globalization*. New York: Oxford University Press.
Klasen, S. (2005) 'Economic Growth and Poverty Reduction: Measurement and Policy Issues', OECD Development Centre Working Paper no. 246. Paris: OECD.
Klasen, S. (2006a) 'Macroeconomic Policy and Pro-Poor Growth in a Dualistic Economy: The Case of Bolivia', in G. Cornia (ed), *Macroeconomic Policy and Pro-Poor Growth*. London: Palgrave Macmillan.
Klasen, S. (2006b) 'Gender and Pro-Poor Growth', in L. Menkhoff (ed), *Pro Poor Growth. Policies and Evidence*, Schriftenreihe des Vereins für Socialpolitik. Berlin: Duncker & Humblot, in press.

Kraay, A. (2006) 'When is Growth Pro-Poor? Evidence from a Panel of Countries', mimeo, Word Bank, Washington, DC. *Journal of Development Economics*, 80(2): 198–227.

Ravallion, M. and Chen, S. (2003) 'Measuring Pro-Poor Growth', *Economics Letters*, 78: 93–9.

Ravallion, M. and Chen, S. (2004) 'China's (Uneven) Progress Against Poverty', Poverty Research Working Paper no. 3408. Washington, DC: World Bank.

Ravallion, M. (2005) 'A Poverty–Inequality Trade-Off?', *Journal of Economic Inequality*, 3/2: 169–81.

United Nations Development Programme (UNDP) (2005) *Human Development Report*. New York: Oxford University Press.

White, H. and Anderson, E. (2000) 'Growth versus Distribution: Does the Pattern of Growth Matter?', mimeo, Institute of Development Studies, Brighton.

World Bank (2000) *World Development Report*. New York: Oxford University Press.

World Bank (2005a) *World Development Report*. New York: Oxford University Press.

World Bank (2005b) *Pro Poor Growth in the 1990s*. Washington, DC: World Bank.

2
Introduction to Methods for Analysing the Distributional Pattern of Growth*

Andrew McKay

Introduction

As explained in Chapter 1, the country chapters in this volume are based on several of the case-study papers prepared for the multi-donor Operationalizing Pro-Poor Growth (OPPG) project in 2004–05. To maximize the value of the case-study approach and enable comparability between studies, the OPPG project was explicitly designed such that each country study addressed a common set of questions. Moreover, the country studies used as far as possible a similar set of core analytic techniques in assessing the distributional pattern of growth, and the links to poverty reduction. Inevitably not all methods were feasible or made sense in all cases, but the country studies still retained a strong common core, in particular focused on growth incidence curves and calculations of the rate of pro-poor growth (Ravallion and Chen, 2003).

This chapter provides an introduction to these core methods used in the project, illustrating them as far as possible based on the country case studies represented in this volume. It seeks to provide an intuitive explanation as to why these tools can be useful in practice, as well as providing basic technical detail and follow-up references. In reading this chapter it is important to remember that generic tools are only one part of this analysis; their application needs to be accompanied by a detailed understanding of the country context, and other country-specific analysis.

An understanding of the distributional pattern of growth calls for both macro and micro level analysis. More specifically, it requires a detailed

---

* This chapter is based on an earlier paper prepared as part of the Operationalizing Pro-Poor Growth Project. I am very grateful for detailed comments and suggestions on earlier drafts by Michael Grimm, as well as to others who have given valuable comments: Louise Cord, Ignacio Fiestas, Will Gargent, Stephan Klasen, Manu Manthri, Christian Rogg, and participants at the OPPG Synthesis Conference, Washington, DC, February 2005.

analysis and disaggregation of growth itself; a detailed analysis of the changes in poverty and inequality that accompany this; and an understanding of the factors that link these. This chapter addresses these three different issues in turn. Many of the analytic techniques used in the OPPG project and so discussed here focused on income (in practice often consumption) dimensions of poverty and inequality. But several of the methods can also be applied to non-income dimensions, and some examples of this are also provided in this chapter.

A key concept in this discussion is the meaning of the term 'pro-poor growth', a concept which has been interpreted in many different ways by different authors. It has also been the subject of considerable debate among both researchers and donor agencies. Broadly speaking, it is possible to consider both absolute and relative concepts of pro-poor growth (DFID, 2004). The relative concept of pro-poor growth is one that emphasizes the distributional pattern of growth: growth is pro-poor in relative terms if the incomes of the poor grow at a faster rate than those of the non-poor (such that inequality falls). An absolute concept is that growth is pro-poor if it reduces poverty; the key focus then is on the rate of growth for the poor (the rate of pro-poor growth – see below).

While different commentators and researchers may prefer one concept to another, in reality both are important for this debate. There are many reasons to be concerned with the distributional pattern of growth and the adverse effects of rising inequality on growth and poverty reduction, and the extent to which either high or rising inequality limits pro-poor growth is a key theme in this volume. But the rate of growth itself is also very important for poverty reduction, an issue which may not be sufficiently highlighted by the relative concept of poor-poor growth. In this volume, the case studies confirm that both growth and inequality are important.

The three subsequent sections of this chapter discuss in turn disaggregating growth; examining changes in poverty and inequality in relation to growth; and explaining the links between growth, inequality and poverty reduction, in each case drawing primarily on techniques used in the OPPG project. In these sections the techniques are illustrated drawing primarily on the country case studies included in this volume. The final section of the chapter offers some brief conclusions.

Disaggregating growth

Macro and micro concepts of growth

At the outset it is important to recognize that both macro and micro-based concepts of growth can be defined, and both are relevant in considering pro-poor growth. The standard approach of course is at the macro level, with growth viewed as a change in GDP or GDP per capita, measured as part of the national accounts and generally at the national level (though occasionally at a state level, as for example in India). GDP and its growth over time can generally be disaggregated by productive sector or type of expenditure (consumption versus investment) – but not by poverty or income groups, for example. To look at the distributional pattern of growth (e.g. by location, income group, personal or household characteristics and so on) generally calls for a micro-level concept. It is possible to define growth rates in income or consumption for groups of the population based on household survey data, where these growth rates refer to the specific periods between when (comparable) household surveys are conducted. In such calculations, consumption measures are often preferred for conceptual and practical reasons.

These two concepts of growth (and the income concepts on which they are based) are different from each other.[1] Often they are highly correlated, as for instance in Ghana where the household survey suggests an annual increase in consumption per adult of 3.1 per cent between 1991 and 1998, while the national accounts suggests a 2.9 per cent increase in per capita private consumption over essentially the same period (Aryeetey and McKay, 2004). But this is not necessarily the case. In Romania, where GDP per capita showed an average increase of 0.2 per cent per annum over the period 1996–2002, households surveys showed a 3.0 per cent per annum average decline over the same period (Gheorghiu *et al.*, 2004).

Another distinction between the macro and micro concepts of growth is the frequency with which the information on growth rates is available. GDP growth (or growth in total private consumption) is measured on an annual basis, whereas growth of household income can only be computed between the years when appropriate and comparable household surveys are available – typically two or three instances in time, with intervals of a few years in between (in Zambia twice over the 1990s with a seven-year gap in between). Therefore in looking at growth based on micro data, it is important to know whether these years are in any way 'atypical'. Certainly the growth rates can not be easily extrapolated.

In practice there may be other difficulties in the use of household surveys to analyse the distributional pattern of growth over a period of time. One significant problem – especially when surveys are conducted infrequently – is when survey methodology changes. In this case the consumption or income data may not be comparable over time – or only based on strong assumptions about the likely impact of the change in methodology.[2] In the case of Zambia, a new survey methodology was introduced in the 2002 survey, which meant that it was not possible to compare this with the earlier surveys in 1991 and 1998. A second problem is that household survey data may not be available, or may not cover the entire country. It may be possible to overcome this problem if other nationally representative surveys are available that collect information on household assets which can be used to estimate household income.[3] The Bolivia chapter in this volume provides an important example of this based on Demographic and Health Surveys, as well as an analysis of sensitivity to two different possible approaches. A third problem, specific to the use of household income data, is the presence of zero or negative reported incomes among the poor.

In understanding the distributional pattern of growth the focus is specifically on the relationship between macro-level economic growth and changes in individual household incomes or consumption levels.

Sectoral patterns of growth

In disaggregating growth, a first key question to consider is its sectoral pattern. This enables an initial understanding of the nature of growth (which sectors are driving growth or accounting for the decline?) and how it relates to the sectors in which the poor are predominantly employed.

For example, total and sectoral growth rates for Romania since 1993 are plotted in Figure 2.1 (Gheorghiu *et al.*, 2004). This shows a significant variation in overall growth performance over the period, with negative growth between 1997 and 1999. By sector, the largest variations in growth rates are apparent in agriculture. In general the performance of the industrial and services sectors is strongly associated with the overall pattern or growth, because agriculture accounts for a smaller share of GDP.

This is a highly aggregate level of analysis though may still give some initial clues about likely poverty trends, for example if, as in Romania and in many other countries, the poor are disproportionately working in the agriculture sector. Of course this needs to be complemented by a more detailed disaggregation at the subsectoral level, because for example the relative rates of growth of subsistence and cash crop agriculture is also likely to have

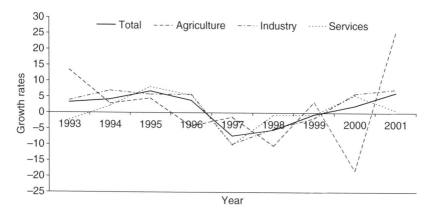

Figure 2.1 Growth rates in Romania by sector, 1993–2001
Source: Derived from Gheorghiu *et al.* (2004).

important implications for poverty. In the case of Ghana (Chapter 3), agricultural growth was much faster among export crops (notably cocoa) than among food crops. While significant numbers of the poor do cultivate cocoa, they are disproportionately engaged in food crop cultivation, especially so for the poorest of the poor. This pattern of agricultural growth gives an initial clue about likely poverty trends, including in this case its spatial pattern.

Growth accounting analysis

It is important to understand the nature and sources of economic growth (or its absence), including the factors that account for it. Growth accounting analysis can provide some initial insights on these questions. It is based on a production function where the level of GDP, or total production (Y_t in period t) in an economy depends on key inputs to that production, in particular physical capital (K_t), and labour/human capital (H_t):

$$Y_t = F(K_t, H_t)$$

Growth can come about through increased levels of these inputs, due to investment in physical capital or human capital formation; or from these inputs being used in a more efficient and more productive manner (including through new technology). Growth accounting analysis allows for an assessment of the relative importance of these different factors in accounting for growth or its absence. It identifies the proportion of growth over a period that is due to increased use of factor inputs, based on the assumption that the production function can be represented by Cobb–Douglas technology with constant returns to scale. Output growth not accounted for by a growth in inputs is attributed to changes in total factor productivity (TFP); this inevitably captures a number of features including changes in technology and institutional changes, as well as measurement problems and deviations from the (strong) assumptions of the underlying implicit model. The decomposition of growth can be represented as follows:

$$\frac{\Delta Y}{Y} = \sigma_K \frac{\Delta K}{K} + \sigma_H \frac{\Delta H}{H} + TFPG$$

where σ_K and σ_H are the shares of physical and human capital respectively in total income, and *TFPG* represented total factor productivity growth.

An example of the application of this method for Ghana, here on a per-worker basis, is presented in Table 2.1. In this example education contributes positively to growth in each period, but the change in TFP is the major factor accounting for the volatility of growth over this period. Poor investment performance also played an important role in accounting for the growth performance in the 1980s.

The value of growth accounting analysis is that it helps identify the extent to which changes in inputs account for the levels of growth and their

Table 2.1 Growth accounting-based decomposition of sources of growth in Ghana

Selected periods	Growth in real GDP per worker	Contribution of		
		Physical capital per worker	Education per worker	Residual (TFPG)
1980–84	−3.94	−0.93	0.66	−3.66
1985–89	2.32	−0.40	0.72	2.01
1990–97	1.27	0.75	0.41	0.11
Total: 1960–97	−0.12	0.52	0.50	−1.15

Source: Aryeetey and McKay (2004).

fluctuations over time. But two important issues in its application are the imprecision of the method, and the difficulty of interpreting the total factor productivity term. This TFPG term is a hybrid, a 'catch-all' for many different factors that could affect growth performance.

Spatial and other subnational growth analysis

It is also important to be aware of spatial patterns to growth in a country, given its relevance for poverty reduction as well as the potential political sensitivity of this issue. Ghana and Vietnam are two examples in this volume that show strong spatial differentiation in growth rates.

Most spatial growth analysis is based on household survey data (so the micro-concept of growth). It can provide valuable insights about differential experiences of growth over a specific period across regions. One straightforward disaggregation is between urban and rural areas as shown in the top panel of Table 2.2 below for the case of Burkina Faso. This shows a positive, though very slow, increase in expenditures in rural areas over this period, but a decline in urban areas.

But given the heterogeneity of urban and rural areas in all countries, it is important to look for much more detailed spatial disaggregation, and in Burkina Faso this reveals significant variations. Selecting predominantly cotton-growing regions (Table 2.2 again), the general pattern is of falling average per capita expenditure in most regions, but to differing extents, and with important exceptions, as in the case of *Cascades*. A comparison between the Center West and Center South shows different trends in adjacent regions. This raises the important question of what underlies these differences in trends. It may also have implications for regional patterns of change in poverty.

In addition to spatial disaggregation, growth data can be disaggregated in many other dimensions, including occupation category, education level, gender, ethnicity, landholding category, among others. In focusing on the

Table 2.2   Growth rates in selected localities of Burkina Faso

Region	Real household expenditure per capita (index, mean=100)		
	1994	*1998*	*2003*
Rural	75	78	81
Urban	227	217	186
Areas with more than 40% producing cotton			
Hautes Bassin	130	120	115
Mouhoun	86	85	68
South West	100	81	73
Cascades	92	113	115
Areas with more than 20% producing cotton			
Centre West	92	95	101
Centre South	75	73	63

Source: Grimm and Günther (2004).

distributional pattern of growth it is important to disaggregate growth to the extent permitted by available data, not just by productive sector as in the national accounts (following standard practice), but also between different groups of households, defined in different relevant dimensions such as location, occupation, and relevant household characteristics (such as gender, size and education level). The relevant disaggregations will vary from case to case, and depending on data availability. Based on such disaggregations, spatial convergence or divergence analyses can be performed as illustrated in Chapter 4 on Vietnam.

Poverty and inequality changes in relation to growth

The analysis of changes over time in poverty and inequality will be based on micro-level information, which will generally be required across the entire country, in other words drawing on a nationally representative sample of households. When looking at pro-poor growth, a significant emphasis is often placed on the income dimensions of poverty and inequality (as in the OPPG project). But income or consumption are not ultimate ends in themselves, and it is important equally to focus on social indicators such as education attainment, life expectancy or child nutritional status, each of which should be able to be enhanced by pro-poor growth. In other words, these indicators are also important measures of the extent to which growth is pro-poor.

Measures of income poverty and inequality are computed from household survey data using data on the total income, or more often consumption, of the household, adjusted for household size and composition and relevant price differences. The importance of adjusting for price differences with relevant price data, an issue often given insufficiently attention in analysis of income poverty and inequality, is strongly emphasized in the Burkina Faso chapter in this volume. To study income poverty requires comparison with a poverty line, reflecting a level of income needed to satisfy minimum consumption needs. To set national poverty lines (as used in the country studies in this volume), the cost of basic needs method is commonly used (Ravallion and Bidani, 1994). Many indicators of non-income poverty and inequality can also be derived from the same surveys (for example in relation to educational attainment), while others may need to be calculated from other surveys such as the Demographic and Health Surveys (DHS). This section discusses some key methods for analysing changes in poverty and inequality.

Profiling changes in poverty and inequality

Just as growth rates vary across different groups of a population, so do levels of poverty and inequality and their changes over time. From a poverty reduction perspective, it is important to build a disaggregated picture of poverty and inequality in a country, and its changes over time. Given the focus on pro-poor growth, the following discussion focuses on these changes over time.[4]

As with the subnational growth analysis, this disaggregation is enabled by household survey data. Estimates of poverty and inequality and their changes over time can be disaggregated across relevant population groups defined along many different dimensions, including location, occupational category, household demographic characteristics, ethnicity, education level and land ownership. For these purposes income poverty is typically calculated relative to a national poverty line, but it is also common practice to report extreme poverty (relative to a lower poverty line), as for example in the Romania chapter in this volume. As is well known poverty is commonly summarized using the P_α class of poverty indices (Foster, Greer and Thorbecke, 1984) defined as follows:

$$P_\alpha = \frac{1}{n} \sum_{i=1}^{q} \left(\frac{z - y_i}{z} \right)^\alpha$$

where n is the total number of individuals surveyed, q the number that are poor, z the poverty line, y_i the household income for individual i, and α a parameter reflecting the weight placed on the depth of poverty. The interpretation of the index depends on the value of α. The extent of poverty is commonly summarized as a headcount measure ($\alpha = 0$; the proportion of a given population that are poor), but is often also reported using the poverty gap index ($\alpha - 1$, taking account of the average shortfall below the poverty line) and a poverty severity index ($\alpha = 2$; placing still greater weight on the

Table 2.3 Selected disaggregations of changes in the poverty gap index in Bolivia between 1994 and 2002 (%)

Category	Moderate poverty		Extreme poverty	
	1994	2002	1994	2002
Proportion of household members aged between 15 and 65 years				
Less than or equal to 0.5	50.2	40.9	32.0	20.0
Greater than 0.5	31.3	23.5	16.6	9.8
Language spoken by household head				
Spanish	32.5	23.0	16.4	8.3
Indigenous	63.8	42.1	45.8	21.8

Source: Klasen *et al.* (2004).

poorest among the poor, and thus being sensitive to inequality among the poor). The depth of poverty is sometimes summarized as the average shortfall of the poor below the poverty line, which is also equal to the ratio P_1/P_0.

As an example of poverty disaggregation, Table 2.3 shows changes in the poverty gap index for both moderate and extreme poverty in Bolivia, disaggregated according to the age composition of the household and language spoken. In this case poverty and extreme poverty, measured by the poverty gap index, are somewhat higher among households with lower proportions of members in the key working age group, and in non-Spanish speaking households. All show reductions in the extent of poverty between 1994 and 2002, though in general the gap between these two groups does not narrow.

It is also possible to consider the statistical significance of differences or changes in poverty levels, where the calculation of the standard errors need to take account of the principles underlying the sample design (Howes and Lanjouw, 1998). In the case of Ghana (Chapter 3, Table 3.3) while poverty headcount measure fell in six out of seven locations, in only two of these was the reduction statistically significantly different from zero at the 5 per cent level.

Income inequality can be measured in different ways including decile or quintile shares, by means of the well-known Gini coefficient, by the generalized entropy class of indices (Sen, 1997), or by a range of other summary indices.[5] But it is also important to disaggregate income inequality. Inequality indices such as Gini coefficients can be computed for groups of the population, and their changes compared over time. Table 2.4 shows changes in Gini coefficients in Bolivia disaggregated between the departmental capital cities, towns and rural areas. Over this three-year period there was a quite large upward movement in the Gini coefficient. By disaggregating it is clear that this reflected a sharp increase in inequality in the capital cities because the Gini coefficients in the remaining locations changed very little.

Table 2.4 Gini coefficients for Bolivia disaggregated by location, 1999 and 2002

Location	1999	2002
Capital cities	0.480	0.540
Towns	0.455	0.452
Rural	0.423	0.421
National	0.525	0.551

Source: Klasen *et al.* (2004).

Table 2.5 Percentage share between group inequality in a decomposition of the mean log deviation for Romania, for different groups

Criterion for defining groups	1994	1998	2002
Place of residence (urban/rural)	8.7	8.4	12.0
Education level of household head	20.6	22.0	27.2
Labour market status of household head	8.7	10.6	15.8

Source: From Chapter 10 of this volume.

What this does not tell us though is how inequality between the capital cities and the remaining locations (an important contributor to overall inequality) changed over this period.

A decomposable inequality index (Sen, 1997) such as the generalized entropy class of indices (which include the Theil index and mean log deviation as special cases; Litchfield, 1999), enables an assessment of changes in inequality between as well as within groups. The decomposition distinguishes within group and between group inequality, the latter capturing differences in mean income values between groups. Table 2.5 below shows the proportion of the mean log deviation in Romania that is accounted for by differences between groups defined according to residence, education level and labour market status. The results show increasing inequality between groups according to each of these criteria over the years considered here.

The focus so far has been on disaggregating income concepts of changes in poverty and inequality but analogous techniques can also be applied to non-income indicators. Thus for instance Figure 2.2 shows change in primary school enrolment rates for girls in Ghana disaggregated by location. Here the fastest rate of growth is in the poorest savannah region, which contrasts with the pattern for income poverty, highlighting the value of looking at non-income dimensions. Non-income concepts of poverty and inequality and their changes can also be disaggregated by groups as part of producing a profile of poverty and distributional change.

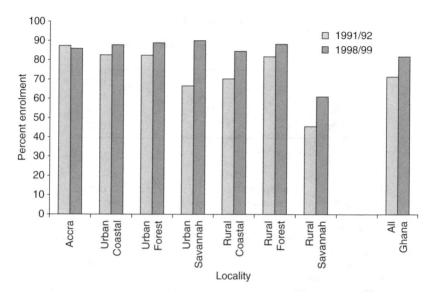

Figure 2.2   Changes in net enrolment rates of girls in primary school in Ghana
Source: Based on Coulombe and McKay (1995).

Summarizing contributions to poverty change: the Ravallion–Huppi decomposition

When changes in poverty are disaggregated by location or other groups, as discussed above, it is valuable to be able to summarize the contribution of each group to overall poverty change, as well as allowing for the poverty impacts of movements between groups (for example, migration between rural and urban areas). The decomposition developed by Ravallion and Huppi (1991) provides a straightforward means of doing this. If the population is divided into m mutually exclusive and exhaustive groups indexed by j ($j = 1, \ldots, m$), then the change in poverty between period 1, denoted by P^1 and that of an earlier period, denoted by P^0, can be decomposed as follows:

$$P^1 - P^0 = \sum_{j=1}^{m} \left(P_j^1 - P_j^0 \right) n_j^0 + \sum_{j=1}^{m} \left(n_j^1 - n_j^0 \right) P_j^0 + \sum_{j=1}^{m} \left(P_j^1 - P_j^0 \right) \left(n_j^1 - n_j^0 \right)$$

where n_j^t is the number of people in group j in time period t (t=0, 1) and P_j^t the value of the poverty index for group j in time period t. The first term on the right hand side of the decomposition is the poverty reduction due to the change in poverty within each group; the second term is the change in poverty due to the aggregate effect of population movements between groups; and the third term is an interaction between these two effects.

Table 2.6 Decomposing poverty reductions in Vietnam, 1993–2002, by urban–rural location (%)

Decomposition components	Contribution to poverty change, 1993–2002
Intra-area affects Urban	82.7
Intra-area affects Rural	14.2
Total intra-group effect	96.8
Total inter-area population shifts	4.3
Interaction effect	−1.1

Source: Chapter 4 of this volume.

This is illustrated in Table 2.6 for the case of Vietnam over the period 1993–2002, distinguishing between urban and rural areas (see also Chapter 4). Over this period, where national poverty fell substantially (from a headcount of 58.1% in 1993 to 28.9% in 2002), the vast majority reflected poverty reduction within the urban and rural areas, within both of which poverty fell substantially. Population movements from rural to urban areas made a positive contribution to the change in poverty, but the contribution of this was small. This dominance of the intra-group effects is also observed in a similar decomposition into five main locations in Ghana (which also experienced significant poverty reduction over the period); but when the decomposition is repeated for the poverty severity index the relative contribution of the migration term increases.

Datt–Ravallion decomposition

A central policy and analytic concern is to understand why poverty levels are increasing or decreasing over a period of time. As a starting point in answering this, a convenient decomposition is the Datt–Ravallion decomposition (Datt and Ravallion, 1992) which helps identify the relative contributions of two proximate determinants: growth (that is changes in the average levels of household incomes) and redistribution (changes in inequality that accompany growth). This initial decomposition will obviously need to be accompanied by a deeper understanding of the factors that account for these changes in average income and inequality.

The technique relies on the definitional relationship between average income (or consumption), inequality and absolute poverty. Where the poverty line remains fixed in real terms (as is reasonable over a few years),[6] then poverty will be lower when average income is higher (for a given level of inequality); and (in most cases) poverty will be higher when inequality is higher (for a given average income). The Datt–Ravallion decomposition uses this fact to decompose a change in absolute poverty into three terms:

1. a growth effect: the change in absolute poverty which would have occurred if the observed growth in the average income level had been the same for everyone;
2. a redistribution effect: the change in absolute poverty which would have happened if the observed change in inequality had occurred without the mean income changing; and
3. a residual term, representing the inexact nature of the above decomposition in practice.[7]

If the poverty index in periods $t+1$ and t is denoted by P_{t+1} and P_t respectively, and if the index is written as a function of the mean income, μ, and its distribution summarized by its Lorenz curve L, then if period t is taken as the reference period this decomposition can be written as follows:

$$P_{t+1} - P_t = \left[P\left(\mu_{t+1}, L_t\right) - P\left(\mu_t, L_t\right)\right] + \left[P\left(\mu_t, L_{t+1}\right) - P\left(\mu_t, L_t\right)\right] + R$$

where R is the residual. The first term in square brackets on the right-hand side is the growth effect: the impact on the poverty index of the change in the mean income between period t and $t+1$ assuming that distribution had not changed. Analogously, the second term captures the effect of the change in distribution assuming that the mean income had not changed. The growth and redistribution effects are artificial constructs (because both average income and inequality will change in any real situation), but this decomposition does allow an assessment of the relative importance of growth and inequality in accounting for changes in poverty.

In the case of rural Zambia (Table 2.7), poverty fell between 1991 and 1998, with the poverty severity rate showing the fastest percentage point decrease. For all indices the growth and redistribution effects served to reduce poverty. For the headcount measure the growth effect dominates. But once the indices start to place weight on the depth of poverty, the relative importance of the redistribution component increases substantially, such that this effect dominates for the poverty severity measure. This is expected given the fall in rural inequality over this period which accompanied the growth. Here

Table 2.7 Changes in different indices of poverty in rural Zambia decomposed into growth and redistribution effects (in percentage points)

Poverty measure	Change in poverty	Growth component	Redistribution component	Residual
P_0	−6.8	−5.2	−0.1	−1.5
P_1	−14.7	−4.9	−8.5	−1.3
P_2	−16.3	−4.9	−8.5	−1.3

Source: Chapter 9, Table 9.4, of this volume.

the growth and redistribution components operated in the same directions. But there is no standard pattern for this across OPPG case studies.

The same information provided by the Datt–Ravallion decomposition could be demonstrated in another manner, as shown by the example of poverty reduction in urban Bangladesh. Urban poverty fell sharply in the first half of the 1990s, but rose slightly in the second half of the decade. Urban inequality also rose over this period, offsetting the growth effect in the first half of the decade and contributing to the increase in poverty in the second half. The simulation summarized in Table 2.8 demonstrates the extent to which urban poverty would have fallen faster in the first half of the decade if it had not been accompanied by increasing inequality. It also shows that poverty would not have risen in the second half of the decade had inequality not increased.

The Datt–Ravallion decomposition is a convenient summary of the extent to which changes in poverty relate to growth and distributional change but it needs to be complemented by an understanding of the factors accounting for the distributional pattern of growth.

Growth and inequality elasticities of poverty

The importance of growth for poverty reduction is widely accepted by researchers and policy-makers. But nevertheless there is a substantial variation in the extent to which growth translates into poverty reduction. The poverty elasticity of growth gives a measure of how effectively growth is translated into poverty reduction – and can be used as a starting point to try to identify the factors that might enhance this effectiveness.

If a measure of poverty is represented as P and average income by μ, then the growth elasticity of poverty is simply:

$$\varepsilon_{P,\mu} = \frac{\partial P}{\partial \mu} \frac{\mu}{P}$$

It measures the percentage change in a poverty measure in response to a one per cent increase (or decrease) in average income. This elasticity can be

Table 2.8 The effect of inequality on urban poverty in Bangladesh (%)

	1991/92	1995/96	2000
Gini coefficient	36.2	38.6	40.5
Headcount index – actual	38.2	29.8	31.3
Headcount index – simulated if inequality unchanged	38.2	25.8	25.3

Source: Sen *et al.* (2004).

computed for different poverty indices. Note that this is a total elasticity of growth; it does not assume that the distribution has been held constant. The elasticity can in principle therefore be positive if inequality increased enough to offset the positive effect of growth on poverty reduction. But of course in general it will be negative: absolute poverty will generally fall if average income increases, and rise if average income decreases. It is also possible to compute growth elasticities of poverty assuming an unchanged distribution (based on the first component of the Datt–Ravallion decomposition above for example); such elasticities will be negative by definition for an unchanged poverty line (and assuming price changes have been adequately allowed for).

For the specific case of Zambia, estimates of the growth elasticity of poverty (Table 2.9) show that the magnitude of this is modest for the headcount index of poverty, but slightly higher for the poverty gap and poverty severity indices. Nonetheless these growth elasticities are small compared to many other countries considered in the OPPG programme and more generally. These low values will be influenced by the high level of inequality in Zambia.

The same table shows an analogous concept, the inequality elasticity of poverty:

$$\varepsilon_{P,G} = \frac{\partial P}{\partial G} \frac{G}{P}$$

where G represents the Gini coefficient. The effect of a reduction in inequality on the headcount measure of poverty is very modest, but it has a very big impact on the poverty gap and poverty severity measures. Again this is a total elasticity because the mean income can change; therefore the elasticity can be positive or negative. As with the growth elasticity, it is possible to compute a partial elasticity about an unchanged mean income. Again this is analogous to the second term of the Datt–Ravallion decomposition.

Growth elasticities of poverty can change significantly over time, as illustrated by the case of Indonesia during and following the East Asian crisis (see Table 2.10).

In general, many factors will influence the size of the growth elasticity of poverty. These include the initial level of inequality (where inequality

Table 2.9 Estimated growth and inequality elasticities of poverty for Zambia

Poverty index	Growth elasticity of poverty	Inequality elasticity of poverty
P_0	−0.62	0.25
P_1	−0.87	1.70
P_2	−0.99	3.10

Source: Thurlow and Wobst (2004).

Table 2.10 Growth elasticity of poverty in Indonesia over the 1990s

Year	Annual % change in per capita income	Growth elasticity of poverty
1993–96	5.2	−1.2
1996–99	−3.2	−3.0
1999–2002	2.5	−3.3

Source: Timmer (2005).

is higher initially, the elasticity will tend to be lower) and the distributional pattern of growth itself (where growth is associated with increasing inequality, this will mean less poverty reduction), but is also depends on many other factors including the average income level, the poverty line and the extent to which the poor are located close to, or far from, the poverty line. As such cross-country comparisons of the growth elasticity of poverty can be hard to interpret. However, such comparisons may be more valuable across regions within a country, as demonstrated in the OPPG case studies of Brazil and India; this then prompts an analysis of why elasticities are higher in some locations than others (see Besley, Burgess and Esteve-Volart, 2005).

Growth incidence curves

A key question of interest in this volume is to understand how different individuals in a population fared over a period of time – how their living conditions changed over time and how this varied across different groups of the population. The growth incidence curve (GIC) is a graphical technique that allows us to look at this. GICs were developed for income-based measures of well-being, but as will be discussed below can also be extended to non-income indicators.

The analytic foundations for GICs were set out by Ravallion and Chen (2003). Their interpretation is most clearly explained by considering some examples, as presented in Figure 2.3. The GIC is based on a comparison between survey data at two points in time, in the case of Bangladesh for instance 1992 and 2000. The horizontal axis of the graph represents the different percentile groups of the population: the first percentile (the poorest 1% of the population), the second percentile, and so on up to the 100th percentile (the richest 1%). The graph represents on the vertical axis the annual change in the consumption measure between these two points in time for each percentile group.[8]

The shape and position of the GIC will vary from case to case, and this provides important insights into changes in poverty and distributional patterns of growth. If the GIC is always above zero (as in the example of Bangladesh), then this indicates that there has been growth (incomes or consumption levels have increased) at all points of the distribution.

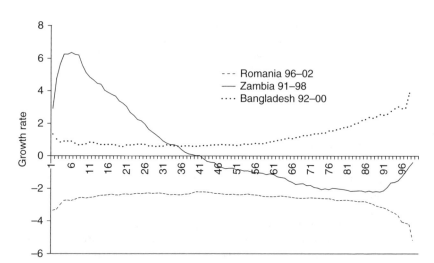

Figure 2.3   Selected examples of growth incidence curves

This will also imply that absolute poverty has fallen over this period for all conceivable absolute poverty lines (and all conventional measures of poverty). The same obviously applies in reverse if the GIC is always below zero (example of Romania in Figure 2.3). On the other hand if the GIC is sometimes above and sometimes below zero (example of Zambia in Figure 2.3), whether or not poverty has fallen will depend on where the poverty line is drawn.

In addition, the shape of the GIC provides information about the distributional pattern of growth. In the example of Vietnam in Figure 2.4, the GIC is broadly upward-sloping. Thus consumption levels increased in all percentile groups over this period, but they increased at faster rates in higher percentile groups compared to lower percentile groups. Therefore inequality increased over this period. In the example of Indonesia (Figure 2.4), consumption levels slightly fell in the majority of percentile groups over this period (presumably reflecting the impact of the East Asian crisis), but the curve is broadly downward-sloping. The crisis hit higher percentile groups harder than lower percentile groups. Thus inequality fell over this period. These examples highlight the difference between absolute and relative concepts of pro-poor growth. In Vietnam growth was pro-poor in an absolute sense, and poverty fell; but it was not pro-poor growth in a relative sense. In Indonesia inequality fell (pro-poor change in a relative sense), but growth was negative and poverty increased. Thus growth was clearly not pro-poor in an absolute sense.

In general GICs will show both upward and downward-sloping intervals across the range from the lowest to the highest percentile. But this still

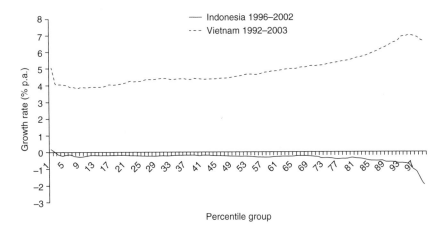

Figure 2.4 Examples of upward and downward-sloping income growth incidence curves
Source: Relevant OPPG case studies.

provides important information about the distributional pattern of growth or decline. However, it is important to discount the patterns at the extreme ends of the distribution because here the effects of measurement error are most severe. When the curves are computed using income data, the presence of zero or negative values at the lower end of the distribution also causes problems for interpretation.

While the GICs presented so far all relate to the national level, it can be very valuable to apply the same technique to subgroups of the population, for example distinguishing urban and rural areas, or different regions. In practice there are often important regional variations in levels and distributional patterns of growth, which are not revealed in the national-level GICs. For example, in the case of Zambia over the period 1991–98 (Figure 2.5), the national GIC shows positive consumption growth up to the 35th percentile, and negative thereafter. But plotting separate rural and urban GICs shows a very different pattern between these locations. The rural GIC shows positive growth up to the 94th percentile; whereas the urban GIC shows decline throughout the entire distribution. This pattern partly accounts for the shape of the national GIC, but this crucial information about the differential urban and rural experiences is not evident from the national GIC alone. Similarly, in the case of Ghana, the national level GIC suggested positive growth in all percentile groups over the period considered. But computing GICs for subnational groups revealed that there has been negative growth for substantial

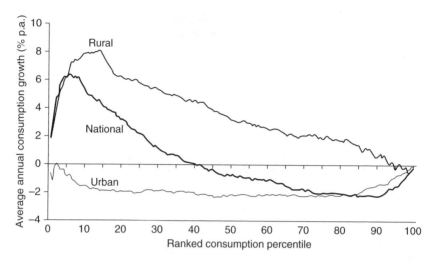

Figure 2.5 Urban and rural growth incidence curves for Zambia

numbers of households in the northern savannah region (see Chapter 3). This information was not revealed in the national GIC because of the averaging it implies.

Rate of pro-poor growth

The rate of pro-poor growth is a summary measure of the extent to which the poor are participating in, or benefiting from, growth. There are both absolute and relative concepts of this. The country studies in the OPPG project focused more on the absolute concept, developed by Ravallion and Chen (2003). This is therefore discussed in more detail below. But for many purposes analysts may prefer to compute relative concepts instead or in addition; examples of such concepts are discussed by Kakwani and Pernia (2000), and Kakwani, Khandker and Son (2004), among others.

The Ravallion–Chen concept of the rate of pro-poor growth is the average growth rate for percentiles which were poor in the first period. This is a direct measure of whether and to what extent growth is benefiting the poor (or decline is hurting the poor). This relates to an absolute concept of pro-poor growth, by answering the question of whether growth reduces poverty. It is also closely related to the growth-incidence curve; the rate of pro-poor growth is equal to the average growth rate of all percentiles up to the poverty line, which is not the same as the growth rate of mean income of the poor. However, in interpreting this measure, it is important to compare it with the mean growth rate for the whole population (ordinary growth rate). If the rate of pro-poor growth is higher than the ordinary growth rate, this indicates that growth is pro-poor in a relative sense; if it is less this indicates that growth is associated with increasing inequality between poor and non-poor households.

The rate of pro-poor growth can also be computed for groups of the population. Regionally disaggregated rates of pro-poor growth are presented in Table 2.11 (here for example for Vietnam), along with the corresponding mean growth rates. Both show significant variations across regions. The rates of pro-poor growth are positive in all regions, except for the North West. But in most cases they are substantially less than the mean growth rate, the only exception being the South Central Coast. This shows that the latter is the only region in which growth was pro-poor in a relative sense; in all others it was not (at least for this poverty line and index).

The relationship between the rate of pro-poor growth and the mean growth rate can be illustrated by adding to the GIC a horizontal line for the overall growth rate. This is shown in Figure 2.6 for the case of Zambia. The GIC lies above the ordinary growth rate up to the 37th percentile and below it thereafter. This means that the consumption growth of the poorest 37 per cent of all households exceeded the ordinary rate of growth.

Rates of pro-poor growth can be computed for different poverty lines, and will be specific to the poverty line chosen. This can be of value in looking at rates of growth among the poorest. Again experiences vary. In the case of Bolivia, those lying below the extreme poverty line experienced a faster rate of pro-poor growth between 1989 and 2002 (2.2%) than those below the moderate poverty line (1.8%). In the case of Ghana those below the 20th percentile had a pro-poor growth rate of 1.3 per cent between 1991 and 1998, compared to a rate of 2.1 per cent for the poor as a whole.

Table 2.11 Rates of pro-poor growth, and mean overall growth rates in Vietnam, by regions, 1998–2002 (% per annum)

	Rate of pro-poor growth (headcount, national poverty line)	Mean growth rate
North West	−1.6	4.0
North East	4.4	7.0
Red River Delta	1.4	3.9
North Central Coast	0.5	1.6
South Central Coast	4.6	3.5
Central Highlands	5.0	5.1
South East	2.6	4.1
Mekong River Delta	2.6	4.5

Source: Chapter 4, Table 4.5, of this volume.

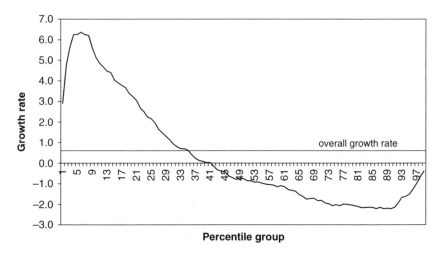

Figure 2.6   Growth incidence curve for Zambia compared to mean growth rate
Source: Based on data for OPPG Zambia case study.

Non-income growth incidence curves

The growth incidence curves discussed above were based on income or consumption indicators, but it is equally important to know about the distributional pattern of changes in non-income indicators of living standards. A corresponding concept has been defined for such indicators by Klasen (2005) and Grosse *et al.* (2005) – the non-income growth incidence curve (NIGIC).

There are two variants of this: the conditional NIGIC considers changes in the non-income indicator with reference to income percentile groups, and the unconditional NIGIC considers changes in the non-income indicator with reference to percentile groups of that indicator. Though these were not used in OPPG case studies, it is a straightforward extension. Consider as an example Figure 2.7, which shows conditional and unconditional NIGICs for years of education completed by young adults in Bolivia.

The conditional NIGIC for average number of years of education is plotted in Figure 2.7 as the solid line. This shows the percentage increase in years of education in each income percentile group. The curve lies above zero everywhere (average educational levels improve in all income percentile groups), and is broadly downward-sloping (faster growth in education among the income poor). A comparison of this curve with the income GIC (Klasen, 2005) shows that the percentage growth in education is less than the percentage growth in income among almost all income percentile groups (the conditional NIGIC lies almost always below the income GIC; Klasen, 2005).

The dashed line in Figure 2.7 above shows an unconditional NIGIC for the same indicator, where here the percentiles on the horizontal axis are

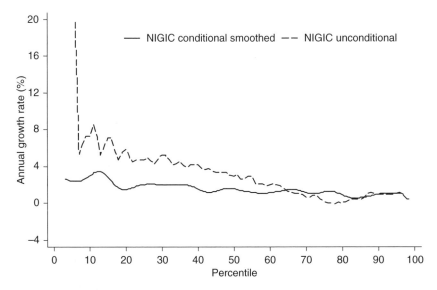

Figure 2.7 Growth incidence curves for years of education for adults aged 20–30 years in Bolivia

defined based on a ranking of years of education from the lowest on the left to the highest on the right. The interpretation of the NIGIC is entirely analogous to the income GIC. Because the curve lies above zero almost everywhere, this indicates positive growth in the average number of years of education throughout (with the exception of two or three percentiles in the eighth educational decile group). The growth rates are very fast in lower percentiles, reflecting a very low base to begin with, and are not defined when the starting value was zero. The broadly downward-sloping pattern of the curve, especially strong in the lowest percentiles, shows that growth rates have been faster for those that had fewer years of education to start with. In other words educational inequality in Bolivia according to this indicator has fallen; there has been pro-poor growth in a relative sense – as well as an absolute sense – in the average number of years of education.[9] This is much more strongly the case here compared to the income GIC (Klasen, 2004). In addition because the unconditional NIGIC has a much steeper slope than the corresponding conditional NIGIC, the growth in education is much more strongly related to initial education level than it is to the initial income level.

The same technique can be applied to other non-income indicators which show sufficient variation across different groups of the population; however they are unlikely to be informative in the case of indicators which are zero-one in nature (such as whether someone is literate or not).

Explaining the links between growth, inequality and poverty reduction

Having discussed ways in which patterns of growth and changes in poverty and distribution can be analysed; the next step is to understand the factors underlying the relationship between growth and poverty reduction – beyond the proximate determinants discussed above. This is a very large area of investigation; two areas are briefly reviewed below with illustrations from the country studies included in this volume.

A third very valuable approach, though not used in the country case studies in this volume, is the use of intra-country regression analysis. This involves seeking to model growth rates or changes in poverty across states, provinces, districts or other disaggregated population groups, as a function of the characteristics of these groups, such as demographic characteristics, infrastructure, institutional characteristics, gender differentials, unemployment rates and other average characteristics of the groups. This technique is much more powerful than cross country econometric analysis, including because the explanatory variables are likely to be much more comparable and to have been measured in the same way. However, the data requirements are demanding, including the need for a sufficiently large sample size to enable meaningful disaggregation to the state or district level, and the need for separately available data on the characteristics to be used as explanatory variables. Where such analysis can be undertaken it can be very informative in understanding for example, factors influencing the poverty elasticity of growth, as in the OPPG case studies of Brazil (Menezes-Filho and Vasconcellos, 2004) and India (Besley, Burgess and Esteve-Volart, 2005).[10] The study by Besley *et al.* is particularly informative in this respect (Besley and Cord, 2006).

Labour market analysis

The labour market plays a key role in the links between growth, inequality and poverty reduction. Labour is a key asset for many of the poor, as the central means of earning their livelihood, and the labour market has played a key role in many successful poverty reduction experiences. Migration has also frequently been an important factor in poverty reduction, including through remittances sent back by migrants. The labour market here needs to be interpreted sufficiently broadly to include not just working for an employer but also own account work in agriculture or non-farm businesses, the latter being the dominant form of employment in many low income countries.

A straightforward starting point is to examine the relationship between employment status and poverty, shown for example in Table 2.12 for Romania. Clearly poverty levels are much lower in households where the head works outside of the agricultural sector, and where the head is a skilled

Table 2.12 Poverty headcount in Romania by employment status of household head, 1999 to 2002 (%)

Category	1999	2002
Non-employed	39.2	34.0
Agriculture	55.4	49.0
Non-Agriculture	21.5	14.7
Skilled	11.5	8.9
Unskilled	42.9	39.1

Source: Chapter 10.

worker (these two factors being correlated with each other). Poverty levels are high where the head is not-employed and more so when the head works in the agricultural sector. For each category poverty levels fell over the period, but the reduction was largest for households where the head was employed in a non-agricultural activity.

Another important starting point is to examine sectoral employment trends alongside sectoral growth trends: are workers moving out of declining sectors and into expanding sectors? Unfortunately this is difficult to do in practice because of the poor quality – or simple absence – of employment data in many low and even middle-income countries. Sometimes survey data can be used to examine employment trends. In the case of Zambia, survey-based employment data (Figure 2.8) show an increase in employment in the agricultural sector and in trade services over a period of stagnant growth and increasing poverty (1991–98). This shift into agriculture appears

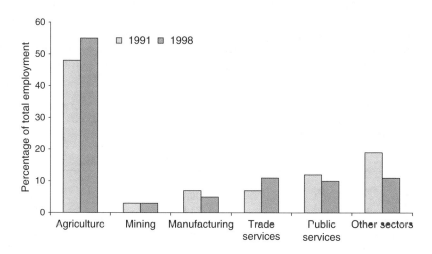

Figure 2.8 Sectoral distribution of employment in Zambia, 1991 and 1998

to be associated with a reduction in employment in the public sector and in manufacturing. In Romania as well there was a significant shift of employment into the agricultural sector against a background of weak economic performance and a sharp decline in industrial employment. In both cases these movements in employment are likely to be associated with increases in poverty over the period, but of course poverty may have increased even more in the absence of these movements.

It is also of interest to look at growth in income or expenditure levels by occupational category of the household head. Table 2.13 shows such a disaggregation for Burkina Faso derived from the household surveys. Average expenditure levels of subsistence farmers and cotton farmers – the poorest groups by some way to begin with – increased modestly over this period, while the expenditures of the other three categories fell. This resulted in reduced inequality between these groups. These average data though provide no information on the distribution within these groups. It also hides the fact that households often derive income from several distinct sources and that therefore the occupation of the household head is only one among several determinants of household income.

As already seen the composition of employment categories changes over time as households move out of one category into another. This may be contributing to the changes in average expenditure levels such as shown in Table 2.13. The Ravallion–Huppi decomposition discussed above can be informative in separating out the changes due to increasing income or expenditure levels within groups from the effects due to movements between groups. Thus in the case of Ghana, disaggregating households according to their main type of employment (Table 2.14) shows that movement between sectors has made an important contribution to poverty reduction. The largest contribution to poverty reduction though has been made by intra-group effects in areas that are large employers (food crop agriculture, various non-farm self employment activities) or fast growing sectors (export farming). The application of this decomposition allows a preliminary identification of

Table 2.13   Disaggregation of growth rates in Burkina Faso by main occupation

Region	Real household expenditure per capita (index, mean = 100)		
	1994	*1998*	*2003*
Public	351	306	314
Private	274	296	228
Informal	199	213	163
Subsistence	71	73	75
Cotton	75	86	85

Source: Grimm and Günther (2004).

Table 2.14 Decomposition of poverty reduction in Ghana by sector of activity

Household main economic activity	Population share (1991) (%)	Population share (1998) (%)	Percentage point change in poverty	Share of poverty reduction (%)
Food crop farmers	43.6	38.6	8.6	30.6
Export farmers	6.3	7.0	25.4	13
Private informal employ.	3.1	2.9	13.3	3.3
Public sector employment	13.5	10.7	12	13.2
Private formal employ.	3.9	4.9	19	6.1
Non-farm self-employ.	27.6	33.8	9.8	22
Not working	2.0	2.1	1.6	−0.2
Total intra-group effect				88.0
Total migration effect				10.6
Residual				1.4

Source: Aryeetey and McKay (2004).

the extent to which different occupational categories were able to participate in growth.

Changes in expenditure levels within employment categories are most likely to reflect changes in earnings in those activities; hence it is of value to look at earnings data directly where such data are available. Frequently earnings data are only available for wage employees, being much more difficult to compute for those working for themselves. Table 2.15 presents a summary of growth of wage earnings in different sectors in Vietnam. The

Table 2.15 Levels and changes in mean levels of real monthly (net) earnings in Vietnam, 1993–98, annual averages (thousand dong)

	1993 '000 dong	1998 '000 dong	% change Monthly earnings	% change Hourly earnings
Total	**335.1**	**548.7**	**10.4**	**8.3**
Formal industry	377.5	619.9	10.4	10.9
Formal services	230.3	594.1	20.9	13.8
Informal industry	378.1	609.6	10.0	9.2
Informal services	343.1	483.0	7.1	1.1

Source: Bernabé and Krstić (2005), from their table 9. Note that this table is based on wage employees only.

fastest earnings growth is observed in the formal services sector and the slowest in the informal services sector. The fact that monthly earnings in the formal services sector are growing faster than hourly earnings implies that hours worked have increased in this sector.

Finally, where longitudinal or panel data are available this can be very valuable in examining labour market transitions for individuals, not just for groups of workers. Among OPPG case study countries, panel data with quite good quality labour market information was available for Vietnam. Table 2.16 presents a disaggregation of those escaping poverty between 1993 and 1998 (the time period of the panel data) according to the sectors in which they worked initially (1993, in the rows) and finally (1998, in the columns). 64.3 per cent of those escaping poverty worked in the agricultural sector in both years, but nearly 14 per cent of those that worked in agriculture in 1993 and escaped poverty had changed occupation by 1998, mostly moving into the informal industry or services sectors.

CGE modelling and related techniques

In many respects the ultimate interest of this analysis of pro-poor growth (for researchers and policy-makers) is in identifying and understanding the likely impact that specific current and proposed policies have on growth, poverty and distribution. In practice such impacts can be very difficult to identify and quantify, especially when many factors can change simultaneously. One promising approach to addressing this is through economy-wide modelling approaches. These can be applied both in an *ex post* sense, seeking to explain what factors underlay changes in the past; but they are most powerful used in an *ex ante*, forward-looking context, trying to simulate the impact of future policy scenarios. The latter was more commonly used in the OPPG project and will be the focus of discussion here; but the same techniques can equally be applied in an *ex post* sense. Both are relevant in the analysis and understanding of pro-poor growth.

Table 2.16 Vietnam percentage of employed that moved out of poverty by employment status and sector (1993–98) (population over 15yrs)

1993	Agriculture	Industry formal	1998 Services formal	Industry informal	Services informal	Total
Agriculture	64.3%	0.6%	0.9%	6.4%	6.0%	78.2%
Industry formal	1.0%	0.2%	0.1%	1.0%	0.6%	2.8%
Services formal	1.0%	0.1%	0.6%	0.3%	2.4%	4.2%
Industry informal	3.0%	0.2%	0.0%	3.8%	1.3%	8.4%
Services informal	2.2%	0.1%	0.2%	0.8%	3.2%	6.5%
Total	**71.4%**	**1.1%**	**1.8%**	**12.2%**	**13.5%**	**100.0%**

Source: Bernabé and Krstić (2005).

A number of different modelling approaches are available, two of which are discussed here.[11] One is essentially an accounting based approach, the Poverty Analysis Macroeconomic Simulator (PAMS) model developed by the World Bank for looking at the poverty impact of macroeconomic policy (Pereira da Silva *et al.*, 2002). PAMS combines the World Bank's RMSM-X framework (reflecting sectoral patterns of growth) with a labour market module (distinguishing different groups and focusing on employment and earnings) and with household survey data in a simple top-down fashion. Thus, the model can be used to simulate the poverty effects of macroeconomic shocks and policy change at a relatively high disaggregated level. This model is applied here in the chapter in Romania, and a variant of this model was also used in the Burkina Faso OPPG case study (Grimm and Günther, 2004).

The second widely used approach is based on computable general equilibrium (CGE) modelling. This approach is used in the chapters on Bolivia and Zambia in this volume. The CGE modelling approach incorporates behavioural modelling in a way that the PAMS approach does not. It is characterized by strong microfoundations, based a representation of the behaviour of key actors in the economy, including consumers, producers, government and the rest of the world. The model allows the interactions between these agents through different market and non-market channels, and is solved as a general equilibrium. It allows for the possibility of disaggregation, including by household groups. Simulations using the model enable linkages to be made between macro or sectoral policy changes, and outcomes at a more micro level. While many classic CGE models were static in nature, for looking at growth-related issues this needs to be extended to a dynamic model, in particular incorporating the modelling of investment. Many recent CGE models are explicitly dynamic, including those applied in the Bolivia and Zambia chapters.

CGE models offer many advantages, but also some limitations. Construction of a CGE model, especially one that captures dynamics, is a significant undertaking in its own right. The results also depend highly on the assumptions underlying the model (e.g. about market clearing, and about the way dynamics are modelled).

In the present context an important drawback of CGE model approaches is that they are not well-suited for assessing the distributional effects of macroeconomic shocks and policy reforms given that they usually distinguish only a small number of representative households. Empirically it is well known that intra-group heterogeneity is then still very high (see Table 2.5 above). In addition, depending on the shock considered, intra-group inequality may change much more than inter-group inequality.

To capture such effects, CGE models, as well as models such as RMSM-X, can be linked directly to household surveys, forming a micro-simulation approach.[12] This is the broad approach used in the Bolivia and Zambia chapters in this volume. Allowing for intra-group heterogeneity can be done in several ways. The easiest way is to classify households in the household sample and in the CGE according to the same groups and then to expand household incomes in the sample by the group-specific growth rates given by the CGE. Doing this implies accounting for intra-group heterogeneity but not for *changes* in intra-group heterogeneity. This approach is used in the PAMS framework as well as in the CGEs used in the chapters on Bolivia and Zambia. Going a step further implies using the method suggested by Bourguignon, Robilliard and Robinson (2003). In this approach not only growth rates but also employment changes are transmitted to the house-hold survey. Labour supply and earnings are modelled using a reduced-form household income generation model. The intercepts of these equations are then adjusted until the employment structure and the group-specific mean earnings in the household survey match the numbers in the CGE model. Through the changes in the employment structure this approach accounts also, at least partly, for changes in intra-group inequality. One could also say that this approach accounts to some extent for the behaviour or response of households to shocks. The most sophisticated form of such a macro-micro linkage is to build a so-called integrated macro-micro model. In such a model the CGE and the household survey are not linked in a top-down fashion, but all household related aggregates are rather simulated on the household level and interact directly and in an iterative way with the other aggregates. However, the integrated approach needs to be based on a structural model of household income generation requiring very detailed household data and on a relative simple CGE framework to be tractable. Such an integrated model has recently been used to study poverty alleviation strategies in Madagascar (Cogneau and Robilliard, 2004).

Where micro-simulation models based on CGE models can be constructed, they represent a very useful technique to simulate expected future growth and poverty trends. For example, in the Zambia chapter, the authors consider a number of different future policy scenarios, and simulate the impacts on sectoral growth of these different scenarios using a CGE model, comple-mented by a micro-simulation model to look at poverty and distributional effects in some detail. The baseline scenario and two alternative future policy scenarios are summarized in Table 2.17, looking at the estimated impacts of the different scenarios on growth (level and sectoral pattern) and on the poverty measure for urban and rural areas.

The baseline scenario is based on a 4 per cent overall growth rate, with export crops playing a key role in this. The estimated poverty reduction impact of this growth pattern though is modest. Different alternative scen-arios are distinguished depending on the lead sector for growth. Of the two presented here, the agricultural led strategy is much more effective in redu-cing rural poverty and not much less effective at reducing urban poverty than the industry led strategy. The authors are also able to simulate estimated future GICs for the different scenarios (Thurlow and Wobst, 2004).

Table 2.17 Simulated future sectoral growth rates for Zambia under different scenarios

	GDP share or poverty rate (%), 2001	Baseline scenario	Agriculture-led scenario	Industry-led scenario
Real annual compound growth rate (%) 2001–15				
GDP (factor cost)	100.0	4.0	5.0	5.0
Agriculture	24.7	4.6	7.7	4.5
Staple crops	22.6	4.1	7.3	4.2
Export crops	1.4	10.2	13.2	7.7
Industry	27.3	3.6	3.5	6.1
Mining	11.0	1.9	1.9	4.8
Manufacturing	16.2	4.5	4.5	6.9
Services	48.0	3.9	4.2	4.5
Final year poverty incidence rate (%) 2015				
Rural	73.3	63.7	50.4	61.0
Urban	37.3	30.9	25.2	24.4

Source: Chapter 9 of this volume.

The estimates for future growth and distributional changes (including poverty reduction) need to be considered with caution, especially over this time horizon. But these estimates are still valuable. For example, they high-light the relatively modest poverty reduction that is likely to occur in the current scenario in Zambia. In addition they help to identify the relative impact of different scenarios and their anticipated distributional effects. They also form a starting point for a discussion about why different scenarios produce divergent results.

Using the PAMS framework, simulations can be conducted in an analogous manner to CGE models. Figure 2.4 in the Romania chapter presents some forward-looking simulations on the impacts of different labour market and sectoral growth scenarios on poverty. Again, the PAMS model does not incor-porate behavioural modelling in the way that a CGE model does, and it is not based on an equilibrium analysis; but PAMS can also be linked to household surveys as the CGE models discussed above to enable a relatively highly disaggregated distributional analysis. The model is based on a much less detailed representation of the economy, but as such is easier to construct compared to a CGE model.

Conclusions

This chapter has summarized a number of important techniques for analysing the relationships between growth, poverty reduction and inequality, which have been used in the cross-country Operationalizing Pro-Poor Growth Project. The country chapters in this volume apply many of these techniques, and more are used in the reports on which these chapters are based. Of particular importance perhaps is the growth incidence curve, and the associated rate of pro-poor growth, and their use in looking at both the level and the distributional pattern of growth. Of course the techniques by themselves are only helpful when combined with country-specific contextualization, insight and knowledge, which the country chapters also provide.

There remains considerable scope to develop techniques further in future. The GICs are sensitive to data quality issues, especially at the extremes of the distribution. They also do not look at household mobility over time, which would require longitudinal data. Another important area for development relates to the relationships between growth and non-income dimensions of poverty; growth can play an important role in enabling progress in core social indicators, and that is a key dimension of what a pro-poor pattern of growth should mean. Another important area relates to developing a better understanding of the links between growth and poverty reduction which goes beyond the labour market analysis and simulation models discussed earlier in the chapter. Intra-country regressions can be a valuable technique here. A final important issue relates to questions of data availability; there is still a significant number of countries where the household survey data is not yet available, and these are often precisely the countries where the need for pro-poor growth is most urgent, because they have had little recent experience of either growth or poverty reduction. However, as shown in the Bolivia case study, even in such cases this limitation can often be overcome, given that Demographic and Health Surveys are now available for many countries worldwide.

Notes

1. See Deaton (2005) and Ravallion (2001) for debates on comparability between survey and national accounts-based concepts of average income, an issue which has been particularly discussed with reference to India.
2. For instance, Coulombe and McKay (1995) and Appiah *et al.* (2000) make assumptions to try to draw conclusions about trends in poverty in Ghana over a period when the questionnaire was revised significantly. This predates the period considered in the Ghana chapter in this volume.
3. This requires the availability of a single cross-section survey which can be used to establish the econometric relationship between household income and the assets it owns, so that knowledge of the latter can be used to predict the former.
4. Thus for example we do not discuss poverty-mapping here, a very valuable technique for building a much more detailed picture of the spatial pattern of poverty but which has not yet been applied to looking at changes in poverty at this level. Elbers, Lanjouw and Lanjouw (2003) provide a detailed discussion of this important technique.
5. McKay (2002) provides an introduction to the measurement of inequality, including an explanation of the Gini coefficient.
6. See Chapter 6 for a case where this assumption does not hold.

7. The residual term is difficult to interpret, reflecting an index number problem. In practical terms the overall results of the Datt–Ravallion decomposition become difficult to interpret when the residual term is large relative to either the growth and inequality components (as for example in the Indonesia case study due to the effects of large price changes). It is common practice to use procedures to eliminate the residual by doing forward and backward decompositions (setting the reference period in turn to $t-1$ and t), and averaging the results. But there is no scientifically rigorous justification for this.
8. Note that what is being compared is the averages for the corresponding percentile groups in each of the two years; the same households or individuals are not being compared.
9. Of course this reduction in inequality in years of education in Bolivia partly reflects the fact that there are practical upper limits to the likely level of education for many people. Moreover, it may also reflect relatively high levels of educational attendance to start with; this result will not necessarily apply to poorer countries with low levels of educational attendance to begin with.
10. Neither of these case studies though is included in this volume, which is why the technique is not discussed in more detail here.
11. Various other approaches have been developed; Essama-Nssah (2005) provides a helpful summary of different approaches.
12. Cogneau *et al.* (2003) provide a very useful survey of microsimulation approaches able to assess the poverty impact of macro-economic shocks and policy reforms.

References

Appiah, K., Laryea-Adjei, S.G. and Demery, L. (2000) 'Poverty in a Changing Environment', Chapter 16 of E. Aryeetey, J. Harrigan and M. Nissanke (eds), *Economic Reforms in Ghana: The Miracle and the Mirage*. Oxford: James Currey.

Aryeetey, E. and McKay, A. (2004) 'Operationalizing Pro-Poor Growth: Ghana Case Study', October, Paper commissioned by AfD, BMZ (GTZ and KfW), DFID and the World Bank.

Bernabé, S. and Krstić, G. (2005) 'Labour Productivity and Access to Markets Matter for Pro-Poor Growth. The 1990s in Burkina Faso and Vietnam', OPPG Synthesis Paper, June.

Besley, T. and Cord, L. (2006) *Delivering on the Promise of Pro-Poor Growth: Insights and Lessons from Country Experiences*. London: Palgrave Macmillan.

Besley, T., Burgess, R. and Esteve-Volart, B. (2005) 'Operationalizing Pro-Poor Growth: India Case Study', January, Paper commissioned by AfD, BMZ (GTZ and KfW), DFID and the World Bank.

Bourguignon, F., Robilliard, A.-S. and Robinson, S. (2003) 'Representative Versus Real Households in the Macro-Economic Modelling of Inequality', Working paper DT 10, DIAL.

Cogneau, D. and Robilliard, A.-S. (2004) 'Poverty Alleviation Policies in Madagascar: A Micro-Macro Simulation Model'. DIAL Working paper DT 11. Paris: DIAL.

Cogneau, D., Grimm, M. and Robilliard, A.-S. (2003) 'Evaluating Poverty Reduction Policies — The Contribution of Micro-Simulation Techniques', in J.-P. Cling, M. Razafindrakato and F. Roubaud (eds), *New International Poverty Reduction Strategies*. London: Routledge Books, pp. 340–70.

Coulombe, H. and McKay, A. (1995) 'An Assessment of Trends in Poverty in Ghana, 1988–92', PSP Discussion Paper no. 81. Poverty and Social Policy Department, November, Washington, DC: World Bank.

Coulombe, H. and McKay, A. (2003) 'The Evolution of Poverty and Inequality in Ghana over the 1990s: A Study Based On The Ghana Living Standards Surveys', paper prepared for World Bank Poverty Dynamics in Africa Project, final draft, December.

Datt, G. and Ravallion, M. (1992) 'Growth and Redistribution Components of Changes in Poverty: A Decomposition with Application to Brazil and India', *Journal of Development Economics*. 38:275–95.

Deaton, A. (2005) 'Measuring Poverty in a Growing World (or Measuring Growth in a Poor World)', *Review of Economics and Statistics*, 87/1:1–19.

DFID (2004) 'What is Pro-Poor Growth and Why Do We Need to Know?', Pro-Poor Growth Briefing Note 1, February.

Elbers, C., Olson Lanjouw, J. and Lanjouw, P. (2003) 'Micro-Level Estimation of Poverty and Inequality', *Econometrica*, 71/1:355–64.

Essama-Nssah, B. (2005) 'Assessing the Distributional Impact of Public Policy', World Bank Policy Research Working Paper no. 2883. Washington, DC: World Bank.

Foster, J., Greer, J. and Thorbecke, E. (1984) 'A Class of Decomposable Poverty Indices', *Econometrica*, 52/3:761–6.

Gheorghiu, R., Paczynski, W., Radziwill, A., Sowa, A., Stanculescu, M., Topinska, I., Turlea, G. and Walewski, M. (2004) 'Operationalizing Pro-Poor Growth. A Country Case Study on Romania', report prepared for *Operationalizing Pro-Poor Growth* work programme, a joint initiative of AfD, BMZ (GTZ, KfW Development Bank), DFID and the World Bank.

Grimm, M. and Günther, I. (2004) 'How to achieve pro-poor growth in a poor economy. The case of Burkina Faso', report prepared for Operationalizing Pro-Poor Growth work programme, a joint initiative of AfD, BMZ (GTZ, KfW Development Bank), DFID and the World Bank, Eschborn: GTZ.

Grosse, M., Harttgen, K. and Klasen, S. (2005) 'Measuring Pro-Poor Growth in the Non-Income Dimension', mimeo, University of Göttingen.

Howes, S. and Lanjouw, J.O. (1998) 'Does Sample Design Matter for Poverty Comparisons?', *Review of Income and Wealth*, 44/1:99–109.

Kakwani, N. and Pernia, E.M. (2000) 'What is Pro-Poor Growth?', *Asian Development Review*, 18/1:1–16.

Kakwani, N., Khandker, S. and Son, H.H. (2004) 'Pro-Poor Growth: Concepts and Measurements with Country Case Studies', International Poverty Centre (IPC) Working Paper no. 1, Brazil.

Klasen, S. (2005) 'Economic Growth and Poverty Reduction: Measurement and Policy Issues', OECD Development Centre, Working Paper 246. Paris: OECD.

Klasen, S., Grosse, M., Lay, J., Spatz, J., Thiele, R. and Wiebelt, M. (2004) 'Operationalizing Pro-Poor Growth – Country Case Study Bolivia', report commissioned by AfD, BMZ (GTZ and KfW), DFID and the World Bank.

Litchfield, J.A. (1999) 'Inequality: Methods and Tools', note prepared for World Bank PovertyNet Website available at: http://www1.worldbank.org/prem/poverty/inequal/methods/litchfie.pdf

McKay, A. (2002) 'Defining and Measuring Inequality', DFID-ERC Briefing Paper on Inequality No. 1 available at: http://www.odi.org.uk/PPPG/publications/briefings/inequality_briefings/01.pdf

Menezes-Filho, N. and Vasconcellos, L. (2004) 'Has Economic Growth Been Pro-Poor in Brazil? Why?', paper commissioned by AfD, BMZ (GTZ and KfW), DFID and the World Bank as part of Operationalizing Pro-Poor Growth project, October.

Pereira da Silva, L., Essama-Nssah, B. and Samaké, I. (2002) 'A Poverty Analysis Macroeconomic Simulator (PAMS): Linking Household Surveys with Macro-Models', *The World Bank Working Paper Series*, no. 2888.

Ravallion, M. (2001) 'Should Poverty Measures be Anchored to the National Accounts?', *Economic and Political Weekly*, 08/09:3245–52.

Ravallion, M. and Bidani, B. (1994) 'How Robust is a Poverty Profile?', *World Bank Economic Review*, 8/1:75–102.

Ravallion, M. and Chen, S. (2003) 'Measuring Pro-Poor Growth', *Economics Letters*, 78/1:93–99.

Ravallion, M. and Huppi, M. (1991) 'Measuring Changes in Poverty: A Methodological Case Study of Indonesia during an Adjustment Period', *World Bank Economic Review*, 5/1:57–82.

Sen, A.K. (1997) 'On Economic Inequality', Oxford University Press, Clarendon Paperbacks.

Sen, B., Mujeri, M.K. and Shahabuddin, Q. (2004) 'Operationalizing Pro-Poor Growth: Bangladesh as a Case Study', November, paper commissioned by AfD, BMZ (GTZ and KfW), DFID and the World Bank.

Son, H.H. (2004) 'A Note on Pro-Poor Growth', *Economics Letters*, 82/3:307–14.

Thurlow, J. and Wobst, P. (2004) 'The Road to Pro-Poor Growth in Zambia: Past Lessons and Future Challenges', paper commissioned by AfD, BMZ (GTZ and KfW), DFID and the World Bank as part of Operationalizing Pro-Poor Growth project, October.

Timmer, C.P. (2005) 'Operationalizing Pro-Poor Growth: Indonesia', paper commissioned by AfD, BMZ (GTZ and KfW), DFID and the World Bank, June.

Part I

Pro-Poor Growth and Regional Inequality

3
Growth with Poverty Reduction, but Increased Spatial Inequality: Ghana over the 1990s

Ernest Aryeetey and Andrew McKay

Introduction

In a continent with tragically few success stories over the last quarter century, Ghana stands out as a country that has managed to achieve sustained economic growth over the last 20 years. This has been accompanied by significant reductions in the proportion of the population living in absolute poverty, as well as improvements in several non-monetary dimensions of well-being. This has been achieved in an environment of political stability, including transition to democracy. The achievement is impressive given Ghana's record over the immediately preceding 1965–83 period, which was a time that knew severe political instability and economic decline.

The availability of nationally representative household survey data towards the beginning and end of the 1990s enables a disaggregated analysis of the pattern of growth and poverty reduction over this decade. Over this period income poverty fell and many other dimensions of wellbeing improved, a finding supported by other surveys and data. But one striking message from the survey results analysed here is the highly spatially differentiated pattern of growth and income poverty reduction over this period. Some locations have experienced reasonable growth and significant income poverty reduction over the period, while others have experienced little of either.

This pattern has contributed to increased spatial inequality over the period, a fact also confirmed from other sources (Vanderpuye-Orgle, 2002; Shepherd *et al.*, 2004). One aspect of this is widening of an already large north–south differential, an issue with deep historical roots and which is politically sensitive in Ghana, as in many West African countries (Shepherd *et al.*, 2004). But the picture is more complex than this. There are significant variations in economic performance within the north and the south.

Analysis of the survey data allows a better understanding of the factors underlying this pattern, in particular by linking the spatial pattern of change to the economic activities in which individuals and households are engaged.

This confirms that the spatial pattern of growth is strongly related to the sectoral pattern of growth, which in turn reflected various factors including policy, infrastructure, resource endowments and external factors. In addition the ability of the poor to participate in growth has varied across locations in Ghana.

An analysis of these issues forms a key focus for this chapter, which is structured as follows. The next section provides the relevant background, including a summary of growth performance over the period. This is then followed by a summary of the aggregate changes in poverty over this period, looking at both income and non-income dimensions and considering the distributional pattern of change. We then present the spatial disaggregation of change over this period, followed by a more detailed understanding by linking to the sectoral pattern of change over this period, looking at the different income earning activities of households. A final section concludes.

Country background

Ghana is an independent republic in West Africa bordering Côte d'Ivoire, Burkina Faso and Togo, and covering an area of 238,537 sq km. The total population of Ghana was counted at 18.9 million in the 2000 census and is expected to grow annually at 2.1 per cent for the period 2000–15. The proportion of children under 15 years is still large at 44.2 per cent, reflecting faster population growth in the recent past. The population is ethnically quite diverse, an important issue given recent history of tensions and conflict with ethnic dimensions in other West African countries, including neighboring Côte d'Ivoire.

At Independence in 1957 Ghana was regarded as a beacon in Africa, with much potential and having comparable levels of per capita income to countries such as South Korea and Malaysia. Yet by 2002 Malaysia's per capita income exceeded that of Ghana by a factor of around 12. This is a striking contrast between sustained fast growth in Malaysia (in common with many other East and Southeast Asian countries) over this period compared to its absence in Ghana, notwithstanding recent recovery. In the case of Ghana, after initial growth following Independence, the years 1965–83 saw considerable economic and political instability and a trend decline in per capita income.

This is widely regarded as a consequence of inappropriate and highly inconsistent state-led policies to attain import-substituting industrialization, financed in part by high taxation of cocoa, a key export commodity (Frimpong-Ansah, 1991). This period saw frequent changes of power (often by coup d'état) between predominantly military governments. Instability was particularly severe in 1970s and early 1980s (Figure 3.1), with Rado (1986) characterizing the 1977–83 period as one of 'acceleration towards the abyss'. Ghana's performance from the mid-1960s through the 1970s

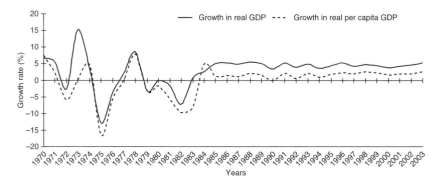

Figure 3.1 Real GDP growth and real per capita GDP growth, 1970–2003, Ghana

contrasts starkly with neighbouring Côte d'Ivoire, which has a very similar economic structure and resource endowment. Over this period Côte d'Ivoire enjoyed positive sustained growth, pursued more consistent economic policies, and maintained political stability. Côte d'Ivoire is also an important cocoa producer and competitor for Ghana; and in the period of decline in Ghana there was significant cross-border smuggling of cocoa into Côte d'Ivoire. Côte d'Ivoire (and other West African countries) enjoyed the benefits of membership of the CFA franc zone, while Ghana's exchange rate was frequently seriously overvalued.

The situation since the mid-1980s has changed markedly in Ghana. Since 1985 Ghana has enjoyed sustained economic growth (Figure 3.1) of around 4.5 per cent per annum (or 2% to 2.5% per capita). The country has had political and economic stability, making important moves towards liberalization in both the economic and political spheres, and has also become a substantial aid recipient. There is also evidence of significant progress in poverty reduction over this period.

Of course there is an important element of catching up lost ground. By contrast from the 1980s onwards, Côte d'Ivoire has experienced economic decline and political instability. A comparison of growth rates with other West African countries (Table 3.1) shows that in the 1990s Ghana has been among the fastest growing economies in West Africa, and it has now become a leading economy in the subregion, to some extent taking over the mantle previously held by Côte d'Ivoire (the direction of cocoa smuggling has now reversed).

1983 saw the launch of the IMF/World Bank Economic Recovery Programme as the government realized the situation was unsustainable. The details of this programme have been widely documented elsewhere (Aryeetey *et al.*, 2000). The reforms, in combination with the large resource inflows which accompanied them, did succeed in relaunching growth, and there was strong initial recovery in both the domestic and external sectors

Table 3.1 Average annualized per capita growth rates of West African countries

	1980–89	1990–99	2000–02	1980–2002
Benin	0.0	1.6	2.9	1.1
Burkina Faso	1.1	1.3	1.1	1.2
Cape Verde	4.6	2.8	2.3	3.4
Côte d'Ivoire	−3.8	−0.5	−3.4	−2.3
Gambia, The	0.3	−0.4	−0.3	−0.1
Ghana	**−1.3**	**1.6**	**2.4**	**0.5**
Guinea	1.6	1.5	1.1	1.4
Guinea-Bissau	0.2	−0.9	−2.6	−0.6
Liberia	−7.1	−1.3	6.7	−2.8
Mali	−1.9	1.0	2.3	−0.1
Mauritania	−0.2	1.0	1.4	0.5
Niger	−3.0	−1.5	−0.3	−2.0
Nigeria	−2.1	0.2	−0.3	−0.9
Sao Tome and Principe	−1.0	−0.8	1.6	−0.4
Senegal	−0.4	0.6	1.5	0.3
Sierra Leone	−1.0	−6.4	3.1	−2.8
Togo	−0.6	−1.0	−1.9	−0.9

Source: World Development Indicators, 2004.

(Hutchful, 2002). The fiscal situation improved significantly between 1984 and 1992, but then deteriorated with the transition to democracy in 1992, with a clear link to electoral cycles in the 1990s. This led to a sharp increase in the domestic debt burden. Moreover, and partly linked to this poor fiscal performance, private investment has consistently been poor, savings rates have remained very low, the financial sector remained highly under-developed, and the government consistently struggled to control inflation. The exchange rate has remained unstable and interest rates have been very high. There has though been some improvement in fiscal management and inflation control in recent years.

Exports played an important contributory role in growth over the post-1984 period, although their composition has changed little until recently, dominated by the traditional (colonial) exports of cocoa, gold and timber. The rehabilitation of gold and cocoa production has been very important. They benefited from the elimination of the substantial anti-export and other biases against these sectors in the past (taxation, overvalued exchange rates and import tariffs). Only in recent years has there been significant growth in non-traditional exports, the majority of which are still agricultural or processed agricultural products such as pineapples, yams, wood products, cocoa products, canned tuna and oil palm products. The agricultural sector itself though remains predominantly oriented to subsistence or transactions in local markets, and there has been little transformation of this sector over the period. Import liberalization over this period has also had a substantial impact, both positive (increased inputs for production; large inflows of consumer goods which were then traded, much in the informal sector) and negative (for example increased competition from imported agricultural products such as rice). The move towards a market determined exchange rate was another important factor, after many years over which the exchange rate had been highly overvalued.

However, despite the positive growth rates of the last two decades, it is important to emphasize the point that there is no evidence of significant structural change in the economy. There is some decline in the share of industry and agriculture, and a growing share of services in GDP, but the magnitudes are small. Much of the increase in services seems to derive from the relatively lower-order service sectors, notably wholesale and retail trade, and also restaurants and hotels (Aryeetey and Fosu, 2003). The shares of mining and construction in GDP have also increased over the last decade, but that of manufacturing has not. Of particular importance for poverty reduction, there has been very little employment creation in the formal sector; the growing sectors are mostly own account activities. These changes are not suggestive of structural transformation, or a likely step change in growth performance. Establishing a strong performance in manufacturing will be of central importance in sustaining and accelerating growth in Ghana, though the challenges in doing so are substantial (World Bank, 2004; Teal, 1999a, 1999b).

The post-reform period was one of sustained growth, reversing the previous decline. Further, increased revenues, including significantly from aid, enabled significantly increased levels of public spending, including for the provision of key services (education in particular), and investment in infrastructure (for example roads, electrification). This would be expected to have translated into poverty reduction in both income and non-income dimensions, the issue to which this chapter now turns.

Patterns of change in poverty in the 1990s

Since the late 1980s onwards, there are now many sources of data on different dimensions of poverty in Ghana, both qualitative and quantitative. Important qualitative sources include a participatory poverty assessment carried out in several rural and urban communities in 1994/95 (Norton *et al.*, 1995); the Ghana 'Voices of the Poor' study (Kunfaa, 1999); participatory poverty consultations conducted in 36 communities as part of preparing the first Ghana Poverty Reduction Strategy (GPRS; Government of Ghana, 2003, section 3.3); plus a number of other local-level studies. Main sources of survey data include the Demographic and Health Survey (DHS; conducted in 1987, 1993, 1998 and 2003); the Core Welfare Indicators Questionnaire (CWIQ; 1987 and 2003); and the Ghana Living Standards Survey (GLSS;

Table 3.2   Recent trends in different dimensions of poverty in Ghana

Indicator	Data source and year			
	GLSS		CWIQ	
	1991/92	1998/99	1997	2003
Poverty headcount index	51.7	39.5		
Gini coefficient	0.373	0.388		
Net primary school enrolment rate – girls	71.5	81.9		
Net primary school enrolment rate – boys	76.5	84.9		
Net secondary school enrolment rate – girls	33.7	39.0		
Net secondary school enrolment rate – boys	40.9	42.4		
Literacy rates			48.5	53.4
Child stunting			29.9	32.4
Percentage of those ill consulting health personnel	49.3	43.8		
Percentage of households having access to potable water	64.8	75.1		
Percentage having safe sanitation facilities			45.8	55.0
Percentage of households connected to electricity	29.8	41.4		

Source: GLSS and CWIQ surveys.

1987/88, 1988/89, 1991/92 and 1998/99 with another round currently in process).

These sources provide information on a variety of different dimensions of poverty. Some core quantitative poverty indicators are presented in Table 3.2. Indicators are taken from the two most recent GLSS surveys where possible, because this is the only source that can be used to compute spatially disaggregated indicators of consumption growth and therefore it is of most interest to look at the trends in indicators over the same period.[1] The GLSS surveys are also the only source for computing the poverty headcount and the Gini coefficient which are of specific importance in discussing pro-poor growth.

The general patterns revealed by Table 3.2 are of reductions in income poverty over this period, improvements in educational indicators, improvements in access to drinking water, sanitation and electricity; but of an increase in income inequality and deterioration in health indicators. Health indicators available from other sources, including the DHS surveys, support this latter assessment. Life expectancy fell slightly over the 1990s, from 57.2 in 1990 to 57.0 in 2000. While the infant mortality rate fell from 74 in 1990 to 58 in 2000, the recent DHS survey suggests an increase to 64 per 1,000 births in 2003. The 2003 CWIQ results also show that use of health services has not improved since 1997, and shows a significant increase in wasting among under five children as well. There is quite strong evidence then for a worsening of health indicators over the 1990s, into the early years of the current decade.

The estimates of income poverty are constructed from GLSS data. The monetary standard of living measure is computed based on total house-hold consumption expenditure per adult equivalent,[2] adjusted for price differences between different months and regions using a Paasche cost of living index. This measure is then compared to an absolute poverty line established using the cost of basic needs method developed by Ravallion and Bidani (1994). More details of these calculations are provided by GSS (2000). The observed decline in the incidence of poverty is statistically significant at the 1 per cent level, and is also qualitatively robust to a wide variety of different choices that can be made in constructing income poverty estimates (for example the choice of the adult equivalent scale, or the data used to adjust for price changes between the two periods; Coulombe and McKay, 2001). The improvements in education enrolments, and in access to potable water and electricity are confirmed by other data sources from those reported in Table 3.2 (even though the definitions and so the levels sometimes differ between surveys). The GLSS surveys also show large improvements in ownership of many household assets (Coulombe and McKay, 2004).

Qualitative sources though indicate a less-positive picture. In Ghana qualitative studies frequently report widely held perceptions of worsening poverty levels and increasing livelihood insecurity (Norton *et al.*, 1995; Kunfaa, 1999). It is inevitably difficult to identify the time horizon over which this assessment applies. Further, the concepts of poverty used by respondents are frequently different, with a stronger focus on vulnerability and food insecurity. So the results are not necessarily in direct conflict. Further, individual perceptions of poverty also often focus on absolute numbers of the poor, while the results here focus on population propor-tions (Kanbur, 2001). In addition, the quantitative results only concern the average; even if wellbeing in some dimensions has improved on average, many may still be worse off. It is also important to remember that quantit-ative surveys compare indicators at two points in time that are not neces-sarily indicative of longer term trends. This is especially an issue in relation to income poverty. That said, there is no reason to think that the years of the third and fourth GLSS surveys are in any way exceptional in terms of climatic conditions or agricultural harvests.

In summary there is quite strong evidence that growth over the 1990s has been associated with poverty reduction in most, but not all dimensions. The 2003 CWIQ survey shows that some indicators such as education and asset ownership have continued to improve into the early years of the current decade and there is some tentative, indirect evidence based on the use of poverty predictors (Cavalcanti, 2005) that this may be the case for income poverty as well.

The distributional pattern of growth in household consumption levels is shown in Figure 3.2 by means of a growth incidence curve. It is important to remember that this only looks at growth in consumption between two specific points in time. With this caveat, the curve shows that at the national level all percentile groups in 1998/99 had higher average consumption levels than their counterparts in 1991/92, and so absolute poverty falls whatever the poverty line. Consequently, Ghana has experienced pro-poor growth in an absolute sense over this period; the rate of pro-poor growth (Ravallion and Chen, 2003) is 2.1 per cent at the poverty line, though would be less at lower poverty lines (the poorest therefore seem to have participated somewhat less in growth). The growth incidence curve shows higher average rates of growth in higher percentile groups, indicating an increase in inequality over this period (consistent with the Gini coefficient above); this is not pro-poor growth in a relative sense. The mean growth rate over

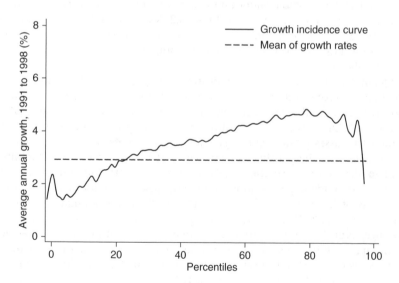

Figure 3.2 Growth incidence curve: Ghana

this period is 3.1 per cent, somewhat higher than the rate of pro-poor growth.

Disaggregation of the pattern of growth and poverty reduction provides an important explanation of the changes that have taken place over this period.

Spatial differentials in growth and poverty reduction

An analysis of the spatial pattern of growth and income poverty reduction in Ghana over this period shows a sharply spatially differentiated pattern (Table 3.3). The disaggregation in this table follows common practice in Ghana, distinguishing urban and rural areas and the three main ecological zones; it also maintains adequate sample size to enable analysis. The survey results show that growth rates in household consumption levels are highest in Accra, the capital city, and the Rural Forest region, the production base for the key export commodities (cocoa, gold, timber) which as argued above have played an important role in growth in Ghana over this period. There was also reasonable growth in the average consumption level of households in the other urban areas in the southern half of the country (coastal and forest zones), but growth in the rural coastal zone and particularly in the northern savannah zone (urban or rural) was much slower over this period. The northern savannah, which was significantly poorer to start with, fell further behind in relative terms over this period – one dimension of the increase in inequality observed in the Gini coefficient above.

The spatial pattern of changes in income poverty follows this pattern of growth. At the disaggregated level, only for Accra and the rural forest region did statistically significant reductions in poverty occur, this being the case for both the incidence and severity measures. There were also reductions in poverty indices in other urban areas in the south (coastal and forest zones) reflecting increases in average consumption levels there, but these changes are not statistically significant at conventional levels; a similar analysis applies to the rural coastal zone. By contrast in the northern savannah region increases in several measures of poverty are observed (poverty incidence in urban areas, where average consumption levels fell; poverty severity in rural areas, notwithstanding a small increase in average consumption). In general it is clear that there has been a clear link between the rate of growth in a locality and its progress in poverty reduction.

A Ravallion–Huppi decomposition of poverty change distinguishing intra-locality and migration impacts (Aryeetey and McKay, 2004) shows that it is the poverty reduction within the rural forest region that has been by far the largest contributor to the national poverty reduction (57.2% of the reduction in the incidence of poverty and fully 86.3% of the poverty severity index). The migration impact of movements between localities has been small.

Table 3.3 Indices of poverty in Ghana by locality, 1991/92 and 1998/99

	Population share		Average growth rate in mean	Incidence of poverty, P_0 (standard errors in parentheses)		Severity of poverty, P_2 (standard errors in parentheses)	
	1991/92	1998/99	1991/92 to 1998/99	1991/92	1998/99	1991/92	1998/99
Accra	8.2	8.8	4.2	23.1 (3.7)	3.8 (1.7)**	1.7 (0.3)	0.2 (0.1)**
Urban Coastal	8.7	7.8	3.1	28.3 (4.0)	24.2 (4.8)	2.4 (0.5)	2.8 (0.8)
Urban Forest	11.0	11.8	3.1	25.8 (3.8)	18.2 (3.9)	2.2 (0.5)	2.0 (0.6)
Urban Savannah	5.3	4.8	−1.5	37.8 (7.2)	43.0 (6.8)	6.9 (3.0)	4.2 (1.0)
Rural Coastal	14.2	14.6	2.0	52.5 (3.4)	45.2 (3.6)	6.7 (0.9)	6.0 (1.0)
Rural Forest	29.6	31.6	4.5	61.6 (2.2)	38.0 (2.8)**	10.6 (0.7)	4.4 (0.6)**
Rural Savannah	23.1	20.6	1.2	73.0 (2.7)	70.0 (5.1)	16.1 (1.4)	17.8 (2.2)
All	100.0	100.0	3.2	51.7 (1.7)	39.5 (2.3)**	8.8 (0.5)	6.6 (0.7)**

Source: Authors' calculations from the Ghana Living Standards Survey, 1991/92 and 1998/99.
Notes: Sample share is expressed in per cent. P_0, P_2 denote values of the P_α poverty indices for $\alpha = 0.2$ respectively. ** denotes changes in poverty between the two years that are statistically significant at the 1% level.

Growth incidence curves at the locality level provide more detailed information by focusing on the distributional pattern of change within localities. Aryeetey and McKay (2004) present the full set of growth incidence curves (though aggregating the three urban regions together because of the small sample size for the urban savannah); those for the rural forest and rural savannah zones are reproduced here as Figures 3.3 and 3.4 respectively. The curves for Accra and the rural forest zone show positive consumption growth throughout the distribution; and in Accra growth was in fact higher in lower percentile groups. In these localities it is evident that many poor households were able to participate in growth.

The shapes of the GICs in the other localities suggest some increase in inequality within the locality in each case, with bigger growth rates in higher percentile groups. The increases in consumption were very modest for households in the lower decile groups in the other urban and rural coastal groupings, implying very limited participation of poor households in growth there. In the rural savannah (Figure 3.4) average consumption levels fell over this period for five of the lowest six decile groups despite reasonable growth performance at the national level and even an increase in average consumption within this locality.

A decomposition of the change in the incidence of poverty into growth and redistribution effects (Table 3.4) highlights the dominance of growth effects in Accra and the rural forest, as well as in the increase in poverty in the urban savannah region. However, adverse distributional change in

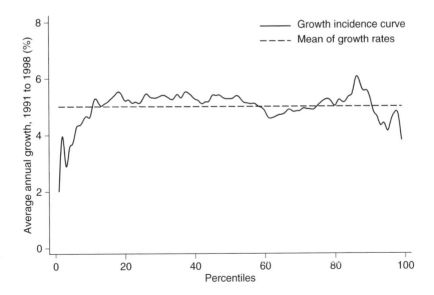

Figure 3.3 Growth incidence curve: Ghana, rural forest

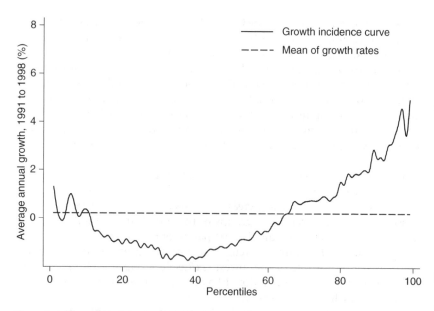

Figure 3.4 Growth incidence curve: Ghana, rural savannah

Table 3.4 Changes in the incidence of poverty, Ghana 1991/92–1998/99, decomposed into growth and redistribution effects, by geographic locality

	Total change	Growth effect	Redistribution effect	Residual
Accra	−19.4	−10.1	−9.3	0.0
Urban Coastal	−4.1	−12.2	+8.1	0.0
Urban Forest	−7.5	−11.2	+3.6	0.0
Urban Savannah	+5.2	+7.6	−2.4	0.0
Rural Coastal	−7.3	−10.5	+3.2	0.0
Rural Forest	−23.7	−22.5	−1.2	0.0
Rural Savannah	−3.0	−4.5	+1.5	0.0
Ghana	−12.3	−13.1	+0.9	0.0

Note: Authors' calculation from the Ghana Living Standards Survey, 1991/92 and 1998/99. The figures presented for the growth and redistribution terms are the average of the 'forward' and 'backward' decompositions, and so the residual term is zero by construction.

other localities reduced the impact of the growth that took place on poverty reduction. The importance of adverse distributional effects for the change of poverty becomes much more important in relative terms when the depth of poverty is taken into account. For example, adverse distributional effects in the urban coastal and rural savannah zones are sufficiently large that the poverty gap and poverty severity indices both increase in the urban coastal and rural savannah regions.

The consequence of these adverse distributional effects within some localities is that the pattern of poverty reduction varies more between localities than does the rate of growth, and the latter is already quite unequal comparing the savannah zone with the rest of the country in particular.

The pattern of change of non-income dimensions of poverty shows less consistent patterns of spatial differentiation (GSS, 2000; Coulombe and McKay, 2004), and for some indicators the northern savannah fares better than other regions. Thus the reduction in health consultations by those ill or injured is not observed in the savannah zone, in contrast to most of the rest of the country. And the biggest increase in net enrolment rates in primary school is observed in this zone, though this partly reflects a significantly lower starting point. The same does not extend to secondary education though. On the other hand the improvements which have occurred throughout the country in household access to drinking water and to electricity have been much less in the savannah zone compared with the rest of the country. Clearly the pattern of change in these non-income indicators is much less directly linked to the spatial pattern of growth. This is expected as the impact growth would have on these indicators is indirect, operating through public revenue and spending. Some of the improvements in these indicators though have reflected aid spending, channeled through government or NGOs.

The spatial pattern of growth in many ways is likely to reflect its sectoral pattern, given spatial concentration of activity. Among the factors identified above as being important for growth in Ghana over this period has been growth in production of export commodities, many of which are currently concentrated in the forest zone. The wider distributional pattern of growth of course depends in part on the fortunes of the sectors in which individuals or employed or can move into; though within sectors of course there is a range of experience. The impact of growth on consumption poverty also depends on other factors such as transfers between households or benefits resulting from increased public spending. The next section analyses the sectoral pattern of growth, trying to link this to the spatial pattern of consumption growth, and considers the factors that have enabled – or not enabled – individuals and households to participate in growth.

Linking spatial trends to the sectoral pattern of growth

It is important to note that Ghana does not publish spatially disaggregated data on economic growth. Neither does it publish material on the spatial allocation of public resources. Determining what investments have been made in Ghana's regions and how these may be linked to growth is currently not possible from the available material. Hence inferences about the spatial distribution of growth can only be drawn from sectoral patterns to the extent that sectoral activities overlap with the regions of the country.

Over the period between the third and fourth rounds of the GLSS surveys, growth was fastest in the services and industrial sector, and slower – though still positive – in the agricultural sector on which the largest number of households are primarily reliant.

The GLSS surveys also collect information on household incomes (Coulombe and McKay, 2004) and so allow an analysis of households' main income sources. The data show that in 1991/92 a majority of all households relied primarily on earnings from agricultural activities, and the proportion of households for whom this was the case had declined only slightly by 1998/99. Analysis of poverty by sector of main employment (Table 3.5) shows that poverty levels are highest by far for households reliant on

Table 3.5 Trends in incidence of poverty by industry of main occupation of household (national accounts classification), Ghana 1991/92 and 1998/99

Main economic activity	Sectoral growth rate	Population share		Incidence of poverty, P_0	
		1991/92	1998/99	1991/92	1998/99
Agriculture	3.0%	53.3	49.3	65.8	54.7
of which:					
Agriculture and livestock	2.8% (cocoa 5.4%)	51.6	46.9	66.8	55.8
Forestry and logging	5.8%	0.8	0.2	20.0	34.4
Fishing	1.8%	0.9	2.2	48.6	33.6
Industrial	4.8%	11.4	13.9	41.4	27.2
of which:					
Mining and quarrying	6.5%	0.8	1.2	29.2	7.1
Manufacturing	3.7%	8.7	10.5	42.6	28.8
Electricity, water & gas	5.1%	0.2	0.3	13.0	23.7
Construction	5.9%	1.6	1.9	45.0	31.8
Services	6.0%	33.3	34.8	34.4	23.8
of which:					
Wholesale and retail trade	7.7%	17.0	18.6	35.2	26.7
Transport, storage & comms	6.3%	2.8	3.4	32.6	10.8
Finance, real estate and business services	5.3%	0.7	1.0	16.6	14.7
Public admin, defense and other services	5.2%	12.8	11.9	34.8	23.6
Non-working		2.0	2.0	24.2	21.0
All		100.0	100.0	51.7	39.5

Sources: Authors' calculation from the Ghana Living Standards Survey, 1991/92 and 1998/99. Growth rate data from IMF Statistical Abstract, 2000.

agriculture compared to those primarily working in the industrial or service sectors.

Looking at changes over this period, in broad sectoral terms the pattern of growth has favoured (i) those in the industrial or services sector, who were less poor to begin with, compared to those in agriculture; or (ii) those (relatively few) households that have been able to move from agriculture into the industrial or services sectors. In spatial terms there were few such households in the northern savannah region.

There are, though, important variations in growth rates by sub-sectors. Within the agricultural sector, there was fast growth in the (export-oriented) cocoa and forestry and logging sub-sectors, but food crop cultivation and fishing have fallen far behind. Given the continued central role of agriculture in the Ghanaian economy, this is clearly one factor behind the fast growth in the forest zone compared to the coastal and savannah zones. Growth over this period was also fast in the mining and quarrying subsector, another export oriented activity much of it conducted in the forest zone of the country, although one with low employment levels. These patterns are clearly linked to a policy stance focused on export promotion and increasing incentives to produce cash crops, but which emphasized much less non-cash crop agriculture. Other fast-growing sub-sectors over this period included construction and most sub-sectors of services, especially wholesale and retail trade. Many of these activities are predominantly urban-based, and much more developed in the southern half of the country compared to the north (which is anyway much less urbanized). Increased imports – received predominantly in the southern coastal ports – have been one important stimulus to the growth of wholesale and retail trade, along with increasing incomes in Accra and other areas. Trade liberalization has been an important factor here.

Quite good progress on poverty reduction is observed in all sectors, including agriculture. Focusing on sub-sectors with sufficiently large numbers of employees, growth in agriculture and livestock; manufacturing; public services; transport and wholesale and retail trade have all made important contributions to poverty reduction over this period. Application of a Ravallion–Huppi decomposition to this data suggests that intra-subsector effects have been much more important in accounting for the poverty reduction than migration effects between locations. Over this period there has also been some movement of households into poverty reducing subsectors, notably wholesale and retail trade, but there has been movement out of other important poverty reducing sub-sectors such as public services. The reduced employment in the latter is a consequence of some retrenchment over this period as part of the structural adjustment programme to reduce the size of public employment and the fiscal deficit. But the government also raised civil service salaries in 1992 (an election year, obviously having an adverse impact on the fiscal deficit), and this was an important factor contributing to the reduction in poverty among this group over the period.

Table 3.6 Trends in incidence of poverty among rural agricultural households, by locality and export position, Ghana 1991/92 and 1998/99

Type of farming	Proportion of households within locality		Incidence of poverty, P_0	
	1991/92	*1998/99*	*1991/92*	*1998/99*
Food crop farmers				
Rural coastal	51.6	44.4	58.0	51.9
Rural forest	48.0	40.7	67.8	47.0
Rural savannah	78.0	72.7	76.7	76.8
Export farmers				
Rural forest	18.1	19.3	67.6	37.4

Source: Coulombe and McKay (2004), computed from the Ghana Living Standards Survey, 1991/92 and 1998/99.

The data for Table 3.5 did not disaggregate poverty change among those working in agriculture by different crops, because households typically cultivate a range of crops. However, if a distinction is drawn between those households cultivating any export crops (chiefly cocoa) from those that do not (Table 3.6), important differences are apparent. First, and unsurprisingly, producers of the main export crops are almost exclusively in the rural forest zone. Second poverty reduction among agricultural households was much greater over this period in the rural forest zone compared to the other rural areas. The reduction in poverty was greatest among export farmers, consistent with the fast growth in the cocoa sub-sector. But there was also a sharp reduction in poverty among food crop farmers in the rural forest zone. By contrast, poverty among food crop farmers in the rural coastal area fell relatively modestly, while it did not fall at all in the savannah zone. Third, over this period there was some movement out of agriculture in all zones as some households obtained more income from other livelihood activities (chiefly a range of non-farm self employment activities), but in the rural forest region more households were harvesting main export crops in 1998/99 compared to 1991/92. This will partly have reflected past replanting decisions, with many households that neglected or removed their cocoa trees in the 1970s, only returning to cocoa cultivation from the late 1980s onwards reflecting better prices and a more favourable policy environment.

A growth incidence curve for export farming households (Figure 3.5) confirms the strong and disproportionate participation by the poor in the fast growth among this group. By contrast a growth incidence curve for food-crop farming households (Figure 3.6) shows (i) a much lower overall level of growth in consumption; and (ii) that what growth did occur was disproportionately in higher percentile groups, with little or no growth in the poorest quintile. This of course partly reflects the spatial patterns discussed above.

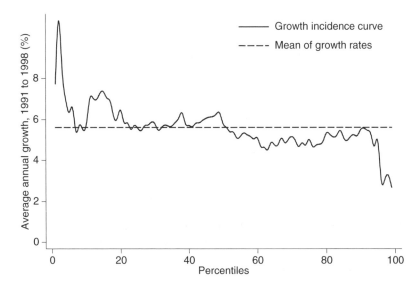

Figure 3.5 Growth incidence curve: Ghana, export farmers

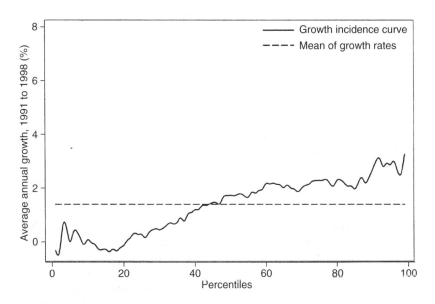

Figure 3.6 Growth incidence curve: Ghana, food farmers

But it also highlights how large numbers of food crop farmers, one of the poorest occupational categories, were unable to participate in growth over this period, so limiting its pro-poor impact.

The analysis of Table 3.6 suggests that there was a significant increase in production levels in food-crop agriculture in the rural forest zone; but further analysis based on income data from the GLSS survey (Coulombe and McKay, 2004) shows that this is not the main driving force of the growth in consumption levels there. Even where food crop farmers were able to participate in growth, income data from the GLSS survey[3] shows that increased agricultural income was not the main driving force. One significant change apparent over the 1990s is the increased receipts by households of remittances from within and outside the country.[4] A sharp increase in remittance income by food farmers in the rural forest, much more than increased agricultural production levels, appears to be the driving force behind poverty reduction among this group. The increase in remittance income is much less in the other rural areas, but it is not clear why this is the case. Thus, where food farmers have been able to participate in growth, much of this has reflected non-agricultural factors.

In Accra, where substantial income poverty reduction occurred over this period, the major household economic activity changes that took place were a significant movement out of public sector wage employment (largely due to retrenchment) and a corresponding increase in self-employment activities (from 51% of the employed workforce in 1991/92 to 63% in 1998/99). The formal private sector expanded little over this period. One of the biggest growth areas was wholesale and retail trade, traditionally a predominantly female activity but which saw increased male participation over this period. There was also an expansion in those working in transport and communications. As well as this increase in participation in these sub-sectors, predominantly on a self-employment basis, earnings also increased substantially, much more so than in other sub-sectors in Accra (Coulombe and McKay, 2004). Between 1991/92 and 1998/99 earnings in trading and transport/communication activities increased in real terms by around 7 per cent and 6 per cent per annum respectively. Important driving factors behind this appear to have been import liberalization and high levels of demand within Accra (reflecting various factors including higher public sector salaries, increased public spending in general, foreign inflows). A corresponding change though is not observed in other areas in Ghana, where the structure of income sources and economic activities is much more stable.

In sharp contrast with Accra and the rural forest, the northern savannah zone saw little progress with poverty reduction over this period, and regress according to some measures. In rural areas where poverty is most severe, households were reliant predominantly on food crop and subsistence agriculture for which growth was slow over the period, and where the savannah zone faces uncertain climatic conditions in some areas, notably the upper east region. Vulnerability and food insecurity are high for many households in this region (a point stressed in the study discussed above by Norton *et al.*, 1995). In 1991/92 three-quarters of households in the rural savannah obtained their livelihood from food crop farming, with limited participation in markets, and around 60 per cent of household income came from agriculture. In each respect the situation had scarcely changed by 1998/99. Market participation in this area is limited. The slow growth in non-export agriculture on which the rural savannah relies, combined with its more difficult environment for farming (greater climatic uncertainties than elsewhere in Ghana, and limited opportunities for many for dry season cultivation in some areas), limited non-farm opportunities and low receipts of remittance income are all key factors accounting for the lack of growth and poverty reduction.

There is some evidence, too, that low growth in the rural savannah zone over this period was strongly associated with remoteness. The savannah region as a whole is more distant from ports which were of central importance in Ghana's export growth over this period (given that exports were predominantly to countries outside Africa), but also important for access to imports (including agricultural inputs and goods for trading). The population in the north is more dispersed than in the south, and households and communities are more remote in terms of access to key facilities (health, education, markets, and roads) than elsewhere in Ghana. But within the savannah zone there is some evidence that growth performance was negatively associated with remoteness. Factor analysis was used to construct a summary index of remoteness of locations based on distance to key facilities as obtained from a community questionnaire: the nearest market, health clinic, junior secondary school, motorable road and location for public transport. Distinguishing more remote areas (index score above the median value) and less remote areas (below the median) shows a clear difference; the average growth rate was negative in the more remote areas, but positive in less remote areas.[5] While tentative, this conclusion makes intuitive sense.

Conclusions

Ghana has now attained 20 years of sustained growth, which is an impressive achievement in relation to other countries in West Africa and especially given the long period of economic decline and political stability that preceded this. Growth in the 1990s was associated with quite significant reductions in income poverty, and in that sense was pro-poor; moreover many non-income indicators also improved over this period. Important policy changes over this period, plus impacts of aid inflows and increased public spending, played an important role in accounting for this growth.

The policy and institutional environment, though, resulted in a pattern of growth with strong sectoral patterns. Export-oriented sectors grew relatively fast in response to the improving incentives over this period, but still with a strong reliance on the traditional exports of cocoa, gold and timber. There was also fast growth in wholesale and retail trade and allied activities such as transport, this being partly a consequence of import liberalization, as well as growth in the construction sector. But in other areas growth was slow, including manufacturing and the large majority of the agricultural sector in which the poor are disproportionately represented. This uneven sectoral growth translated into a highly spatially differentiated pattern of growth. It was also a pattern of growth associated with limited employment creation, reflecting low levels of private investment.

The spatial pattern of income poverty reduction over this period strongly reflects the pattern of growth, with poverty reduction predominantly in Accra and the forest zone. This pattern led to increased spatial inequality over the period, with the northern savannah zone and parts of the southern coastal zone lagging behind. The increase in the income differential between northern and southern Ghana is a matter of concern, given the political sensitivity of this issue in Ghana and the wider West African context. Slow growth and income poverty reduction in the lagging regions seem to reflect a number of factors, including weak performance in agriculture and fisheries, infrastructure weaknesses, import competition and limited scope for non-agricultural activities. There has been though more progress in human development dimensions, in particular in northern Ghana.

There is a sense too that much of the poverty reduction that was achieved over the 1990s in Ghana may have been that which was easiest to achieve, and that continued poverty reduction will be more difficult to achieve. For continued poverty reduction in Ghana and a more inclusive pattern of pro-poor growth in Ghana in the future (which will potentially also be a faster growth as well), much more focus needs to be placed on the growth potential of lagging sectors and regions. In the case of northern Ghana, the largest lagging area, a report by ODI and CEPA (2005) argues that there is considerable potential for growth based on the agriculture and related processing activities, trade with neighbouring countries, mining and tourism; but to date these areas have often not been adequately prioritized in national level policy (agriculture), or where they have the emphasis has been more on locations in the southern half of the country (mining, tourism, trade). To realize the growth potential though, key infrastructure, notably road connections, will be required, as well as investment in effective irrigation schemes. This is likely to be a major challenge, including in political terms, but recent successful experiences in Burkina Faso (whose resource endowment is no better than northern Ghana) can offer important lessons (Grimm and Günther, 2004).

It is also important though for Ghana to create secure employment opportunities outside agriculture, something on which the country had a weak record over the 1990s; the growth in employment was almost exclusively in informal self-employment activities, with limited spillovers. The recovery of the manufacturing sector is important, including in processing activities linked to agriculture. In both cases the continued weak response of private investment (more than 20 years after reform began) is a major underlying cause. This is not due to a lack of investable resources in Ghana or abroad; rather it is associated with other factors such as continued weaknesses in the financial sector; fiscal instability and its macroeconomic consequences; and a long tradition of ambivalent government attitudes to the private sector. Such investment spending may not directly provide many employment opportunities for the poorest, but it does increase the scope for labour movement into higher return sectors, a potentially important aspect of poverty reduction but one which has been limited in Ghana to date.

It is worth noting that some attention is being paid to a number of these issues in the latest Ghana Poverty Reduction Strategy (GPRS II) for 2006–08. The new GPRS II aims to 'achieve accelerated and sustainable shared growth, poverty reduction, gender equity, protection and empowerment of the vulnerable and excluded within a decentralized, democratic environment' (GoG, 2005). It is planned to raise per capita income to at least US$1,000 by 2015. The document highlights the need for structural transformation with a lot of emphasis on modernizing agriculture. Modernized agriculture is indeed expected to serve as the catalyst for structural transformation. It is clear that a more equal faster growth is seen as the way forward, except that no clear new strategy is currently articulated for the task.

But the issue of achieving structural transformation is indeed high on the agenda of government. That will explain why, following the endorsement of GPRS II by parliament in March 2006, the National Development Planning Commission has embarked on a new process of bringing stakeholders together to consider strategies for achieving accelerated growth and structural transformation, with a larger scope than the GPRS. The most significant difference between the proposed new initiatives and earlier interventions of the last two decades is the increasing attention being paid to equitable regional development using private resources. In this regard, the observations made here should help strengthen the process.

Finally, from a methodological point of view, this chapter (like that for Vietnam in this volume) has highlighted the importance of a regionally and sectorally disaggregated analysis in applying core techniques such as growth incidence curves and poverty and inequality decompositions. This then forms a basis for trying to understand the economic, political or institutional factors which cause spatial differentiation. It can also provide a clearer understanding of the national level pattern. Growth is often spatially unbalanced. When the slowest growing regions are also the poorest then this has important implications for pro-poor growth, and its political and economic stability. Slower regional growth may reflect various factors such as resource endowments, proximity to the coast or population density, but some of these factors are endogenous, and the impact of some disadvantages can be reduced by infrastructure investment if growth potential exists (as in this case in northern Ghana). Panel data can help to provide a richer understanding of what enables individuals to participate in growth in more successful regions, and the extent to which households are prevented from making favourable transitions (for example in labour market status, use agricultural inputs or sell more output in the market) in lagging regions. This enables an analysis of individual mobility to complement the insights from growth incidence curves. Panel data can also provide a much richer understanding on vulnerability and its impact on household behavior, clearly a key factor in northern Ghana, as in Burkina Faso and throughout the Sahel region in West Africa.

Notes

1. Note that the analysis focuses only on the third and fourth rounds of the GLSS surveys, and does not consider the first two conducted in the late 1980s. This is because the first two rounds were done with a significantly different questionnaire, so raising concerns about comparability. Adjustments can be made to try to take account of the likely effect of the different questionnaire structure (fundamentally the change in the recall period used to collect consumption data), and this has been done in studies by Coulombe and McKay (1995) and Appiah *et al.* (2000); but concerns always remain about how reliable such adjustments are. For this reason this chapter focuses on the two most recent surveys that were done using essentially the same questionnaire.
2. The adult equivalence scale used here adjusts for differences in calorie requirements according to age and gender using a scale commonly used in nutritional studies in Ghana (National Research Council, 1989). The use of alternative adult equivalence scales, which also try to take account of differences in non-food requirements and which do not make distinction by gender do not change the results presented here significantly (Coulombe and McKay, 2001).
3. There is evidence that income data is underestimated in the GLSS survey in line with many similar household surveys (McKay, 2000). But in this case it still appears to provide a reasonably reliable picture of the composition of household income and its changes over time. Coulombe and McKay (2004) discuss this in more detail.
4. This sharp increase in remittances from within and outside the country is evident from the GLSS surveys, and evidence from other sources (including but not limited to data on external inflows or remittances) attests to the importance of this phenomenon.
5. We are grateful to Louis Boakye-Yiadom for assistance in constructing this index.

References

Appiah, K.S., Laryea-Adjei, G. and Demery, L. (2000) 'Poverty in a Changing Environment', Chapter 16 of E. Aryeetey, J. Harrigan and M. Nissanke (eds), *Economic Reforms in Ghana: The Miracle and the Mirage*. Oxford: James Currey.

Aryeetey, E. and Fosu, A. (2003) 'Economic Growth in Ghana: 1960–2000', mimeo, African Economic Research Consortium, Nairobi.

Aryeetey, E., Harrigan, J. and Nisanke, M. (eds) (2002) *Economic Reforms in Ghana: The Miracle and the Mirage*. Oxford: James Currey and Woeli Publishers.

Aryeetey, E. and McKay, A. (2004) 'Operationalising Pro-Poor Growth: Ghana Case Study', available at http://www.dfid.gov.uk/pubs/files/oppgghana.pdf

Cavalcanti, C.B. (2005) 'Ghana: Recent Trends in Growth and Poverty Reduction', Paper presented at the International Conference on shared Growth in Africa, 21–22 July, Accra, Ghana.

Coulombe, H. and McKay, A. (1995) 'An Assessment of Trends in Poverty in Ghana, 1988–92', PSP Discussion Paper no. 81, Poverty and Social Policy Department, Washington, DC: World Bank, November.

Coulombe, H. and McKay, A. (2001) 'Assessing the Robustness of Changes in Poverty in Ghana Over the 1990s', mimeo, UK Department for International Development and World Bank.

Coulombe, H. and McKay, A. (2004) 'Selective Poverty Reduction in a Slow Growth Environment: Ghana in the 1990s' Paper presented at ISSER-Cornell International Conference on Ghana at the Half Century, Accra, July.

Frimpong-Ansah, J. (1991) 'The Vampire State in Africa. The Political Economy of Decline in Ghana', London: Currey.

Government of Ghana (2003) 'Ghana Poverty Reduction Strategy 2003–2005: An Agenda for Growth and Prosperity', Vol. 1, Accra: Ghana Publishing Corporation, Assembly Press.

Grimm, M. and Günther, I. (2004) 'How to Achieve Pro-Poor Growth in a Poor Economy. The Case of Burkina Faso', Report prepared for Operationalizing Pro-Poor Growth work programme, a joint initiative of AFD, BMZ (GTZ, KfW Development Bank), DFID and the World Bank, Eschborn: GTZ.

GSS (Ghana Statistical Service) (2000) 'Poverty Trends in Ghana in the 1990s', Accra: Ghana.

Hutchful, E. (2002) 'Ghana's Adjustment Experience: The Paradox of Reform', Oxford: James Curry Limited for the United Nations Research Institute for Social Development.

Kanbur, R. (2001) 'Economic Policy, Distribution and Poverty: The Nature of Disagreements', *World Development*, 29/6: 1083–94.

Kunfaa, E. Y. (1999) 'Consultations With The Poor: Ghana Country Synthesis Report', CEDEP, Kumasi, July.

National Research Council (1989) Sub-Committee of the 10th Editions of the RDAs, 'Recommended Dietary Allowances', Washington, DC: National Academy Press.

Norton, A., Bortei-Doku Aryeetey, E., Korboe, D. and Dogbe, D.K.T. (1995) 'Poverty Assessment in Ghana Using Qualitative and Participatory Research Methods', PSP Discussion Paper no. 83, Washington, DC: World Bank.

ODI and CEPA (2005) 'Economic Growth in Northern Ghana', Report for DFID Ghana, prepared by Overseas Development Institute, London and Centre for Policy Analysis, Accra.

Rado, E. (1986) 'Notes Towards a Political Economy of Ghana Today', *African Affairs*, London, 85: 563–72.

Ravallion, M. and Bidani, B. (1994) 'How Robust is a Poverty Profile?', World Bank *Economic Review*, 8/1.

Ravallion, M. and Chen, S. (2003) 'Measuring Pro-Poor Growth', *Economics Letters*, 78/1:93–9.

Shepherd, A., Gyimah-Boadi, E., Gariba, S., Plagerson, S. and Wahab Musa, A. (2004) 'Bridging the North South Divide in Ghana?', Background Paper for the 2005/06 World Development Report, 23 December.

Teal, F. (1999a) 'Why Can Mauritius Export Manufactures and Ghana Not?', *The World Economy*, 22/7.

Teal, F. (1999b) 'The Ghanaian Manufacturing Sector 1991–1995: Firm Growth, Productivity and Convergence', *Journal of Development Studies*, 36/1: 109–27.

Vanderpuye-Orgle, J. (2002) 'Spatial Inequality and Polarisation in Ghana, 1987–99', paper presented at the Conference on Spatial Inequalities in Africa, Centre for the Study of African Economies, University of Oxford, 21–22 September.

World Bank (2004) 'Ghana: Public Policy, Growth and Poverty. A Country Economic Memorandum', Report No. 27656-GH, February 6.

4
Pro-Poor Growth in Vietnam: Explaining the Spatial Differences

*Thomas Bonschab and Rainer Klump**

Introduction

After decades of war, Vietnam was reunited in 1975. But it took another ten years before a comprehensive national development strategy was implemented in 1986 under the name of *doi moi* (renovation). The *doi moi* reforms which paved the way for a transition from a centrally planned to a market economy were remarkably successful. GDP increased between 1987 and 2001 at an average annual rate of 6.8 per cent which made Vietnam one of the fastest growing economies in the world. Over the same period, population growth was significantly reduced leading to the even more impressive rates of per capita growth with a long-term annual average of 5 per cent. Also Human Development Index (HDI) values steadily increased from 0.582 in 1985 to 0.688 in 2000 (Van Arkadie and Mallon, 2003).

The spectacular growth experience was accompanied by a dramatic reduction in aggregate poverty. Before 1986 national poverty in Vietnam stood at over 75 per cent; in 2002 it had fallen below 30 per cent; by 2004 it had further dropped to below 25 per cent. Aggregate income inequality as measured by the Gini coefficient did not increase very much between 1993 (0.34) and 1998 (0.35), but climbed to a value of 0.37 in 2002. All these developments make Vietnam one of the showcases of pro-poor growth, which might serve as model for many other developing countries (Klump, 2006).

Despite its successes on the aggregate level there are signs, however, that pro-poor growth in Vietnam has had strong spatial biases. While poverty has almost been eliminated in some of the dynamically growing urban areas

---

*The authors would like to thank GTZ Hanoi Office and the World Bank Hanoi Office for their support of our field studies in Vietnam, and all members of the OPPG team, in particular Ulrike Männer, Hartmut Janus and Julius Spatz, for many valuable suggestions and comments during the work on the Vietnam case study. Excellent research assistance by Nguyen Thi Thue Anh, Patricia Prüfer and Pham Thai Hung is gratefully acknowledged.

there still remain pockets of extremely high poverty in some of the remote rural parts of the country. It is this spatial pattern of pro-poor growth which is the central focus of this chapter. We start our analysis by looking at the spatial patterns of poverty, growth and pro-poor growth. In this section we calculate explicit rates of pro-poor growth for Vietnam's regions and for urban and rural areas during two sub-periods in the 1990s. It is in these calculations where the regional differences in the pro-poorness of growth in Vietnam become the most obvious, because we even find regions where the rate of pro-poor growth was negative. In the next section we ask for the reasons of the huge spatial differences. Our main analytical tools in this investigation are a statistical decomposition of the change in poverty rates for urban and rural areas and for Vietnam's regions as well as an income convergence analysis conducted for Vietnam's provinces.

The following section then asks for the particular reasons for the pronounced spatial differences in pro-poor growth. We assess a series of factors and policies which have influenced the sub-national development of growth, inequality and poverty. Drawing on results from a spatial Bayesian Model Averaging (BMA) analysis of the effects of potential policy variables on growth and poverty we are able to derive guidelines not only for the most promising policy measures but also for the most effective policy packages in order to achieve higher pro-poor growth. Our last section investigates the policy implications of the spatial imbalances.

Spatial patterns of poverty, growth and pro-poor growth

General spatial patterns and the national household surveys

Vietnam has a total land area of about 331,000 square kilometres, stretching from China in the north to the Gulf of Siam in the south. With a population of 79.7 million in 2002 this means an average density of 240 inhabitants per square kilometre. The country has three major geo-climatic zones: north, central and south. It is composed of over 60 provinces and cities dispersed over seven regions: Northern Uplands (sometimes further divided into North-West and North-East), Red River Delta (including Hanoi), North Central Coast, South Central Coast, Central Highlands, South-East (including the main economic centre Ho Chi Minh City – Saigon) and Mekong River Delta. Vietnam is a multi-ethnic country with the Kinh majority as the dominant group. Kinh Vietnamese make up about 65 million people and live in all provinces though they are particularly clustered in the delta areas and urban centres. More than 10 per cent of the total population belong to one of the more than 50 ethnic minorities, predominantly living in rural areas (Bhushan *et al.*, 2001). Overall, some 20 per cent of the population live in urban areas and 80 per cent in rural areas.

Most of our calculations in the following sections are based on the 1992/93 Vietnam Living Standard Survey (VLSS), the 1997/98 VLSS and the 2002 Vietnam Household Living Standard Survey (VHLSS). The VLSS data is obtained from nation-wide nationally representative household surveys conducted in 1992–93 (October 1992 to October 1993) and 1997–98 (December 1997 to December 1998). The VHLSS 2002 gathered expenditure data from 30,000 households and income data from an additional number of 45,000 households, compared to only 4,800 households in 1993 and 6,000 in 1998. Each survey consists of two components, a household survey and a commune survey. The household survey component provides detailed information on schooling, health, employment, migration, housing, fertility, agro-pastoral activities, non-farm self-employment, food expenses and home production, non-food expenditure and consumer durables, credit and saving and some anthropometric variables. The commune questionnaire includes information on demographic variables, economy and infrastructure, education, health and a separate price questionnaire. In 1992–93, 4,800 households in 150 communes were surveyed. The 1997–98 survey includes 6,000 households (approximately 4,300 households from the original 1992–93 sample) and 194 communes. While the 1992–93 and the 1997/8 VLSSs covered 4,300 surveyed households in both periods and thus allow for some panel dimension, the 2002 VHLSS provides no useable panel data-set. We derive from the VLSS and VHLSS an indicator of living standards measured by annual total household consumption expenditure per capita. All expenditures are adjusted using a regional price index and monthly deflators to give expenditure valued in January 1998 prices. Data from the 2002 VHLSS that were supplied by the General Statistics Office (GSO) and World Bank (WB) already contained these adjustments.

Patterns of inequality and poverty

Table 4.1 gives an overview of the spatial pattern of poverty and income inequality in Vietnam. The income distribution for urban and rural areas increased in a rather parallel way from values of 0.35 and 0.28 in 1993, to values of 0.41 and 0.36 in 2002. Regional Gini coefficients in 2002 are the highest in the South-East (0.42), Red River Delta (0.39) and Mekong River Delta (0.39) reflecting growing income differences in the urban centres and the booming agricultural regions, but they are also quite high in the North-West (0.37) and Central Highlands (0.37).

As the figures reveal, some regions like South-East, Mekong Delta and South Central Coast (all located in the south) had lower incidences of poverty than the national average throughout all periods. Red River Delta joined this group in the second phase of growth. North Central Coast, North-West and North-East (important parts of the north) and Central Highlands in the south are characterized by incidences of poverty higher than the national average in all periods. Red River Delta, South-East and Mekong River Delta, which unite more than 50 per cent of Vietnam's population, have witnessed a dramatic increase in inequality during the last phase of growth.

Table 4.1 Spatial dimensions of poverty and inequality in Vietnam

	Poverty rates (headcount index in %)			Share of population (in %)			Gini coefficients		
	1993	1998	2002	1993	1998	2002	1993	1998	2002
National dimension	58.1	37.4	28.9	100	100	100	0.34	0.35	0.37
Regional dimension									
Northern Uplands	81.5	64.2	43.9	15.6	18	15	0.25	0.26	
North-East	86.1	62	38.4	–	–	12			0.36
North-West	81.0	73.4	68.0	–	–	3			0.37
Red River Delta	62.7	29.3	22.4	21.6	20	22	0.32	0.32	0.39
North Central Coast	74.5	48.1	43.9	12.8	14	13	0.25	0.29	0.36
South Central Coast	47.2	34.5	25.2	12.6	11	8	0.36	0.33	0.35
Central Highlands	70.0	52.4	51.8	3.2	4	6	0.31	0.31	0.37
South-East	37.0	12.2	10.6	12.6	13	15	0.36	0.36	0.42
Mekong Delta	47.1	36.9	23.4	22.4	21	21	0.33	0.30	0.39
Area dimension									
Urban areas	25.1	9.2	6.6	19.9	20.9	23.23	0.35	0.34	0.41
Rural areas	66.4	45.5	35.6	80.1	79.1	76.77	0.28	0.27	0.36

Source: World Bank (2003).

The Northern Uplands also recorded a pronounced jump in Gini coefficients. Only in South Central Coast Gini coefficients grew rather slowly.

Regional poverty incidences are closely related to area poverty rates, since the regions with disproportional reduction in poverty are those with a higher share of urban areas, whereas Central Highlands and North-West are mainly rural regions. The figures show that poverty is still significantly higher among rural households which are the overwhelming majority in Vietnam. After falling slightly during the mid-1990s, the Gini coefficient rose significantly both in rural and in urban areas.

Poverty in Vietnam also has an important ethnic dimension. The regions with the higher poverty rates in 2002, North-West (68%) and Central Highlands (52%), are mainly rural and have a high share of ethnic minorities. The regions with the lowest poverty rates, South-East (11%) and Red River Delta (22%), are located around the main economic centres, Ho Chi Minh City and Hanoi. They are dominated by the Kinh, the ethnic Vietnamese, and to some extent also by an important Chinese minority. However, the development of the North-East region does not fit into this pattern. The North-East is populated by more than one-third of Vietnam's ethnic minorities. Poverty has fallen there quite in line with the national trend from 86 per cent in 1993 to only 38 per cent in 2002. Ethnicity alone can therefore not explain the persistence of extreme poverty.

Spatial trends of pro-poor growth

Real per capita expenditures in Vietnam grew at an annual average rate of 5.5 per cent between 1993–2002. Together with the strong reduction of poverty this results in a growth elasticity of poverty of −0.77. The same message can also be taken from a look at the growth incidence curve in Figure 4.1. As can be seen from the growth incidence curve, all percentiles experienced income growth, even if the increase of income for the rich quantiles was significantly higher than for the poorer quantiles. From the growth incidence curves one can directly calculate the rates of pro-poor growth following the definition by Ravallion and Chen (2003), measuring the average income growth for those quantiles below the poverty line. We find that the rate of pro-poor growth for Vietnam, which is as high as 4.1 per cent per year of the whole period 1993–2002 stood at a value of 5.7 per cent per year for the first sub-period 1993–98 and then fell sharply to only 2.2 per cent per year over the second sub-period 1998–2002 (Bonschab and Klump, 2005).

Since the three Vietnamese household surveys provide data on a spatially disaggregated basis we are able to also calculate spatially differentiated rates of pro-poor growth. First, we look at the rates of pro-poor growth for the urban and rural areas which are presented in Table 4.2. We find that with the relatively stable income distribution in the first sub-period the rates of pro-poor growth do not deviate very much from the mean growth rates. In the second

86

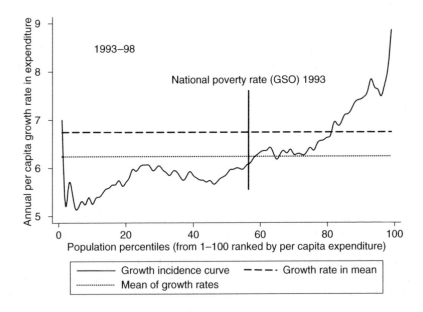

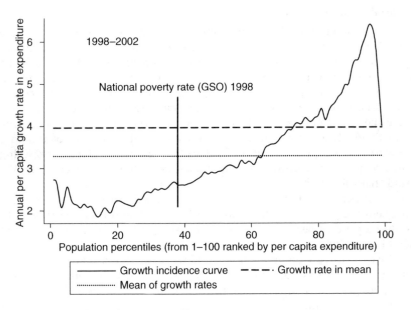

Figure 4.1 Growth incidence curves, Vietnam

Table 4.2 Urban and rural rates of pro-poor growth, Vietnam

Annual area growth rates (%)	1993–98		1998–2002	
	Urban	Rural	Urban	Rural
Growth rate in mean	10.1	5.74	4.74	3.09
Mean percentile growth rate	9.68	5.55	4.25	2.8
Rate of pro-poor growth	8.86	5.25	1.61	2.21
Change in Gini coefficient	−2.8	−3.5	20.6	33.3

Source: Bonschab and Klump (2005).

sub-period we obtain the remarkable result that the mean growth rate is still higher in urban areas than in rural areas, whereas the ranking has changed for the rates of pro-poor growth despite a stronger increase in inequality for the rural areas. The pronounced reduction in the rate of pro-poor growth for urban areas reflects the difficulty to further reduce already low levels of poverty and the rise of new forms of urban poverty. The latter is fuelled, as we will further show below, by the restructuring of urban industries, the volatility of the urban service sectors and a continuous inflow of migrants from poor rural areas.

As can be seen in Table 4.3, the regional variance in the rates of pro-poor growth over the two sub-periods is even more extreme. During the first period it ranges between 12.3 per cent in the South-East and 4.4 per cent in the Mekong River Delta, whereas in the second period the highest value is 5 per cent in the Central Highlands and the lowest is –1.6 per cent in the North-West, both mainly rural regions. While the ranking of the rates of pro-poor growth in the first sub-periods follows almost perfectly the ranking of the mean growth rates, the pattern in the the second sub-period is much more complex, underlining again the very diverse patterns of regional development in Vietnam.

Looking for determinants of spatial differences: spatial decomposition of poverty reduction and provincial income convergence analysis

Spatial decomposition of poverty reduction

Monica Huppi and Martin Ravallion (1991) have proposed a statistical decomposition of poverty reduction which has a particular focus on the spatial dimensions. We applied this method to Vietnam with two different aims; first to distinguish between urban and rural areas, and second to look at the eight Vietnamese regions. Both decompositions indicate the relative gains to the poor within the specific spatial units and the contribution of changes in the distribution of the population across these units. Population

Table 4.3 Urban and rural rates of pro-poor growth, Vietnam

Annual regional growth rates (%)	1993–98							1998–2002							
	Northern Uplands	Red River Delta	North Central Coast	South Central Coast	Central Highlands	South-East	Mekong River Delta	North-West	North-East	Red River Delta	North Central Coast	South Central Coast	Central Highlands	South-East	Mekong River Delta
Growth rate in mean	5.89	9.5	8.12	5.45	4.79	12.37	3.56	4.0	6.95	3.86	1.64	3.51	5.12	4.12	4.53
Mean percentile growth	5.22	8.87	7.06	5.16	4.59	12.42	3.77	1.53	5.69	2.63	1.45	3.73	4.74	3.41	3.41
Rate of pro-poor growth	4.49	8.06	6.23	4.86	4.57	12.32	4.38	−1.64	4.42	1.39	0.47	4.62	5.02	2.55	2.55
Change in Gini coefficient	4	0	16	−8.3	0	0	−9.1	38.5	42.3	21.2	24.1	6.1	19.4	16.7	30

Source: Bonschab and Klump (2005).

Table 4.4   Spatial decomposition of poverty reduction, Vietnam

	1993–1998	1998–2002	1993–2002
Intra-area effects (%)			
Rural	82.2	90.07	82.72
Urban	16.3	6.78	14.16
Total	99.1	96.85	96.78
Inter-area population shifts (%)	1.07	3.84	4.31
Interaction effect (%)	−0.17	−0.69	−1.09
Total intra-regional effects (%)	103.7	93.79	101.09
Inter-regional population shifts (%)	−3.42	14.91	−0.14
Interaction effect (%)	−0.29	−8.7	−0.95

Source: Bonschab and Klump (2005).

shifts between geographical units reflect different patterns of population growth and internal migration, whereas the intra-area and intra-regional effects are calculated as if no population shifts had happened during the period of observation. After adding up both types of effects, a residual can occur which is interpreted as a measure of the correlation between populations shifts and the effects within the spatial units.

The intra-sectoral effects are much higher than the inter-sectoral shift effects, and the interaction effects are all negative (see Table 4.4). The negative sign of the interaction effect means that more pronounced population shifts had a negative impact on the internal factors of successful poverty reduction, because the economically more active among the poor migrated to other locations. However, the pattern is different for the two sub-periods. In the second sub-period the urban contribution to total poverty reduction is more than halved, while the rural contribution has further increased. Also the contribution of population shifts has more then tripled. At the regional level the growing contribution of population shifts, pointing to increasing migration, is even more pronounced. While being negative in the first period, it becomes positive in the second. However, at the same time, the interaction effect has also increased.

A provincial convergence analysis

The three national household surveys are not able to provide reliable data for a dynamic analysis of pro-poor growth on the level of Vietnam's over 60 provinces. This is why in Bonschab and Klump (2004) we used a different data set which allowed at least to analyse the speed of provincial income convergence. As Shupp (2002) has demonstrated for the case of South Africa, there is a natural contribution of regional convergence analysis to the spatial aspects of the pro-poor growth debate. The higher is the rate of provincial convergence, the faster the income differences between provinces are eliminated.

Our provincial convergence analysis is based on a data-set that covers the growth performance of Vietnam's 61 provinces in the period 1995–2000, compiled by Nguyen Van Chinh *et al.* (2002). Based on the accounts of the provincial statistical offices this data-set makes necessary adjustments so that the adjusted gross regional product (GRP) of the 61 provinces and cities sum up to the gross domestic product (GDP) and the regional implicit price indices are compatible with the national implicit price indices.

In order to work with a richer data-set we supplemented our data for real provincial GRP with information on Vietnam's provinces from various other sources. These include regular official information from the GSO as well as internal reports from the Ministry of Planning and Investment (MPI) and the Ministry of Labour, Invalids and Social Affairs (MOLISA). In particular, we used data from the Survey of Labour-Employment 2001, from the Population and Housing Census Vietnam 1999 and from Socio-Economic Statistical Data of 61 Provinces and cities in Vietnam 2001. One data-set on total investment ratios is taken from the 1999 *Human Development Report* of Vietnam published by the National Institute for Social Science and Humanities. Given the problems with data availability and reliability we consulted, wherever possible, data from different sources.

Our first test addresses absolute convergence across Vietnam's provinces. By absolute convergence we mean that – ideally – the forces of a market economy generate higher growth rates in the poorer provinces since capital mobility guarantees that the factors of production react at differences in the relative factor prices[1] With our data for Vietnam the estimate for the speed of convergence of real GRP per capita is as low as 0.3 per cent implying a half-life of 230 years. The convergence rate for real GRP per worker, however, is 1.4 per cent, implying a half-life of 50 years. The results for absolute convergence can be further refined by adding a dummy for provinces in the metropolitan centres. With this simple modification the speed of adjustment for output per capita increased to a level of 1 per cent, implying a half-life of 68 years. This result indicates that the fast growing centres and the poor other provinces belong to two completely different 'convergence clubs'. Using the same dummy together with data for output per worker leads to a speed of convergence of 2.8 per cent and a corresponding half-life of 25 years. Again, the result for GRP per worker is about triple the values for GRP per capita.

This result has two important implications for the assessment of Vietnam's development in the 1990s. First, it is a strong proof of the existent, but still extremely low inter-provincial capital mobility in Vietnam. After more than a decade of transformation neither private capital markets and financial institutions nor the redistributive activities of the central government have been able to overcome the problem of the strong regional clustering of investments. Second, the extreme difference between the convergence rates per capita and per worker must be emphasized. Even more so than in South

Africa, the immediate implication of these finding is that 'the fastest and surest way of reducing income inequality is to promote employment in low income regions' (Shupp, 2002, p. 1713).

Whereas our tests for absolute convergence only compare the level of GRP per capita in the baseline year and the successive growth record, the tests for conditional convergence also consider other possible determinants of growth in a cross-provincial perspective. Important determinants are investment in real and human capital across provinces as well as the growth of the population or the working force. In addition (Table 4.5), we look for particular influences of some interesting structural parameters such as infrastructure and geographical advantages (measured by the availability of electricity and a location dummy variable), the impact of ethnical differences (measured by the ratio of ethnic minorities in the total population) and the impact of asset inequality (measured by the percentage of households living in solid houses). We look for those determinants of provincial growth that are statistically significant and contribute to a faster convergence of the poorer provinces compared to the values in our absolute convergence analysis.

Table 4.5 Test for conditional convergence, Vietnam

Variable	Dependent variable: log difference GRP per worker 1995–2000		
	Coefficients		*t-statistics*
Constant	−0,094		−0,289
ln(YW1995)	−0,072**		−2,361
ln(I/GRP)	0,029*		1,733
ln(School)	0,109*		1,750
ln($nw+g+\delta$)	−0,234***		−3,953
Electricity	0,43***		3,447
Urban	0,134**		2,619
House index	−0,304**		−2,219
Ethnic	0,174*		2,150
Geographical dummy	0,074*		1,794
Adjusted-R^2		0,59	
Standard error		0,09	
Observations		61	

Notes: *** (**) (*): Coefficients are significantly different from zero at 1% (5%) (10%) level; YW 1995 is GRP per worker in 1995; I/GRP is total investment as a share of GRP in 1999; School indicates the percentage of working-age population in the education system in 1999; ($g+\delta$) is the sum of growth of technical progress and rate of depreciation; it is assumed to be 0.06; nw is the growth rate of workers averaged for the period 1995–2000; Electricity indicates the percentage of rural communes having electricity in 1998; Urban indicates the percentage of urban population in total population averaged for the period 1998–2000; House index indicates the percentage of households having permanent houses in 1999; and Ethnic indicates the percentage of minorities in total population in 1999.

The influence of income per worker in 1995 (the pure convergence effect) is about the same as in the absolute convergence analysis, whereas the growth effect of total investment is weak but significantly positive. Again, this result underlines that the capital mobility across Vietnam's provinces is extremely low so that most provinces can only converge to a steady state that is conditional on their own rate of investment. On the other hand, we find a high, and also highly significant, positive effect of human capital formation and a high and significantly negative effect of labour-force growth. Infrastructure, measured by the access to electricity and the adherence to an urban area, are significant variables. The ethnical variable is positive and significant, but is highly correlated with the growth of the working population. A significant dummy variable finally measures the effects of special geographical advantages such as being a coastal province or being close to one of the metropolitan centres.

Assessment of factors and policies contributing to sub-national development differences

Various factors and policies have been identified as potential determinants of sub-national differences in income and poverty levels. In the first part of this chapter we give a short overview of their effects. We start with the factors of production, then continue with sectoral strategies, specific regional policies and the effects of migration. Finally, we analyse the effects of targeted social policy measures.

Earlier analyses were not able to decide which factors and policies, individually and in combination, were the most important ones and should thus be regarded as key elements of future development efforts. This is why we make use of a new analytical tool; Klump and Prüfer (2006) have applied a method of Bayesian econometrics, the so-called Bayesian Model Averaging, to Vietnam's provinces in order to find out the most probable determinants of pro-poor growth. We use their results in order to determine the most effective policy package for further growth and poverty reduction.

Population and birth rates

As for most other developing countries, unskilled labour is the most abundant asset of Vietnam's poor. This asset is mostly utilized in agricultural employment, which means that land is the dominant complementary factor of production. Indeed, much of Vietnam's early success in pro-poor growth was exactly owed to the increased employment of unskilled labour in the agricultural sector. However, since the shortage of arable land sets natural limits to this development strategy, further achievements in broadly shared growth had to rely much more on complementing unskilled labour by skilled labour and/or capital.

The availability of unskilled labour is determined by the growth of the population. In a very general perspective Vietnam's achievements in aggregate per capita growth and poverty reduction relied on a drop in population growth from a yearly average of 2.2 per cent in the early 1980s to 1.5 per cent in the late 1990s. The slow-down of fertility and population growth can be traced back to the combined effects of the economic reforms, which raised the opportunity costs for having children, the higher mobility of the population and the introduction of special measures of family planning (White *et al.*, 2001). In 1988 the Vietnamese government officially proclaimed the 'two-child policy' and adopted a comprehensive population policy under the Family Planning Programme (FPP). FPP became a national target programme, under which specialized health centres at the level of commune or districts were financed. Total public expenditure for FPP, as a percentage of total public health costs, increased from 3.5 per cent (1992) to 10.2 per cent (1999). However, the birth rate in rural areas is higher than in the urban centre; and it is much higher among the poor ethnic minorities creating some kind of Malthusian poverty trap.

Land reform

Throughout the 1990s, significantly more than 50 per cent of the poor lived in rural areas and depended primarily or exclusively on employment in agriculture. Estimations as to the exact share of the agricultural employment in total employment differ, but range between around 60 per cent and some 50 per cent (Glewwe, 2004). This made land the strategic complement for a successful pro-poor growth strategy. One of the pivotal steps in the *doi moi* reform process towards a market economy was therefore the decollectivization of farmland. Following Resolution 10 in 1988, land-use rights were granted to individual households, and the land was distributed in a remarkably egalitarian way (Ravallion and Van de Walle, 2001). Later on, the new Land Law of 1993 laid the foundations for the growth of a market for land in rural Vietnam. The new law instituted the issuance of land-use certificates to all rural households, enabling them to inherit, transfer, exchange, lease and mortgage their land-use rights. By the year 2000 nearly 11 million land titles have been issued, making this one of the largest titling programmes in the developing world, not only in scope but also in the speed of implementation (Quy Toan Do and Iyer, 2004). However, the implementation of the new Land Law was characterized by pronounced provincial differences reflecting not only differences in bureaucratic capacities, but also interprovincial differences in the handling of disputes. Where it happened, the improvement of land-related property rights had strongly pro-poor effects since it contributed to a higher diversification of rural incomes. It could be shown that in provinces with a more advanced issuance of land-using rights farmers invested more long-term (in multi-year industrial and fruit crops) and could also devote more labour to non-farm activities (as a result of higher productivity in farming) (Quy Toan Do and Iyer, 2004). In contrast, the lack of secure property rights on forestry land is another important reason for the persistence of poverty among those ethnic minority groups who live in mountainous areas where the use of forestry land is the main source of income (Swinkels and Turk, 2004).

Geographic reasons set natural limits in Vietnam to a development strategy which is purely based on agriculture. Although new arable land could be gained between 1980 and 2000, rural population growth and the extension of agricultural employment led to an overall worsening of the labour–land ratio. The rapid expansion of agricultural production in the early reform period has already induced greater scarcity of sown area and considerable erosion and pollution. The problem of erosion is particularly visible in the sloping-hill soils in central and northern Vietnam. More intensive research for cultivar development and crop and land management, which would raise the productivity of given arable land, is highly needed (Fan *et al.*, 2003).

Human capital

Given the relatively high scarcity of land, broad-based growth in Vietnam had to be based also on other complements to unskilled labour, namely skilled labour and capital. One heritage of the socialist era is a literacy rate which is very high by international standards. Even in the poorest quintile more than 70 per cent of adults can read. The literacy rate dropped for the first two quintiles between 1993 and 1998. Illiteracy became more and more concentrated in the bottom quintiles, leading to a higher concentration of poverty, whereas the top quintiles were able to take better advantage of their new opportunities. Enrolment rates of the poorest quintile and of ethnic minorities started from such low values that even with high growth rates they have not been able to catch up with the national average. Other data show signs of growing inequality in lower secondary schools across the provinces and a gender gap in upper secondary enrolment. Growing regional inequality can be explained by the changing financing structure of education. Whereas communes and districts administrate primary schools, the provinces run the more costly secondary education. Given the high and still growing income differences, financial resources of the provinces differ enormously.

Capital

If we turn to capital formation, it is interesting to note that although gross investment ratios in Vietnam have doubled from 15.0 per cent in 1991 to 30 per cent in 2000, this process went along with an increasing share of state investment, which is now more than 60 per cent of the total. FDI peaked in the mid-1990s with a share of over 30 per cent, but then fell back to less than 20 per cent, which is also the share of domestic non-state investment. The development of a private capital market was the least successful part of the reform programme. In July 2000, Vietnam established a new stock exchange in Ho Chi Minh City, but so far only a few enterprises have been listed and the trading floor is still fairly quiet (Klump and Gottwald, 2003). As our provincial convergence analysis has revealed, intra-provincial capital mobility was so weak that existing differences in capital productivity were not eliminated (Bonschab and Klump, 2004). This result can be explained by the underdevelopment of formal financial institutions and financial markets and the relative inefficiency of informal institutions. It is hard to measure exactly how much money is mobilized through the informal sectors but it is evident that especially the rural sector and small economic activities are facilitated through informal credits. Most informal credits are provided either by wealthy private moneylenders, by mutual lending among family members, friends or neighbours or by so-called ROSCAS ('rotating savings and credit associations', that is family or commercial-based self-help groups pooling money). Whereas mutual family/friend lending and ROSCAS lending is associated with low or zero interest, private moneylenders often take considerable interest rates. However, the informal sector is often considered to be superior to the formal sector. The 1993 VLSS lists that 73 per cent of all households rely on informal credits. Moreover, the emerging private sector often uses the informal sector as a source of capital financing. There are various reasons for the relative persistence of the informal sector. First of all, the formal sector rarely satisfies credit needs for consumption. Poor farmers, for example, who need money due to poor harvest after a natural disaster or due to illness or a wedding, do not easily receive emergency credit from formal lenders. In the absence of available sources of credit, they turn to informal lenders even though these may charge high interest rates (Wolz, 1999).

Agricultural policy

Agricultural policy in Vietnam is traditionally dominated by rice policy. In more recent times, especially after signing the bilateral trade agreement with the USA, fishery and farmed fishery have become more important, both with considerable growth of output value (GSO, 2003). However, rice has a special importance in the agricultural sector, as many households at the bottom of the income distribution chain depend on it as either consumers and/or producers. Moreover, the government has a pronounced interest in issues related to rice since rice policy is associated with ensuring food security, at least since rice had to be imported in large amounts during the near-famine conditions in north Vietnam in 1987. The reform process in the 1990s was marked by crucial shifts in the rice policy. In line with the opening up of the economy and the liberalization of markets, restrictions on rice exports and on internal barriers to trade in rice were relaxed, leading to an increase in real prices of rice. At the same time constraints to import fertilizers were reduced, so that prices for chemical fertilizers fell. Both price changes induced an overall output growth in rice of more than 20 per cent and increased the incomes of farmers (Macours and Swinnen, 2002). This development was backed by the extension of tenure security on land use and Vietnam's further integration into world agricultural markets.

Both the new land policy and the new rice policy spurred a development in which the most readily available factors of production – unskilled labour and land – could be more effectively used in the production process. Rice production has continuously being growing since the late 1980s. Vietnam was the country with the fastest increase of rice output in the world in the 1990s. According to the Food and Agriculture Organization (FAO), Vietnam's growth rate of rice output in the 1990s was 5.3 per cent, as compared to 1.5 per cent in Pacific Asia. The growth in production contributed to rising exports, in volume and value, at least until the Asian crisis, when international demand dropped and export prices fell. Between 1992 and 1998 Vietnam's rice export values increased on average by 9.2 per cent per year.

The overall household income growth during this period had a distinct regional pattern. Most notably, rural households in the south experienced an income growth of 95 per cent, whereas the rural north experienced a considerably lower growth of 55 per cent. The ratio between north and south rural income fell to 0.69. There are various causes which explain the inequality dynamics inherent to the expansion of agricultural production between 1992 and 1998 (Benjamin and Brand, 2004). First, the expansion of output and the integration into world agricultural markets was accompanied by commercialization of the farm sector. This strategy was particularly implemented in the south. As household survey data show, already in 1998 far more than half of crop output was marketed in the south (South Central Coast, Central Highland, South-East and Mekong River Delta), compared to only one-third in the north (World Bank, 2003). Until 2002 the south further increased commercialization of crop output while the north did not proceed very much further. This pattern can be regarded as one explanation for relatively high rates of pro-poor growth in the southern regions of Vietnam in the last survey period. Second, regions producing a rice surplus tend to benefit from increasing rice prices while rice deficit regions lose. The specialization was very pronounced in the south (particularly South Central Coast, South-East and Mekong River Delta), with only the Red River Delta producing some surplus in the north. Third, higher rice prices had ambiguous effects on the poor. On the one hand they generated higher income for rice-producing households, but they also increased the costs of the main food for poor. While such benefits and costs are shared relatively equally among households of the same type, the data suggest that the net benefits are higher for the many southern households specializing on rice production. This last point may partly explain the finding that the drift towards intra-regional inequality is slower than the one for inter-regional inequality.

Industry and services

During the first phase of *doi moi* employment elasticity of growth was highest in agriculture. But agriculture also had to accommodate rural youth without other employment and was burdened by workers retrenched by state-owned enterprises (SOE) reform, so that productivity in agriculture in this period was rather low. Some of the retrenched workers were absorbed by the service sector, which was still very small and grew with high rates and low productivity. In the second period, total productivity growth strongly increased and leading to rising incomes. Highest sectoral productivity growth in this phase was in industry, but employment growth in industry remained moderate since some sectors were capital intensive, state-owned and/or import-substituting. Thus employment elasticity of industry remained low. After the Asian crisis private sector development began to increase employment in industry and services, while productivity in these sectors fell. Agriculture reduced its employment but realized the highest productivity growth. The relative decline of agriculture's share in GDP and the growing shares of industry and services were accompanied by a rise of wage-employment among Vietnam's labour force (Gallup, 2002). In 1998, wage labour was the main source of income for about 18 per cent of households and between 1992 and 1998 average hourly wages increased by an astounding 10.5 per cent per annum. But again, there is a distinct regional pattern to this. The two cities Hanoi and Ho Chi Minh City make up for 25 per cent of the entire wage labour market and allow for a wage premium of upto 80 per cent over rural areas. They are also the areas with the highest wage differentials. In contrast, outside the large and medium-sized cities a decreasing wage inequality between the two surveys could be observed.

Private-sector development

With regard to Vietnam's future growth it is important to look at the dynamics in the private sector. In 1991 the first enterprise law was implemented. Subsequently, a steady stream of firm creations of around 5,600 registrations per year could be observed. In 2000 a significant amendment of the enterprise law was introduced that simplified registration processes and licensing rules. The result was striking, as average yearly registration figures tripled to nearly 19,000 firms between 2000 and 2002. This increase in firm registration led to a shift in the employment structure (Klump, 2003). While in the period from 1995 to 1999 private domestic firms created only 4–5 per cent of jobs, this figure is estimated to have reached 15–30 per cent in the period 1999 to 2001. Importantly, this growth seems to have provoked a shift of job-creation away from household enterprises. However, thus far this shift has had limited impact on overall labour markets. Currently, private domestic enterprises absorb only 2.8 per cent of entire employment. Modelling the job composition with the presently observed 21,000 new firms per year until 2010 shows that this proportion would grow to 8.8 per cent.

Comparing this figure with the performance of other transition economies reveals that this share is too small to achieve effective results.

There is a distinct geographic pattern in the registration of new enterprises. Hanoi and Ho Chi Minh City contributed only 30 per cent of firm creations between 1997 and 1999. After the amendment of the enterprise law in 2000 this figure doubled to 60 per cent. The neighbouring provinces accounted for an additional 15 per cent. Thus, since 2000 only 25 to 28 per cent of new firm creations occurred in genuinely rural provinces where most of the poor live. The main reasons for the shift of firm registration in the urban centres are the better infrastructure of cities (e.g. financing, access to customers) and more capable administrative processes. On the other hand, the spread of new enterprises among provinces is unequal and wider than the spread of FDI, suggesting that more dynamic provinces find it easier to take advantage of this new development (Dapice, 2003).

Development of focal economic areas

Since 1997 the Vietnamese government has given directives for the creation of three focal economic areas in the north, the south and in Central Vietnam. These areas, formed out of particular provinces should produce over-average high economic growth rates and should lead the process of industrialization and modernization of the whole economy. The Prime Minister issued special instructions and directives for the development of these three focal economic areas in 1997, 1998 and 2003:

- The first focal economic area in the north includes Hanoi, Haiphong, Quang Nninh, Bac Nninh and Vinh Pphuc. It is to focus on export-oriented industries and services. High-tech parks should help to boost value-added manufacturing industries and services. Infrastructure should be modernized, including the deep-water sea-port in Cai Lan, airports and highways.
- The second focal economic area in the south initially included in 1997 only Ho Chi Minh-City, Dong Nai, Binh Duong and Baria-Vungtau. In 2003 the Prime Minister extended this area and added the three provinces of Tay Ninh, Binh Phuoc and Long An. It is the most important industrial and service center of the country and should play a role in economic cooperation with Cambodia and other ASEAN economies.
- The third focal economic area in Central Vietnam was established by the Prime Minister in 1997 and includes the provinces of Da Nang, Thua Thieu-Hue, Quang Nam and Quang Ngai. It should link the Central Highlands with deep-water seaports and should serve as an access to Cambodia, Laos, Northern Thailand and Myanmar once an appropriate road infrastructure has been built. While Ho Chi Minh City and Hanoi

were obvious candidates for the development of a growth pole, the development of the central pole is the result of deliberate government activities in order to expand industrial development in the poorer provinces of the central coast. There is some traceable motivation for investing into an additional growth pole in the centre of the country. Historically, the city of Hue was the capital of the Vietnamese empire for over a century and Da Nang has always been one of the most important ports along Vietnam's coast. A major step for the development of the central pole was the decision, taken in 1994, to establish Vietnam's only oil refinery in Dung Quat, in the south of Da Nang. This investment has cost some $130 million a year.

The three focal areas are of central importance for the development record of the country. Their share in GDP rose from 42.5 per cent in 1990 to 46.6 per cent in 1995 and 54 per cent in 2002. Their contribution to GDP growth is 60 per cent, their contribution to the growth of industrial production is 72 per cent and 59 per cent to the growth of the service sector. In the three growth poles 88.5 per cent of domestic investment and 96 per cent of FDI is realized, they are responsible for 80 per cent of Vietnam's exports and 67 per cent of state income (Le Dang Doanh, 2004). The southern pole is responsible for 33 per cent, the northern pole 23 per cent and the central pole only 2.5 per cent of total GDP. It is planned to increase these is figures to 35 per cent, 23.5 per cent and 4.6 per cent, respectively, which would mean almost a doubling of the importance of the central zone.

Migration

As in most comparable countries, a strong, steady flow of *internal migration* constitutes in Vietnam the main link between the three growth poles and the high-poverty rural areas. According to data collected by the 1999 Population and Housing Census, covering all provinces (CCSC 2000), 4.5 million people – 6.5 per cent of the total 1999 population aged five years and older – moved residence between 1994 and 1999. The true numbers would presumably be much higher if non-registered and temporary migrants had been taken into account.

As opposed to pre-reform official measures to encourage migration from the over-populated delta regions, most migration in the 1990s was spontaneous, some of it made easier by the reforms that enabled households to sell farm land and buy urban property to which they moved. The movement came in response to gaps in employment opportunities and income levels, with the young and people from the more educated parts of society making up the majority of the internal migrants. More than half (52 per cent) of all migrants were under 25, and only 10.5 per cent were older than 45, compared with 48 per cent and 20 per cent respectively for the non-migrant population. Not surprisingly, ethnic minorities tend to migrate less and account for only 4 per cent of all the recorded movement. The overwhelming majority, around 60 per cent of the migrants, start to work in the private sector.

By funneling this supply of cheap labour into the growth zones, migration generally helps widen pre-existing spatial growth gaps. Vietnam's rural Central Highlands region, however, provides an example of significant migration drawn by the coffee boom in the late 1990s (Hardy, 2003) serving to generate the highest regional rates of pro-poor growth at that time. Conversely, the tide of migrants has also created new faces of poverty in the urban areas. HCMC and Hanoi especially have been swamped by the large flow of migrants for whom the cities have been unable to provide sufficient infrastructure and other services (World Bank, 2003; ILO *et al.*, 2003). Local governments' efforts to discourage additional migration by denying permanent registration or imposing other administrative barriers channel more and more migrants into living and working in the informal sector where they are not only confined to unskilled, low-paid and low-security jobs, but also are ineligible for public services, exemption from school fees and so on, with a lack of access to housing with water and sanitation infrastructure (Oxfam, 2003; Anh *et al.*, 2003).

Nevertheless, strong positive effects on poverty reduction in poor rural areas stem from the remittances that migrants send back to their families. Survey data for 1998 reveal that those payments constituted 60–70 per cent of the total cash income of rural households (IOS, 1998). The remittances often serve as the most important source of poor, rural families' cash income and significantly reduce such families' vulnerability. The funds are usually used for consumption – like buying basic food – rather than for investment. From this perspective the flow of remittances can be understood as a highly pro-poor redistribution mechanism that builds on Vietnam's strong family ties and the acceptance of migrants to compensate for hardships in crowded cities by improving the well-being of those left in rural villages (Oxfam, 2003).

Public pro-poor spending

Areas of public pro-poor spending with a particular eye on spatial imbalances are the Public Investment Programme (PIP), the special National Programme for Hunger Eradication and Poverty Reduction (HEPR), the Programme 135 for commune-level investments and special programmes for ethnic minorities administered by the Commission for Ethnic Minorities and Mountain Areas (CEMMA). The growth and poverty effects of Vietnam's Public Investment Programme (PIP) between 1996 and 2000 (summing up to more than 200 large-scale investment projects with a value of more than 300,000 billion VND.) have only recently been studied (Larsen *et al.*, 2004). Given the rising state investment ratio in Vietnam after the Asian Crisis together with the reduced annual growth rate a purely macroeconomic analysis would find clear signs of an increasing incremental capital–output ratio. A microeconomic perspective on the level of provinces is able to stress the externalities and network effects that are related to large infrastructure investments. It is estimated that spending an additional 1 per cent of GDP in public investment has been associated with a proportionate reduction in poverty in the order of 0.5 per cent. The study also highlights the high regional imbalances. While more public investment went to the richer provinces the poverty effects of PIP had been much higher in the poorer provinces (between two and three times). Hence a reallocation of public investment to the poorer provinces could improve general poverty.

Despite the provision of special funds for areas with a high share of ethnic minorities, the poverty rate among most ethnic minorities remains high or is even growing. Standard growth strategies seem to miss out the particular needs of these groups that belong to the very poor in Vietnam. Special funds that CEMMA channels to 'minority areas' quite often do not reach the minorities, but rather go to Kinh majority households living in that area. Poor ethnic minorities and the Kinh majority seem to work with fundamentally different models of income generation (Van de Walle and Gunewardena, 2001). If these differences are not taken into account by very specific interventions the effectiveness of the special programmes will remain weak. This is particularly true for the North-West where the rates of pro-poor growth have even been negative during the second sub-period of measurement.

The National Hunger Eradication and Poverty Reduction Programme (HEPR) was officially implemented in 1998 coordinating and integrating various other public initiatives at a central level that had already originated much earlier. Some of the programmes are targeted to poor households directly, other are targeted to poor communes. Examples of the first kind are the provision of 'poor household certificates' and of 'health insurance cards' that both give entitlement to free medical treatment in public hospitals. Other programmes within HEPR provide partial or full exemption to school fees or access to subsidized loans from the Bank of the Poor which has in the meantime been renamed the Social Policy Bank. In 2001, HEPR merged with the Employment Creation Programme to become HEPR-JC. In particular, the education fee exemption programme within HEPR has a high coverage rate, reaching almost one-seventh of all poor and one-fifth of the food-poor and it has a statistically significant effect on school enrollment among the children of the beneficiaries (World Bank, 2003). The selection of the poor households happens in a very decentralized way by commune representatives and village chiefs leading to a high degree of participation and social control.

Programme 135 was also created in 1998. It is a national socio-economic development programme to technically and financially assist poor communes, especially in remote and mountainous areas. Its resources have been used for irrigation, schools, construction of commune centers and so on. It is thus of particular relevance to the implementation of decentralization programmes and for public investment programmes in rural areas. It consists of grants that finance small-scale infrastructure investments in poor and remote communes. It is funded on an annual basis with resources transferred directly to the communes and districts. Problems with participation and control have led to cases of misuse. Funds were positively correlated to the wealth of the regions and most funds went into agricultural production. Only a tiny fraction went into non-farm activities.

An analysis of the static and dynamic incidence of pro-poor spending in Vietnam comes to very sceptical conclusion, though (Van de Walle, 2004). Given that available funds at the local level mainly depend on the relative development level social transfers will not contribute actively to a catching-up of the poorer areas. More is spent relatively and absolutely on the poor in the better-off communes. At the same time, the existing system of social transfers is ineffective in protecting households that are vulnerable to falling living standards. A higher efficiency of social transfers in reducing poverty would require not only a better monitoring at the local level, but also a higher level of risk-pooling at the national level and redistribution via the central state budget. Also in this area the future of pro-poor spending in Vietnam will thus be extremely dependent on future institutional changes in the state sector.

A BMA analysis of the most probable determinants of growth, poverty and pro-poor growth

Based on our spatial growth and poverty analyses we have seen that a wide range of factors seem to exercise an influence on pro-poor growth in Vietnam. What is interesting from a policy perspective, however, is to know which variables, alone or combined with other variables, have most probably the strongest influence. Given the high degree of parameter and model uncertainty in the traditional analyses we would like to base our policy recommendations on a new analytical tool which was developed and implemented to the case of Vietnam by Klump and Prüfer (2006). This new approach relies on the application of Bayesian econometric methods. In particular it applies the method of Bayesian Model Averaging (BMA) which was pioneered by Férnandez, Ley and Steel (2001), Léon-Gonzalez and Montólio (2004) and Mansanjala and Papageorgiou (2004, 2005). Using provincial data from the 2002 VHLSS we first select those variables having the highest solitary impact on growth and poverty and also the most appropriate combination of variables in a model of growth and poverty. Comparing the best regressors and models of the two BMAs for growth and poverty, we are then able to determine the most effective policies for achieving pro-poor growth.

BMA does not require selecting a particular subset of regressors, that is, a special model. All inference is averaged over models, using the corresponding posterior model probabilities (PMPs) as weights. Given a set potential explan-atory variables, BMA separately identifies models that are expedient to explain poverty and growth, by allowing for any subset of the explanatory variables to combine in a regression and to estimate the posterior model probabilities of any such combination of regressors. Conditional on the PMPs, the issue of model uncertainty concerning the most efficient means of poverty alleviation and of growth can be resolved by estimating the posterior probabilities of all possible explanatory variables commonly used.

Table 4.6 presents the results from the growth and the poverty BMA. In combining the relevant informations from both BMAs we find support for birth control, private-sector development, SOE restructuring, promoting metropolitan areas and a further reorganization of the agricultural sector as important instruments of a successful pro-poor growth policy package. The reorganization could happen through a further implementation of the land reform, a broadening of land markets or the intensification and a diversi-fication of agricultural production in order to make the most efficient use of the available land. Regarding the influence of the pro-poor programmes we find some influence on poverty and even growth, but this influence is unclear and not very pronounced, supporting the view that the particular

Table 4.6 Most probable determinants of growth and poverty in Vietnam, 2002

	Growth BMA	Poverty BMA
Most probable parameters	• per capita household expenditure, 1998 • private business implementation • share urban population • birthrate • share locally managed SOEs • life-expectancy • south dummy • population without access to sanitation	• birthrate • land Gini • programme 135 • HEPR • implementation of land reform • south dummy
Additional parameters from most probable models	• share centrally managed SOE • government consumption • public expenditure on health	• share centrally managed SOEs • share agriculture in provincial GDP • share urban population • share ethnic minorities • household expenditures on education

Source: Klump and Prüfer (2006).

pro-poor policies show a significant lack of efficiency and should therefore be reformed.

Conclusions and outlook

The major problem in Vietnam's highly successful growth process emerges from the existing and growing regional imbalances. As we have documented, the three officially recognized growth poles in the South-East, the Red River Delta and to a much more less extent in South Central Coast around DaNang have been the dynamic centres that have attracted most foreign and domestic investment. Vietnam's prospects to catch up with the richer world and to modernize its economy seems to hinge on the development within these growth poles, as they have become the centres of innovation and attract a better-educated labour force. As a matter of fact, policies in favour of less-developed regions will be increasingly difficult to justify on grounds of pure growth objectives. On the other hand, with most of the poor still living outside the growth centres the pro-poorness of growth rather calls for a more even distribution of growth. A study of the spatial dimensions of poverty in Vietnam finds that 96 per cent of the variation in district-level poverty rates can be explained by differences in district-level average per capita expenditure (Minot *et al.*, 2003). Hence poverty reduction in the poor areas can best be achieved by supporting broad-based economic growth in all regions of the country.

The different effects of high, but unevenly distributed growth and more evenly distributed growth on overall poverty reduction have been documented in poverty projections on the basis of data from the VLSS 1997/98 (Agarwal and Beard, 2001). The results under different scenarios can be seen in Figure 4.2 . Under the base-case scenario which assumes an average overall growth rate of 5 per cent real GDP growth, a growth elasticity of poverty as high as 1.3 per cent and a constant regional distribution of poverty, the national poverty can be reduced to 20 per cent by 2010 as has been planned in Vietnam's CPRGS. A higher overall growth rate of 7 per cent with constant regional imbalances would naturally result in a lower national poverty rate of only 15 per cent by the same year. A more uneven distribution of regional growth, with the two most prosperous regions (South-East and Red River Delta) growing at an average of 5 per cent, while South Central Coast (with the third growth pole) grows at half that rate and the remaining other regions grow only at an average of 1 per cent would of course lead to higher poverty imbalances and a reduction of the national poverty rate to only 23 per cent by 2010. The best results in these poverty projections are achieved, however, by a strategy of equally distributed growth. If a uniform growth rate of 5 per cent could be realized over the whole (urban and rural) population of each region, so that the rate of pro-poor growth for all percentiles would be

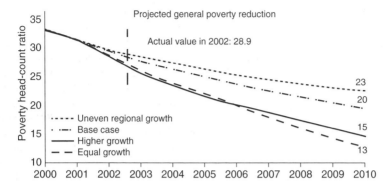

Figure 4.2 Poverty projections, Vietnam 2000–10

Source: Centre for International Development (2002) on the basis of data from Agarwal and Beard (2001).

equal to the mean growth rate, the national poverty rate could be lowered to 13 per cent by 2010.

Today we are able to identify onto which path of poverty reduction Vietnam has moved since 2000. Regional imbalances in growth increased until 2002, with North-West, North Central Coast and Central Highlands increasing their share in total poverty. Average GDP growth over the period 1998–2003 has been more than 6.5 per cent (CIEM, 2004) and hence much closer to the high-growth path than to the base case. On the other hand, the growth elasticity of poverty dropped in Vietnam after 1998. On the basis of an elasticity value of 1.2 per cent the World Bank has calculated that the two effects together would slightly increase the 2015 poverty rate under the high-growth scenario of 7 per cent annual growth to a value of 16 per cent (World Bank, 2003). The same report also develops a 'forward-looking scenario' of the high-growth case, where ethnic minority households in rural areas have a much lower expenditure increase than the rest of the country. This leads to an estimated national poverty rate of 21 per cent in 2010. Given the uncertainty about continuous growth at such high rates as have been realized in Vietnam over the past 15 years, and the high probability of a further fall in the growth elasticity of poverty, the scenarios can only give a very rough idea of the possbile trade-off. However, the projections are supportive of the view that more poverty reductions could be achieved with less growth if this growth is more evenly distributed over the Vietnamese population. This makes it interesting to look at the ways of how existent distributional imbalances can be reducing in the most effective way.

More decentralization of political power and responsibilities was regarded by the Vietnamese government as an important prerequisite for lower regional imbalances. However, the actual implementation of decentralization is still far from optimal. First, the coordination of the fiscal, administrative and political dimensions of decentralization does not seem to be a high priority in the overall planning of the decentralization process. There is no clear vision on how to deal with decentralization in a concerted way, expressed for example in a legal document that would serve all dimensions as a framework for further reforms (Fritzen, 2002; Fforde, 2003). Second, there is almost unanimous complaint about widespread bureaucratic resistance to transferring decision-making authority and resources to lower and lowest levels (Vasavakul, 2002; Fritzen, 2002; Fforde, 2003). Most national poverty-alleviating programmes, like the Programme 135 to assist the poorest communes or HEPR, are implemented in a rather top-down manner. The arguments from government, provincial and district officials resisting to hand over discretionary power to the village level range from the complaint that local people would deviate from agreed plans to the point that the lack of education and required skills to manage decentralized funds is common at communal level. There are probably also some selfish interests involved in such statements as line ministries at each level prefer a strong command-and-control orientation in order to control revenues via state-owned enterprises (Fritzen, 2002). Attitudes might be changing in this regard, but there is some tension between the official government position to promote decentralization and the statements of many relevant government units that communes are incapable of managing their own poverty reduction funds. However, one should not expect decentralized budget planning to work equally efficiently in all provinces and communes without prior training programmes. The lack of knowledge in handling budget issues calls for capacity-building rather than essential scepticism. Third, the increasing regional imbalance resulting from Vietnam's economic growth threatens to make decentralization a reform programme that works in a highly selective manner in favour of better-off areas. Wealthier areas have been more effective in targeting their poor than poorer areas, spending more in relative and absolute terms to their poor (Van de Walle, 2002). Some poor localities, especially in mountainous provinces like the Northern Uplands and the Central Highlands, have difficulty in providing basic standards in education and health due both to a lack of independent opportunities to raise money and limited capacities to make use of the opportunities made available through decentralized managing of national poverty reducing programmes.

Finally, it should be noted that the availability of better spatially differentiated data and of innovative methods for analysing the determinants of spatial imbalances and their implications will be helpful for a successful reshaping of Vietnam's reform programme. However, as we have noted in this chapter, even the existing data allow interesting and deep insights into the growth, inequality and poverty dynamics and into the probably most effective policy packages. The availability of more and better data from the last household survey in 2004 will further improve the preconditions for quantitative analyses in Vietnam.

Note

1. Gundlach (1997) found a speed of convergence of about 2 per cent for output per worker across Chinese provinces which implies a half-life of the reduction in income differences of about 35 years. According to Balisacan and Fuwa (2003) the speed of convergence for per capita expenditures in the Philippines is about 11 per cent per year, implying high inter-provincial capital mobility and a half-life of only 6 years. For South Africa, Shupp (2002) estimates a speed of interregional convergence of around 1.5 per cent for per capita income (half-life of 46 years) and of 2.5 per cent for income per worker (half-life of 28 years).

References

Agarwal, N. and Beard, J. (2001) Halving Poverty and Eradicating Hunger by 2010, Paper prepared for the Poverty Task Force Vietnam, Hanoi.
Anh, D. *et al.* (2003) 'Migration in Vietnam. A Review of Information on Current Trends and Patterns, and their Policy Implications', Hanoi (www.eldis.org/static/Doc).
Asian Development Bank (2001) *Human Capital of the Poor in Vietnam*. Manila: ADB.
Balisacan, A.M. and Fuwa, N. (2003) 'Growth, Inequality and Politics Revisited: A Developing-Country Case', *Economics Letters*, 79: 53–8.
Baulch, B. *et al.* (2003) 'Poverty and Inequality in Vietnam: Spatial Patterns and Geographic Determinants', Washington, DC: (www.ifprl.org/divs/mtid/dr/200312map/dr200312mapall.pdf)
Baulch, B. *et al.* (2004) 'Ethnic Minority Development in Vietnam: A Socioeconomic Perspective', in P. Glewwe *et al.* (eds) *Economic Growth, Poverty, and Household Welfare in Vietnam*, Washington, DC: World Bank Regional and Sectoral Studies: pp. 273–310.
Bhushan, I. Bloom, E. Huu, N.H. and Thang, N.M., (2001) *Human capital of the poor in Vietnam*. Manila: ADB.
Bonschab, T. and Klump, R. (2004) 'Chasing a Better Pro-Poor Growth Strategy for Vietnam: A Provincial Convergence Approach', in M. Krakowski (ed), *Attacking Poverty: What Makes Growth Pro-Poor?* Baden-Baden HWWA-Studies 75, Nomos Verlagsgesellschaft: pp. 171–96.
Bonschab, T. and Klump, R. (2005) *Operationalizing Pro-Poor Growth: Country Case Study Vietnam*, Eschborn: GTZ.
CCSC (Central Census Steering Committee) (2005) *Population and Housing Census Vietnam 1999. Sample Results*, Hanoi.
Centre for International Development (2002) *Vietnam Poverty Analysis*, Canberra and Sydney.
Chinh, N.V., Viet, V.Q. Van T. and Hoang, L. (2002) *Vietnam's Economy in the Years of Reform*, Hanoi.
CIEM (Central Institute for Economic Management) (2002), *Firm Level Survey*, Hanoi.
CIEM (Central Institute for Economic Management) (2004), *Vietnam's Economy in 2003. A Reference Book*, Hanoi.
Conway, T. (2004) 'Politics and the PRSP Approach: Vietnam Case Study', ODI Working Paper 241, London.
Cox, D. (2004) 'Private Interhousehold Transfers in Vietnam', in P. Glewwe *et al.* (eds) *Economic Growth, Poverty, and Household Welfare in Vietnam*, Washington, DC: World Bank Regional and Sectoral Studies: pp. 567–603.
Dang, N.A. (2001) *Migration in Vietnam: Theoretical Approach and Evidence from a Survey*, Hanoi: Communication Publishing House.

Dapice, D. (2003) *Vietnam's Economy: Success Story or Weird Dualism? A SWOT Analysis*, Harvard: Harvard University.

Doanh, L.D. *et al.* (2002) *Explaining Growth in Vietnam*, Mimeo, GDN/CIEM, Hanoi.

Doanh, L.D. (2003) *Options for Managing Revenue Losses and Other Adjustment Costs of CLMV Participation in AFTA: The Case of Vietnam*, Mimeo, CIEM, Hanoi.

Doanh, L.D. (2004) *Vietnam auf dem Weg der Wirtschaftlichen Reform und der Internationalen Integration*, Hanoi.

Fan, S., Huong, P. L. and Long, T. Q., (2003) *Government Spending and Poverty Reduction in Vietnam*, IFPRI/CIEM Project Report, Hanoi.

Férnandez, C., Ley, C.E. and Steel, M.F. (2001) 'Model Uncertainty in Cross-Country Growth Regressions', *Journal of Applied Econometrics*, 16: 563–76.

Fforde, A. (2003) *Decentralization in Vietnam – Working Effectively at Provincial and Local Government Level. A Comparative Analysis of Long An and Quang Ngai Provinces*, report prepared for the Australian Agency of International Development, Canberra.

Fritzen, S. (2002) *The 'Foundation of Public Administration'? Decentralization and Its Discontents in Transitional Vietnam*, Hong Kong: National University of Singapore.

Gallup, J.L. (2004) 'The Wage Labor Market and Inequality in Vietnam in 1990s', in P. Glewwe *et al.* (eds), *Economic Growth, Poverty, and Household Welfare in Vietnam*. Washington, DC: World Bank Regional and Sectoral Studies, pp. 53–94.

General Statistical Office (2003) *Statistical Yearbook*. Washington, DC: GSO.

Glewwe, P., Agrawal, N. and Dollar, D. (eds) (2004) *Economic Growth, Poverty, and Household Welfare in Vietnam*, Washington, DC World Bank Regional and Sectoral Studies.

Goletti, F. and Minot, N. (2000) *Rice Market Liberalization and Poverty in Vietnam*, Washington, DC: International Food Policy Research Institute.

Gundlach, E. (1997) 'Regional Convergence of Output per Worker in China: A Neoclassical Interpretation', *Asian Economic Journal*, 11: 423–42.

Hardy, A. (2003) *Red Hills. Migrants and the State in the Highlands of Vietnam*, Singapore: University of Hawaii Press.

Haughton, J. (2004) *The Effects of Rice Policy on Food Self-Sufficiency and on Income Distribution in Vietnam*, draft version available on http://mail.beaconhill.org/~j_haughton/RiceArt3.pdf

Hung, N. (1999) *The Inflation of Vietnam in Transition*, Centre for ASEAN Studies Discussion paper No 22, Ho Chi Minh City.

ILO, UNDP, UNFPA (2003) *Internal Migration: Opportunities and Challenges for Development in Vietnam*, Discussion Paper, Hanoi.

Institute of Sociology (IOS) (1998) *Migration and Health Survey Vietnam 1997*, Survey Report, Hanoi.

International Monetary Fund (2004) *Vietnam: Evaluation of the Poverty Reduction Strategy Paper (PRSP) Process and Arrangement under the Poverty Reduction and Growth Facility (PRGF)*, Washington DC: IMF.

Justino, P. and Litchfield, J. (2003) *Welfare in Vietnam During the 1990s: Poverty, Inequality and Poverty Dynamics*, PRUS Working Paper No. 8, Sussex.

Kerkvliet, B.J.T. and Marr, D. (eds) (2004) *Beyond Hanoi: Local government in Vietnam*, Singapore: Institute of Southeast Asian Studies.

Klump, R. (2003) *Was Growth Pro-Poor in Vietnam? – Assessments and Policy Recommendations*, Eschborn: GTZ Report .

Klump, R. (2006) 'Pro-Poor Growth in Vietnam: Miracle or Model?', in T. Besley, and L. Cord, (eds), *Pro-Poor Growth – Lessons from the 1990s*, New York (in press).

Klump, R. and Gottwald, K. (2002) 'Financial Sector Reform in Vietnam', in M.J.B. Hall, (ed), *The International Handbook on Financial Reform*, Cheltenham: Edward Elgar.

Klump, R. and Anh, N.T.T. (2005) *Patterns of Provincial Growth in Vietnam, 1995–2000: Empirical Analysis and Policy Recommendations*, Working Paper, University of Frankfurt.

Klump, R. and Prüfer, P. (2006) *How to Prioritize Policies for Pro-Poor Growth: Applying Bayesian Model Averaging to Vietnam*, Working Paper, University of Frankfurt.

Kovsted, J. *et al.* (2003) *Financial Sector Reforms in Vietnam: Selected Issues and Problems*, CIEM and NIAS Discussion Paper No. 301, Hanoi.

Larsen, T. *et al.* (2004) *Vietnam's Public Investment Program and its Impact on Poverty Reduction*, Hanoi.

Macours, K. and Swinnen, J. (2002) 'Patterns of Agrarian Transition', *Economic Development and Cultural Change*, 50: 265–94.

Mansanjala, W. and Papageorgiou, C. (2006) *Rough and Lonely Road to Economic Prosperity. A Re-examination of the Sources of Growth in Africa Using Bayesian Model Averaging*, Working Paper, Baton Rouge: Louisiana State University.

Minot, N. and Baulch, B. (2004) 'The Spatial Distribution of Poverty in Vietnam and the Potential for Targeting', in P. Glewwe *et al.* (eds), *Economic Growth, Poverty, and Household Welfare in Vietnam*, Washington, DC: World Bank, pp. 229–72.

MPI and MOLISA (2001) *National Target Programme*, Hanoi.

MPI (2003) *Vietnam: Growth and Reduction of Poverty*, Hanoi.

Oxfam (2003) *Migration – A Viable Livelihoods Strategy of the Poor Men and Women in Rural Areas*, Draft Report: Hanoi.

Pingali, P.L. and Xuan, Vo.-T. (1992) *Vietnam: Decollectivization and Rice Productivity Growth*, Economic Development and Cultural Change, 40: 697–718.

Ravallion, M. and Chen, S. (2003) 'Measuring Pro-Poor Growth', *Economics Letters*, 78: 93–9.

Ravallion, M. and van de Walle, D. (2001) *Breaking up the Collective Farm: Welfare Outcomes of Vietnam's Massive Land Privatization*, World Bank Policy Research Working Paper 2710, Washington, DC: World Bank.

Ravallion, M. and Huppi, M. (1991) 'Measuring Changes in Poverty: A Methodological Case study of Indonesia during an Adjustment Period', *World Bank Economic Review*, 5: 57–82.

Shupp, F.R. (2002) 'Growth and Income Inequality in South Africa', *Journal of Economic Dynamics and Control*, 26: 1699–720.

Skeldon, R. (1997) 'Rural to Urban Migration and its Implication for Poverty Allevi-ation', *Asia-Pacific Population Journal*, 12/1: 3–16.

Socialist Republic of Vietnam (2002) *The Comprehensive Poverty Reduction and Growth Strategy (CPRGS)*, Hanoi.

Steering Committee of CPRGS (2003) *Vietnam: Growth and Reduction of Poverty: Annual progress Report 2002–2003*, Hanoi.

Swinkels, R. and Turk, C. (2004) *Poverty and Remote Areas: Evidence from New Data and Questions for the Future*, background paper for the PAC Conference, 24–26 November, Hanoi: World Bank.

Tam, L.M. and Vinh, N.D. (1999) 'Remittances and the Distribution of Income', in D. Haughton, J. Haughton, R. Bales, T. T. C. and N. N. Nga (eds), *Health and Wealth in Vietnam. An Analysis of Household Living Standards*, Singapore, pp.167–81.

UNDP (2001) *Human Development Report 2001: Making Technologies Work for Human Development*, New York.

UNICEF (2003) *Reaching Out for Change*, Hanoi.

van Arkadie, B. and Mallon, R. (2003) *Vietnam – A Transition Tiger?*, Canberra.

van de Walle, D. (2004) 'The Static and Dynamic Incidence of Vietnam's Public Safety Net', in P. Glewwe *et al.* (eds), *Economic Growth, Poverty, and Household Welfare in Vietnam*, Washington, DC: World Bank Regional and Sectoral Studies: pp. 189–228.

van de Walle, D. and Gunewardena, D. (2001) 'Sources of Ethnic Inequality in Viet Nam', in *Journal of Development Economics*, 65: 177–207.

Vasavakul, T. (2002) *Rebuilding Authority Relations: Public Administration Reform in the Era of Doi Moi*, Hanoi.

Wagstaff, A. and Nguyen, N.N. (2004) 'Poverty and Survival Prospects of Vietnamese Children under Doi Moi', in P. Glewwe *et al.* (eds): *Economic Growth, Poverty, and Household Welfare in Vietnam*, Washington, DC: World Bank Regional and Sectoral Studies: pp. 313–50.

White, M.J., Djamba, Y.K. and Anh, D.N. (2001) 'Implications of Economic Reform and Spatial Mobility for Fertility in Vietnam', *Population Research and Policy Review* 20: 207–28.

Wolz, A. (1999) *Achievements and Problems of People's Credit Funds in Vietnam*, Diskussionsschrift 71 der Forschungsstelle für Internationale Wirtschafts- und Agrarentwicklung e.V.. Heidelberg.

World Bank, (2003) *Vietnam Development Report 2004: Attacking Poverty*, Washington, DC: World Bank.

Part II

Price Shocks, Policy Reforms and Political Economy

5
Turning Devaluation into Pro-Poor Growth: Senegal (1994–2002)

*Jean-Paul Azam**

Introduction

Senegal is a typical example of a slow-growth/high-stability economy, like many others in the CFA (Communauté Financière d'Afrique) zone. This economy shares some of the features of the Sahelian countries, like its agriculture dominated by groundnut exports, and frequent droughts. Nevertheless, its coastal position gives it a definite advantage for industrial development. It is the closest Sub-Saharan African economy to the main European markets by sea, which has also given rise to a long tradition of out-migration, with a resulting large inflow of remittances (Manchuelle, 1997). Hence, many non-agricultural sources of income have allowed this country to be one of the most urbanized in Africa, with almost 50 per cent of its population living in the urban sector. Its capital city, Dakar, was the capital city of the French AOF (Afrique Occidentale Française) in colonial days, and still plays a prominent role in the UEMOA (West African Economic and Monetary Union). It hosts in particular the headquarters of the BCEAO (Central Bank of West African States). Being a medium-sized country, by the standards of West Africa, Senegal reflects quite accurately the evolutions of the UEMOA economies, as far as its macroeconomic experience is concerned, without affecting them much in return. Nevertheless, its relatively high level of industrial development and of urbanization give this country some relevant idiosyncratic features. In particular, in contrast to many neighbouring countries, agriculture plays here a secondary role in determining growth, while manufacturing and services are playing a central part.

Moreover, it is by far the most democratic country of the region, with competitive elections taking place on schedule with very limited violence (Ka and Van de Walle, 1994; Azam, Dia and N'Guessan, 2002). The first two

*Useful comments by Michael Grimm and Stephan Klasen are gratefully acknowledged. Any remaining errors are obviously mine.

presidents after independence, Leopold Senghor and Abdou Diouf were members of the socialist party. However, the latter was a more technocratic 'modernizer' than the poet-President Senghor, whose development strategy was more focused on cementing national unity through a clientelist regime than on the development of an efficient economy. Until 1993, the ballot was not really secret and a lot of social pressure was exerted on voters, especially in the groundnut basin (Schaffer, 1998). There, the Mouride brotherhood controlled the votes, and benefited from a long-lasting clientelistic relationship with the government (Boone, 2003). The re-introduction of the secret ballot in 1993 improved the working of the democratic institutions. The last presidential elections saw the replacement of the socialist Abdou Diouf by the liberal Abdoulaye Wade, who took over in April 2000.

The only serious stain on the democratic reputation of the Senegalese government since independence has been the problem of lower Casamance (Boone, 2003). This region is predominantly peopled by an ethnic minority, the Diola, whose social system is very different from the hierarchical Sahelian social organization characteristic of the other ethnic groups. The latter is based on a typical caste system with a well-defined ruling elite. The numerically dominant Wolof group is already marginally different from the typical Sahelian type. Their religious leaders overthrew the traditional aristocracy in the course of the eighteenth century, giving rise to the current domination by the Sufi brotherhoods. But the Diola, like the smaller groups also present in the area, are radically different. They have no traditional hierarchy, and resist any type of authority. The Muslim brotherhoods, which play a crucial role in the political control of the rest of the country, are powerless in this region. There is thus no basis on which the typical African system of political management, relying on the co-optation of the traditional elite into the government-sponsored clientelistic system, can be grafted onto such an ethnic group (Boone, 2003). The attempts made by the different governments in Dakar to administratively control this area, with an increasing military presence, ended up in a low-intensity civil war, and many civilians were killed by both sides in the 1980s and 1990s. Hence, this potentially rich region, fit for export agriculture as well as for tourism and fishery, has remained relatively underdeveloped. A peace agreement was signed in March 2001 but lower Casamance is the region of Senegal with the highest incidence of poverty (République du Sénégal, 2004).

This chapter aims at analysing Senegal's medium-run growth experience over the last decade of the twentieth century, with a focus on its impact on the poor. This experience reflects very largely that of the UEMOA, beside some idiosyncrasy as mentioned above. Therefore, the major macroeconomic event that took place over this period is the 1994 devaluation of the CFA franc. In many respects, this draws a clear dividing line between a 'before' and an 'after', that is two periods characterized by a very different macroeconomic adjustment strategy.

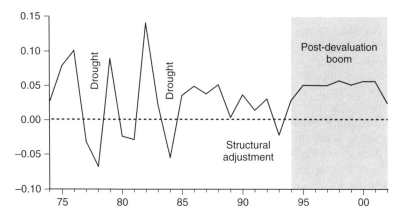

Figure 5.1 Senegal's growth experience, 1974–2002 (GDP, % per annum)
Sources: Berthélemy *et al.* (1996), IMF (2003, 2000, 1996).

Figure 5.1 depicts the growth experience of Senegal over nearly three decades starting in 1974. Three phases can clearly be identified: (i) the instability phase, until 1984, (ii) the 'real-side' structural adjustment phase, 1985–93, and (iii) the post-devaluation boom. Hence, the devaluation was a clear success, from a macroeconomic viewpoint, as it entailed a significant turnaround from low and unstable growth to a sustained boom. The instability phase is marked by a series of external shocks, including the groundnuts and phosphates boom, in the wake of the 1974 oil shock (Azam and Chambas, 1999). The subsequent downturn is punctuated by two severe drought periods, in 1978 and in 1983–84, as well as by the world recession of 1980–81. Although Senegal implemented a first stabilization plan as early as 1979, with some support from the Bretton Woods institutions, it is not until 1985 that the government got seriously involved in the adjustment effort (Rouis, 1994; Ka and Van de Walle, 1994). Moreover, a serious banking crisis occurred all across the UEMOA in 1987 and 1988, which seems to have given a 'wake-up call' to the political elite of the Zone, entailing the emergence of a genuine 'ownership of reforms' in some of these countries (Azam, Biais and Dia, 2004). As a result, structural adjustment really started in Senegal in the late 1980s, and included among other reforms the privatization of several parastatals (Azam, Dia and N'Guessan, 2002).

However, in most countries of the CFA zone, the main problem of the 'real-side' adjustment policy (that is without changing the exchange rate) was the inability of the governments to cut significantly their wage bills. The wages and salaries of the civil servants and the public sector employees were cut only in some countries during that period, and only by a marginal percentage. The high level of these wages was correctly perceived as the main adjustment problem by many analysts (e.g. van de Walle, 1991; Azam, 1995;

Rama, 2000). This problem had two important dimensions. One was that the government wage bill was then consuming an excessive share of fiscal resources, while these wages were also exerting a strong influence on those of the formal sector. Rama (2000) has shown how the wage rates in the civil service and the public sector play a leading role in the determination of the cost of labour for the whole formal sector, and thus significantly affect its competitiveness.

Unfortunately, while reforms were seriously starting in some of the countries of the zone, the terms of trade of the most important CFA economies deteriorated markedly, and for several years from 1987 on (Azam, 1997). In particular, the terms of trade of Côte d'Ivoire deteriorated severely, with a depressing influence on the whole UEMOA area (then UMOA). The early 1990s thus witnessed a relatively disappointing growth experience, which ended in a serious recession in 1993, affecting more or less the whole UEMOA zone. Together with some uninspired policy decisions, which are spelt out in Azam (1997), this made the 1994 devaluation unavoidable. The latter had been postponed for a long period, and was largely anticipated by the relevant agents in the area.

The post-devaluation boom resulted in a sustained growth episode and a significant reduction in poverty. The survey data for Senegal do not allow as thorough an analysis of the dynamics of poverty over the relevant period as that performed on Côte d'Ivoire and Niger in Azam (2004). There are two high-quality surveys, performed in 1994/95 (ESAM 1) and in 2001/02 (ESAM 2), which allow for a correct poverty analysis in this country, but both of them took place unfortunately after the devaluation had taken place. Table 5.1 shows the change in poverty observed between these two dates. These poverty measures are computed from the ESAM datasets using the so-called FGT measure, due to Foster *et al.* (1984).[1]

Table 5.1 thus shows that the response of poverty to the fast recovery of growth was significantly positive over the medium run. The poverty measures are computed separately for Dakar, Other Cities and Rural, in order to control for differences in the relevant consumer price index. They are then

Table 5.1   Change in poverty, Senegal 1994/95–2001/02

	National		Dakar		Other cities		Rural	
	1994	*2002*	*1994*	*2002*	*1994*	*2002*	*1994*	*2002*
Head-count (P_0)	67.9	57.1	56.4	42.0	70.7	50.1	71.0	65.2
Poverty gap (P_1)	23.6	18.3	17.7	12.0	24.4	16.1	25.3	21.4
Poverty depth (P_2)	10.6	7.9	7.4	4.7	10.8	6.9	11.7	9.4

Source: Republique du Sénégal (2004).

aggregated at the national level. The table 5.1 shows that the fall in poverty is significant for each sector and each measure.

The next section brings out the main impact of that devaluation, showing that the first-order effect was a massive cut in the real wages of public-sector employees, which spilt over to the rest of the formal sector. I then show how this entailed a positive growth response, thanks to a timely boost in public investment, before considering the main problem with the Senegalese pro-poor growth policy, namely the lagging response of perceived poverty. This lagged response probably played a part in the democratic ousting of the government that engineered the favourable investment policy mentioned above. A final section concludes by drawing some lessons from the Senegalese experience.

The main impact of the 1994 devaluation

As shown econometrically by Azam and Wane (1999), the devaluation had very little impact on relative consumer prices, and its main effect was a highly significant cut in real wage rates in the formal sector. That analysis was performed for Côte d'Ivoire, Niger and Senegal only. However, it seems quite representative of the events that took place in most countries of the CFA zone. The following discussion gives the flavour of the argument.

Figure 5.2 depicts the real prices of food, clothing and transport and other services in Dakar, in logarithm terms. Taken together, these prices account for 79.8 per cent of the basket of goods included in the CPI. This graph

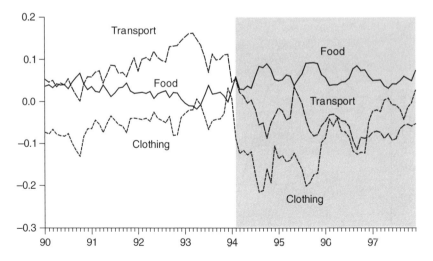

Figure 5.2   Real consumer prices, Dakar (logarithms)
Source: Computed from IMF (1996, 2000).

provides a mixed picture of the effects of the devaluation on relative prices. There is some evidence of real depreciation, if one regards clothing as a non-traded good. Then, we observe an increase in the real price of food, a tradable good, by a few percentage points. There is a more sizable fall in the real prices of transport, more or less representative of the non-tradable service sector, by about 10 per cent. A similar fall had taken place just before the devaluation. However, the real price of clothing falls even further, by more than 10 per cent, while it is hard to believe that this is really a non-traded good. Maybe the trading margins are the dominant component of the price of clothing, explaining this real fall. However, the clothes 'made in Sandaga', the Dakar clothes-producing informal sector, can be found all over West Africa. Moreover, the transport index is in fact mainly comprised of public transports, which account for 40 per cent of this item. The data show that this is the price that mainly lagged behind inflation, because it was fully controlled. Lastly, one observes a convergence of the food and transportation indices at the end of the period, suggesting that the change in relative consumer prices was over at the end of the fourth year after the devaluation. Hence, careful examination of these real prices suggests that putting too much confidence on a story emphasizing real exchange rate adjustment would be unwarranted. Moreover, the relative consumer price changes are at best of short duration, and cannot explain the longer stretch of growth during the post-devaluation boom. Much more significant is the change in real wages and salaries in the formal sector.

Figure 5.3 shows the time profile of the real average wage of civil servants in Senegal. The sharp fall entailed by the devaluation comes out

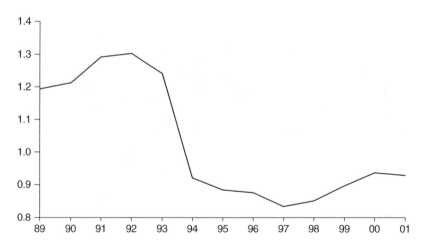

Figure 5.3   Real average wages of civil servants, Dakar (logarithms)
Source: Computed from IMF (2003, 2000, 1996).

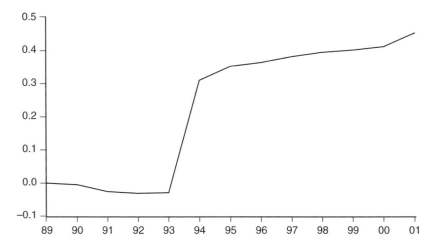

Figure 5.4 Consumer price index, Dakar (end of year, logarithms)
Source: IMF (1996, 2000, 2003).

clearly as well as the subsequent stagnation at a level close to 40 per cent below its peak 1992 value. The 1994–97 period is marked by a continuous decline, as the devaluation was progressively affecting consumer prices, while nominal wages were fixed. A slight recovery, by about 10 per cent, occurred subsequently until the year 2000. Figure 5.4 shows how the consumer price index in Dakar, used for deflating the average wage of civil servants in Figure 5.3, responded to the devaluation. Therefore, beside its obvious macroeconomic dimension, the 1994 devaluation is a remarkable shock affecting the distribution of income, particularly in the urban sector. In the late 1980s, public sector wages were about 10 times higher than average GDP per capita, in Senegal, and in several other UEMOA countries (Azam, 1995). It was even higher in some of them (for example 15 times so in Burkina Faso). This ratio fell drastically in the wake of the devaluation, as public-sector wages fell by about 40 per cent, in real terms, while GDP per capita increased continuously by more than 2.5 per cent per annum.

As Figure 5.1 showed, the post-devaluation boom was remarkably long-lasting. In particular, together with Benin, another democratic regime among the UEMOA countries, Senegal did not experience the recession of the year 2000 that plagued the economies of the zone. The next section shows that a public investment boom, made possible by the improved budgetary situation entailed by the devaluation, played a crucial part in boosting growth and keeping it going after 1997. It is only after this additional impulse was given by the government that private investment picked up significantly, turning the post-devaluation boom into a lasting growth episode. Hence, the expected competitive effect of the devaluation did not materialize entirely, as export agriculture did not respond as expected, as its share in GDP fell. In the meantime, its fiscal effect played the central part, through the fall in the real value of the government wage bill, which in turn freed the resources that financed the increased public investment.

The determinants of pro-poor growth in Senegal

The post-devaluation boom sketched above presents a striking example where a sustained economic recovery ends up pulling a lot of people out of poverty. The present section aims at identifying the main determinants of this overall fall in poverty over the 1994–2001 period, focusing on the determinants of the strong pro-poor growth that dominated the end of the century. It begins by a sectoral decomposition of GDP growth, which brings out some significant structural change. Berthélemy *et al.* (1996) have shown that changes in the allocation of labour among the different production sectors has been the key determinant of aggregate growth in Senegal, and the following analysis provides some support to this view.

Production sector effects

The particularly good performance of rural areas in terms of poverty reduction identified above occurred despite a fairly irregular growth path of the agricultural and livestock sector. The latter experienced a serious depression in 1997 and 1998, discussed further below, followed by a brisk recovery in 2000 and 2001. Figure 5.5 shows a decomposition of GDP (at constant 1987 prices, in log form) over the 1991–2001 decade. It shows that the tertiary sector, which comprises mainly transportation, commerce and other services, experienced a pretty fast growth since devaluation. In real terms, several of its component sectors experienced some very fast growth episodes during this period, like transportation for example which grew by 8.1 per cent per annum on average over 1997–2001. This tertiary sector claims more than half of the total GDP in Senegal (nearly 60% in fact). It also includes the telecommunication sector, which was profoundly reformed during that period in Senegal, and which grew quite fast subsequently (Azam, Dia, and N'Guessan, 2002).

Similarly, the secondary sector experienced a fast growth of output after the devaluation. The chart shows that this sector, which comprises mainly industry and construction and public works (in addition to the relatively negligible mining and oil-milling sectors), benefited markedly from the devaluation. It experienced two years of negative growth in 1993 and 1994, during and just after the recession that affected the whole UEMOA area, and recovered briskly after that. In fact, its growth was uninterrupted until 2001. By contrast, the primary sector, that is mainly agriculture and livestock, experienced a slower growth, and its relative share went down. Its growth rate was negative in 1997 and 1998 (−10.6% and −7.4%, respectively), while

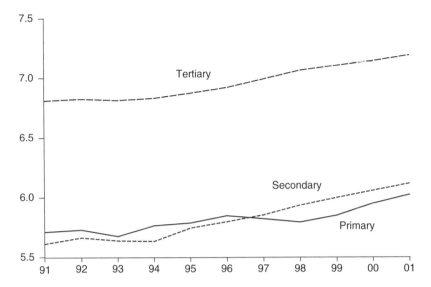

Figure 5.5   GDP per sector, Senegal 1987 (constant prices, logarithms)
Source: IMF (2000, 2003).

it had a very fast recovery in 2000 and 2001 with two-digit growth rates (21.3% and 13.8%, respectively). These wide fluctuations are largely due to the vagaries of the Sahelian climate, while price effects do not seem to have been very significant determinants of the supply response. This is shown pretty clearly from Figures 5.6 and 5.7.

Figure 5.6 shows the level of rainfall on three of the main production areas of the groundnut basin. 1992–93 and 1997–98 were clearly pretty dry years, while 2000–01 were exceptionally good years. By contrast, Figure 5.7 shows that producer prices were recovering from the real shock induced by the devaluation during the period 1997–98. This confirms the well-known result in agricultural economics that price effects on agricultural productions are drawn-out, while climatic shocks have immediate effect. On the other hand, the income effects of these real price changes are felt immediately by the farmers. The deep fall in the real prices of the crops that occurred in 1994 probably entailed a large temporary increase in poverty in the rural areas. However, these producer prices have been deflated using the general consumer price index, which only covers Dakar for most of the period. This might not describe accurately the relevant consumer price changes that affected farmers, as their typical consumption basket comprises a lower share of imported goods, while they consume a large share of their home-produced food. However, there is no suitable price index covering the rural sector.

Figure 5.7 shows that the real price of millet, which is not exported on the international market, except by cross-border trade, fell in 1993, reflecting

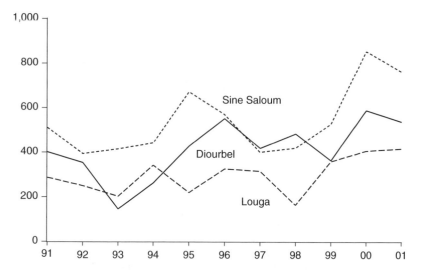

Figure 5.6 Rainfall on the groundnut basin, Senegal (millimeters during the rainy season, May–October preceding the crop year shown)
Source: IMF (2000, 2003).

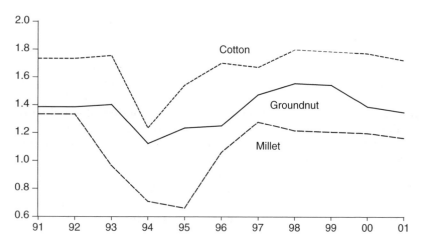

Figure 5.7 Real producers' prices, Senegal
Note: The deflator used only accounts for Dakar over most of the period.
Source: IMF (2000, 2003).

the recession observed that year for the whole UEMOA. The fall in the real price of the two export crops at the time of the devaluation suggests that the pass-through rate was pretty low, so that the marketing sector benefited most from this policy move, rather than the farmers. In other words, the tertiary sector benefited from an implicit subsidy from the farmers, in the wake of the devaluation. This probably explains to some extent the fast growth of the tertiary sector shown by Figure 5.5. Then, real producer prices picked up somewhat, but hardly recovered their pre-devaluation levels. It is only during the drought years that the real price of groundnut went above its pre-1994 level. This probably marginally softened the poverty impact of the drought on the agriculturists.

Therefore, the remarkable reduction in poverty in the rural sector that we described in the introductory section cannot be credited to either a spectacular growth in output or a significant increase in the real price of the produce. Most probably, but the data are lacking to confirm this assertion, it is a demand-driven migration into the urban areas, where industry and services have been thriving, that made a serious dent in rural poverty. The drought that took place at the end of the century, which certainly revived the memories of the 1970s and 1980s, also provided some incentive for labour to migrate to the more progressive sectors.

These results are consistent with those of Berthélemy *et al.* (1996) showing that over the period 1961–90 the increase in total factor productivity, which can be estimated using an aggregate production function, is in fact entirely due to the reallocation of labour from the low productivity primary sector to the higher productivity secondary and tertiary sectors. Poverty thus probably fell in the rural sector because the least productive farmers migrated to the cities, where they found higher productivity jobs. Hence, in the case of Senegal it seems that the rural sector can be viewed as a fairly stagnant reserve of labour, somehow in the spirit of the seminal Lewis model (Lewis, 1954). The difference with the latter is that such a diagnosis is true despite the fact that the primary sector is not just a 'subsistence sector', but also exports a large share of its output. Azam (1993) presents an extension of the Lewis model, motivated by an analysis of Côte d'Ivoire, which brings out the importance for growth of taxation of high wages, assumed to accrue to skilled labour, and the productive use of the resulting tax proceeds by the government. The following analysis suggests that the experience of Senegal provides some support to this view, interpreting the outcome of the devaluation as a massive increase in the taxation of high wages, as suggested above.

The investment boom

Figure 5.8 shows that the post-devaluation recovery was boosted by a major effort concerning public investment. As a percentage of GDP, it went up from an average share of 4.6 per cent of GDP in 1991–93 to an average share of 6.8 per cent of GDP over 1996–2001. The resumption of private investment

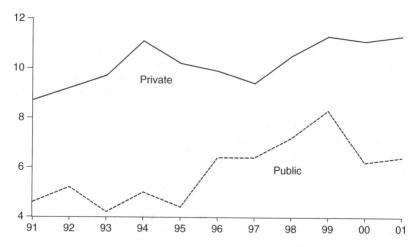

Figure 5.8 Private and public investment, Senegal (% of GDP)
Source: IMF (2000, 2003).

is also quite remarkable, although its time profile is less smooth. It increased from an average share of 8.9 per cent of GDP in 1991–93 to an average of 10.6 per cent of GDP in 1996–2001. It is highly probable that the former played a part in creating the appropriate climate for the latter. The time profile of the private investment share suggests that the devaluation took some time before it elicited a positive response from private investors. This is clearly one of the predictions of the theoretical framework analysed in Azam (2004). In this case, households earning formal-sector wages expect the devaluation to happen, and anticipate its negative effects on their incomes by accumulating savings beforehand with a view to smoothing out consumption later when their incomes are cut by the devaluation. Private saving thus declines in the wake of the devaluation, and because of the low level of intermediation this affects private investment simultaneously. However, other mechanisms have also probably been at work; pre-devaluation slow growth and recession probably left quite a lot of productive capacity idle, so that firms had to make significant cuts in excess capacity before the creation of new capital stock became a priority.

Moreover, the private sector was also waiting for more information to come about the effects of the devaluation, and about the true intentions of the government regarding the management of the post-devaluation boom. The option value of waiting was also probably enhanced by the unprecedented violence taking place in lower Casamance in 1995. This is epitomized by the disappearance of four French tourists between Ziguinchor and Cap Skirring, widely interpreted as a kidnapping by the Casamance rebellion. The military response to this event triggered a lot of violence all over Casamance, with both civilian and military casualties, followed by a relatively calm period until June 1997.

It seems quite likely that the significant increase in public investment which occurred from 1996 onwards, was the true trigger of the private investment recovery. In a financially open economy like Senegal, with a fixed exchange rate, there is no crowding-out effect to be feared, while the demand-boosting and productivity-enhancing effects of public investments are dominant. This central role of public investment, marking the end of a period of falling private investment, does not mean that the devaluation had no useful effect. It means instead that the positive impact took a more roundabout channel than usually expected. The improved situation of the government budget, and in particular the fall in real wages of civil servants and other government employees, due to the devaluation, freed some fiscal resources that the government was able to use for investing. This is the main cause of the investment boom described above. The real wage effect was reinforced by a slight fall in the number of civil servants, which fell from 66,696 in 1994 to 65,259 in 2001, so that the civil service wage bill fell from 7.4 per cent of GDP in 1994 to 5.2 per cent in 2001. However, other policy measures have been taken by the Senegalese government in favour of private investment.

Although it had a self-proclaimed socialist government since independence, until the March 2000 election, Senegal has adopted an investor-friendly policy during the course of the reform period, particularly from the end of the 1980s onwards. A wave of privatization took place, mainly in the utilities sector, sending a good signal to investors (Azam, Dia and N'Guessan, 2002). The main incentive comes from the fiscal burden, which is low by African standards. Table 5.2 represents the scores given to various countries in the UEMOA and its neighbourhood by the Heritage Foundation. This is a composite index that takes into account the highest rate of income tax, as well as the average, and the most relevant marginal income tax rate for

Table 5.2 Fiscal burden scores, Senegal 2003

UEMOA members	Fiscal burden score	Other African countries	Fiscal burden score
Senegal	2.5	Gambia	3
Mali	3	Ghana	3.5
Niger	3	Guinea	3
Togo	3	Nigeria	3.5
Benin	3.5	Algeria	3.5
Burkina Faso	3.5	Morocco	4
Côte d'Ivoire	3.5	Tunisia	4
Guinea-Bissau	4		

Note: The index is coded from 1 (low taxation of profits and incomes) to 5 (high taxation).
Source: Heritage Foundation (http://www.heritage.org/research/features/index/).

the average taxpayer. Additionally, as a check on the credibility of these tax rates, the share of public expenditures in GDP is also taken into account.

Table 5.2 shows that, in general, the UEMOA countries have a slightly more favourable score than the comparison countries, which are taken both from North Africa and from non-UEMOA West Africa. Out of these 15 countries, Senegal has by far the best performance, even among the UEMOA countries. Hence, the boosting effect of the public investment boom described above was supported by a highly favourable tax framework. As a result of the investor-friendly climate created over the last few years of the century, this country's rating has improved significantly. Since 2001, Senegal is rated B[+] by Standard & Poors, a score bettered only by South Africa and Botswana in Sub-Saharan Africa.

Table 5.3 shows the maximum corporate tax rate among the same group of countries. Most of them have a maximum rate of 35 per cent, with the exception of Niger and Togo, within the UEMOA, which have a slightly higher rate, and the oil producing Algeria and Nigeria, which have a lower rate aimed at compensating for the 'Dutch Disease' effect due to oil exports, as well as Ghana. The latter is also a coastal country with a potential comparative advantage in non-traditional exports, like Senegal, which pursues quite an aggressive policy aimed at attracting foreign investors.

A further relevant piece of information regarding the investment incentive structure is provided by Figure 5.9 which shows the ratio of public debt to GDP, which is a major indicator of macroeconomic stability in the CFA zone (Azam, 1997). This ratio can be viewed by investors as a threat of future tax increases, according to the mechanisms described in Cohen (1993) and Eaton (1993). The intuition for this effect is that a high public debt ratio

Table 5.3   Maximum corporate tax rate, Senegal 2003

UEMOA members	Maximum corporate tax rate (%)	Other African countries	Maximum corporate tax rate
Benin	35	Gambia	35
Burkina Faso	35	Ghana	32.5
Côte d'Ivoire	35	Guinea	35
Guinea-Bissau	35 (50 for oil)	Nigeria	30
Mali	35		
Senegal	35	Algeria	30
Togo	40	Morocco	35 (39.6 for banks and insurance)
Niger	42.5	Tunisia	35

Source: Heritage Foundation (http://www.heritage.org/research/features/index/), originally from Ernst & Young *2002 Worldwide Corporate Tax Guide*.

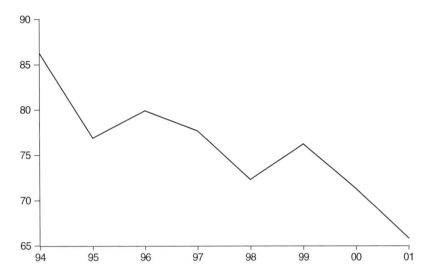

Figure 5.9 Public debt to GDP ratio, Senegal (%)

now may be regarded by potential investors as entailing a future increase in taxation, to finance the corresponding debt service. The figure clearly shows that the Senegalese government made a sustained effort to reduce that threat, the so-called 'debt overhang' effect, as the ratio fell from 86.2 in 1994 to 65.8 in 2001. A major dent in this series shows up in 1998, when Senegal reached a Paris Club agreement worth about CFA francs 23 billion. Moreover, Senegal will benefit from some debt reduction within the HIPC initiative, as decided in June 2000. The latter will be effective only outside the period under analysis, but has probably a positive effect on expectations. All these developments are taking place against a background of sustained reduction of the debt-to-GDP ratio.

Senegal thus comes out as a particularly attractive investment destination among the countries of North and West Africa. It does not seem that the few breaches of privatization contracts, imposed paradoxically by the liberal President Abdoulaye Wade, have much damaged this country's good reputation. An example is provided by the renegotiation of the licenses for the mobile telephone operators Alizée and Sentel (see Azam, Dia and N'Guessan, 2002), which ended up in a surcharge being imposed on them. Its attractiveness is also supported unwittingly by Côte d'Ivoire, whose political instability (the 1999 coup d'état, the 2000 uprising, and the civil war started in 2002 . . .) has destroyed its own attractiveness. In many ways, Senegal is left as the unique investment opportunity among Francophone countries.

It is remarkable that the sustained growth of the post-devaluation boom was not hampered by a shortage of human capital. However, Berthélemy *et al.* (1996) have a fairly negative diagnosis about the education policy pursued by Senegal between independence and the early 1990s. They acknowledge that the enrolment rate increased massively between 1960 and 1990, from 22 per cent to 57 per cent for primary education, and from 2 per cent to 16 per cent for secondary education. But they assessed the quality of education as poor and deteriorating, and not fitted for sustaining economic development. They criticized in particular the Senegalese education policy for putting too much emphasis on classical education. By contrast, Diagne *et al.* (2002) estimate that human capital was not a brake on the resumption of growth after devaluation, finding a positive and nearly significant impact of enrollment in primary education on growth, with a nine-year lag. This effort was not reduced during the post-devaluation boom, and the gross rate of enrolment went from 54.3 per cent in 1993 to 69 per cent in 2000 (Loum, 2001).

Moreover, one may argue that the early effort made by Senegal in favour of education also had an indirect political impact on the government's ability to engineer the timely public investment boom. This comes out clearly by comparison with neighbouring Mali. There, also, the 1994 devaluation of the CFA frame freed a lot of fiscal resources by cutting the government's real wage bill. However, these resources had to be invested in education, as General Moussa Traoré's dictatorship, which fell in 1991, had neglected that sector. The newly established Malian democracy increased the primary enrollment rate from about 30 per cent in 1991 to about 60 per cent in 2000, in response to a strong popular demand. Senegal had made a similar effort much earlier on, and was thus in a position to focus its investment effort on medium-run growth, as described above.

The low political gains from pro-poor growth

The experience of Senegal suggests that engineering pro-poor growth did not benefit the incumbent government. The government was not rewarded for its good performance regarding pro-poor growth, as Abdou Diouf was ousted in the 2000 elections. An important reason for this negative outcome was probably the fall in incomes of the urban elites, while the subjective perception of poverty lagged significantly behind its objective changes. It seems that households perceive a sense of lasting 'crisis', whenever they have experienced poverty. This entails a trade-off between pro-poor growth, with the initial sacrifice that it requires, and political support.

Despite the remarkable fall in poverty documented above, based on the change in consumption experienced by Senegalese households over 1994–2001, perceived poverty has increased significantly in this country. This comes out of the EPPS 2001 survey (Enquête sur la perception de la pauvreté au Sénégal) of the subjective perception of poverty by Senegalese households, which used the same sample as ESAM 2. Figure 5.10 shows that a vast

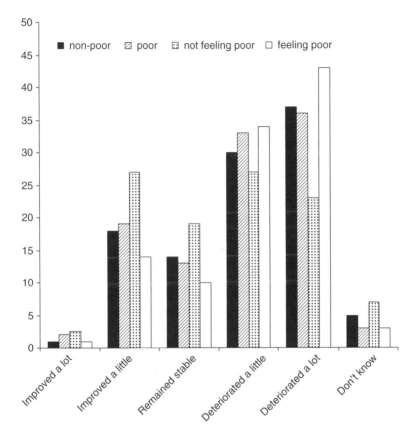

Figure 5.10 Perceived change in poverty, Senegal (%) (EPPS 2001 survey)
Source: République du Sénégal (2004).

majority of the households surveyed did not perceive any improvement in the poverty situation.

More than 85 per cent of households estimated that poverty remained stable or deteriorated during the five years preceding the survey. This is particularly noticeable among the poor or among those who perceive themselves as poor, but the survey shows that these two groups of households are quite different. The overlap between the two categories is highly imperfect; almost two-thirds of the sample households perceive themselves as poor, which is quite a large overestimate, while a significant share of the objectively poor do not perceive themselves as poor (République du Sénégal, 2004). Strangely enough, this divergent diagnosis is not based on a conceptually different view about poverty; more than 50 per cent of the respondents to the survey consider 'the inability to feed one's family' as the main correlate of poverty (ibid.). This is not grossly inconsistent with the consumption-based approach, adjusted by the number of adult-equivalent household members, used in the objective poverty assessment.

Hence, this suggests that there is a strong persistence in the perception of poverty, such that investing in increased poverty now with a view to improve significantly poverty later might be a risky choice from an electoral point of view. This disconnection between the subjective and the objective changes in poverty raises an important political problem. In a democratic country like Senegal, this reduces the incentive for the government to actively fight poverty, as the resulting improvement is not correctly perceived as such by voters. President Diouf, who presided over the implementation of the growth-boosting policy in the late 1990s, was beaten at the March 2000 elections, while a sense of 'crisis' was widespread in the electorate. However, nothing really proves that voter's perception of the change in poverty played any part in determining this outcome. Maybe 'Sopi' – the change, in Wolof – was desired for its own sake, as a way of checking that the elections were not rigged, contrary to the belief shared by many about the previous ones, or for any other reason.

Conclusion

The Senegal case study shows that poverty decreased significantly during the last decade of the twentieth century, from 1994/95 to 2001/02, both absolutely and relatively. The devaluation of the CFA franc that occurred in January 1994 entailed both a major macroeconomic shock, and a major reshuffling of the distribution of income, mainly among urbanites. The latter felt the main blow of the devaluation, as the fall in real wages of civil servants and other public sector employees spilled over onto the incomes of the urban informal sector. Moreover, the change in real producer prices in agriculture (Figure 5.6) suggests that poverty also went up in that sector in the wake of the devaluation, before it improved significantly later on. This fall in the real price of their output, together with the low level of rainfall, probably created a fall in peasants' incomes, which helped provide the incentives to migrate to the cities, where the other sectors experienced quite a high rate of growth after 1996.

During the three years following devaluation, despite the fast recovery of GDP growth, and the fall in real wage rates in the urban sector, private investment did not pick up. It did so only after 1996, when the government used the fiscal resources freed by the reduction in the real value of its wage bill for financing a major increase in public investment. The resulting investment boom stretched out the post-devaluation boom in time, and managed to tide the Senegalese economy over the regional recession of the year 2000. During this third phase, from 1996 to 2001, the poverty effect of the accelerated growth seems spectacular.

This summary description of the growth and poverty process during the last decade of the twentieth century, until 2001, suggests that macroeconomic policy is playing a major role in determining the dynamics of poverty. However, when it involves a huge change in relative incomes, like the 1994 devaluation did, such a policy can also be viewed as a redistribution policy. The real wages of formal-sector workers were drastically cut, falling by about 40 per cent until the end of the period. Its impact was thus akin to that of a major increase in income tax for these people. Nevertheless, the analysis of the time profile of investment suggests that Senegal could only reap the full benefit of the devaluation when its government chose to use this fiscal windfall for financing a boom in public investment. The latter was in turn transmitted to private investment, which also boomed at the end of the century. In other words, the fiscal effect of the devaluation seems to have played a more important part in launching and sustaining the post-devaluation boom than the redistribution effect. Conversely, the success of the pro-poor growth episode of the end of the century, over the half-decade 1996–2001, is due to the combination of two effects: first, the devaluation drastically reduced the government's wage bill, acting in fact like a major increase in income tax affecting these people, and, second, the resources thus freed were wisely used by the government for boosting the economy by an appropriate mix of increased public investment and public debt reduction. The latter combined with various fiscal measures for creating an 'investor-friendly' environment, which invited private investment to follow in the steps of public investment.

In Senegal, thus, the road which leads from a cut in the incomes of the rich to an increase in the incomes of the poor is quite a complex one. This is probably true also in most countries of the world. The bottom line is that pro-poor growth occurred at the end of the century because the government engineered a sustainable change in the *functional* distribution of income, from wages to profits, and not just a transfer of income from the rich to the poor. This change was obtained by an increase in public investment and the creation of an investor-friendly environment based on low corporate taxation and low public debt.

This is the core lesson of Senegal's pro-poor growth experience: profitability fuels private investment, and the latter is the engine of sustained growth. This simple message has been emphasized time and again in the literature (see for example Malinvaud, 1980). As the former Chancellor of West Germany Helmut Schmidt used to say: 'The profits of today are the investments of tomorrow and the investments of tomorrow make the employment of the day after tomorrow' (cited in Malinvaud, 1980, p. 4). Therefore, as poverty is liable to lag significantly behind growth, it takes a sustained effort in favour of profitability to pull a significant number of people out of poverty. The Senegalese experience described above shows that devaluation is only one of the possible means that can be used for that purpose, acting like a tax on formal-sector wages. It suggests that timely and efficient public investment is also quite important, and cutting the public debt overhang is important as well. These are probably not the only ways that profitability can be supported, and other means to the same end should be sought in different institutional and political settings. The unprecedented stretch of fast economic growth that resulted from this strategy managed to pull a large share of the Senegalese population out of poverty. Unfortunately, from the point of view of the incumbent government, the objective reduction in poverty was not correctly perceived by voters, as shown by the survey performed in 2001 on the subjective perception of poverty. It might also have played a part in determining the election results of the year 2000, where the incumbent government was ousted. Although it is not certain that the misperception of the change in poverty played a significant part in this outcome, it might have had some impact. Maybe, in a democratic polity like Senegal, the true political challenge is to find a strategy for reducing the subjective perception of poverty. The latter probably affects electoral outcomes, and no genuine 'ownership' of pro-poor growth policy will emerge without it in democratic countries.

The Senegalese experience thus suggests that pro-poor growth was triggered by a fall in the real wages of civil servants, which was engineered by devaluation. This raises an important issue regarding why such a cut was impossible to implement by other means during the 'real-side' adjustment phase. Probably, Keynes' (1936) relative wage theory would go a long way in explaining this fact. The devaluation made it highly plausible that nobody would escape from the real wage cut, while a political decision of cutting nominal wages would raise the suspicion that some 'happy few' would escape, and would thus be resisted. The Senegalese experience also suggests that the benefit of such a cut would not have materialized without a timely decision by the government to use the fiscal resources thus freed for boosting public investment rather than letting the wage bill catch up on prices. However, its subsequent electoral defeat suggests retrospectively that it might be politically preferable for the incumbent government to choose a policy mix more in favour of the urban elite's wages, as the poor do not accurately perceive how they benefit from pro-poor growth. Nonetheless, 'Sopi' made the Senegalese proud of their democracy, thus producing an additional public good that should be added to the national accounts.

Note

1. Denote y_i individual i's level of income, usually measured by his (her) consumption level, assuming that the individuals are ordered by increasing income, and denote by z the poverty line. Then, individual i's consumption gap may be defined as the percentage shortfall of his (her) consumption level below the poverty line: $G_i = (z - y_i)/z$. The FGT measure is then given by:

$$P_\alpha = \left(\frac{1}{n}\right) \sum_{i=1}^{q} \left(\frac{z - y_i}{z}\right)^\alpha, \tag{5.1}$$

where n is the size of the population, q the index of the individual whose consumption level lies just on the poverty line, and α is a parameter capturing the analyst's concern for the depth of poverty. If $\alpha = 0$ is chosen, then this index is just the head-count index $H = q/n$. If $\alpha = 1$ is chosen instead, the poverty measure that we get is the product of the headcount index by the average consumption gap among the poor $H\bar{G}$, where $\bar{G} = \sum_{i=1}^{q} G_i/q$. This index thus takes into account not only the incidence of poverty, but its average depth also. More emphasis can be put on the depth of poverty by weighing each individual's consumption shortfall by itself, i.e. by choosing $\alpha = 2$. These three measures are computed for Senegal in Table 5.1 for 1994 and 2001, and are respectively presented under the three headings described above: 'Head-Count', 'Consumption Gap' and 'Poverty Depth'.

References

Azam, J.-P. (1993) 'The "Côte d'Ivoire" Model of Economic Growth', *European Economic Review*, 37: 566–76.

Azam, J.-P. (1995) 'L'Etat auto-géré en Afrique', *Revue d'économie du développement*, 1–19/4.

Azam, J.-P. (1997) 'Public Debt and the Exchange Rate in the CFA Franc Zone', *Journal of African Economies*, 6/1: 54–84.

Azam, J.-P. (2004) 'Poverty and Growth in the WAEMU after the 1994 Devaluation', *Journal of African Economies*, 13/4: 536–62.

Azam, J.-P., Biais, B. and Dia, M. (2004) 'Privatization versus Regulation in Developing Economies: The Case of West African Banks', *Journal of African Economies*, 13/3: 361–94.

Azam, J.-P. and Chambas, G. (1999) 'The Groundnuts and Phosphates Boom in Sénégal (1974–1977)', in P. Collier and J.W. Gunning (eds), *Temporary Trade Shocks in Developing Countries, Vol. 1*. Oxford: Oxford University Press, pp. 226–58.

Azam, J.-P., Dia, M. and N'Guessan, T. (2002) 'Telecom Sector Reform in Senegal', World Bank Working Paper, WPS 2894, Washington DC. (www.worldbank.org/html/dec/Publications/Workpapers/home.html)

Azam, J.-P. and Wane, W. (1999) 'The Impact of the Devaluation of the CFA Franc on Poverty in the WAEMU', unpublished. Washington DC: World Bank.

Berthélemy, J.-C., Seck, A. and Vourc'h, A. (1996) *La croissance au Sénégal: un pari perdu?*. Paris: Études du centre de développement de l'OCDE.

Boone, C. (2003) *Political Topographies of the African State*. Cambridge: Cambridge University Press.

Cohen, D. (1993) 'Low Investment and Large LDC Debt in the 1980s', *American Economic Review*, 437–49.

Diagne, A. and Daffé G. (eds), (2002) *Le Sénégal en quête d'une croissance durable*, CREA – Karthala: Paris.

Eaton, J. (1993) 'Sovereign Debt: A Primer', *World Bank Economic Review*, 7: 137–72.

Foster, J., Greer, J. and Thorbecke, E. (1984) 'A Class of Decomposable Poverty Measures', *Econometrica*, 52: 761–6.

International Monetary Fund (1996) 'Senegal – Statistical Annex, SM/96/138'. Washington DC: IMF.

International Monetary Fund (2000) 'Senegal – Recent Developments', Washington, DC: IMF.

International Monetary Fund (2003) 'Senegal – Statistical Appendix', IMF Country Report No. 03/168, Washington, DC: IMF.

Ka, S. and Van de Walle, N. (1994) 'Senegal: Stalled Reform in a Dominant Party System', in. S. Haggard, and S.B. Webb (eds), *Voting for Reform. Democracy, Political Liberalization, and Economic Adjustment.* Oxford: Oxford University Press, pp. 290–359.

Keynes, J.M. (1936) *The General Theory of Employment, Interest and Money*, London: Macmillan St Martin's Press.

Lewis, W.A. (1954) 'Economic Development with Unlimited Supplies of Labour', *Manchester School*, 22: 139–91.

Loum, M.L. (2001) *Le Sénégal au 1er avril 2000*, EXCAF Editions: Dakar.

Malinvaud, E. (1980) 'Profitability and Unemployment', Cambridge: Cambridge University Press.

Manchuelle, F. (1997) *Willing Migrants. Soninke Labor Diasporas, 1848–1960*, Athens: Ohio University Press.

Rama, M. (2000) 'Wage Misalignment in CFA Countries: Were Labour Market Policies to Blame?', *Journal of African Economies*, 9 /4: 475–511.

République du Sénégal (2004) 'La pauvreté au Sénégal: de la dévaluation de 1994 à 2001–2002', Ministère de l'économie et des finances, Direction de la prévision et de la statistique, version préliminaire, Dakar, January.

Rouis, M. (1994) 'Senegal: Stabilization, Partial Adjustment, and Stagnation', in Ishrat Husain and Rashid Faruqee (eds), *Adjustment in Africa: Lessons from case Studies.* Washington, DC: The World Bank, pp. 286–351.

Schaffer, F.C. (1998) *Democracy in Translation*, Ithaca: Cornell University Press.

van de Walle, N. (1991) 'The Decline of the Franc Zone: Monetary Politics in Franco-phone Africa', *African Affairs*, 90: 383–405.

6
Pro-Poor Growth in Burkina Faso: The Role of Price Shocks

Michael Grimm and Isabel Günther *

Introduction

Burkina Faso is one of the poorest countries in the world. In 2004, real GDP per capita was estimated at only US$384 (IMF, 2005) and according to the Human Development Index, the country was ranked 175th out of 177 countries (UNDP, 2004). Burkina Faso is a landlocked country with a population of roughly 12.5 million. It has a very low human capital base and only very few natural resources. More than 80 per cent of the Burkinabè population lives in rural areas working predominantly in the agricultural sector, which suffers from very limited rainfall and recurrent severe droughts. The country depends highly on cotton exports, which account for almost 60 per cent of total export earnings, as well as on international aid.

Despite these rather unfavourable conditions, Burkina Faso experienced relatively strong economic growth and showed a good macroeconomic performance during the last 10 years. Since 1991 the country has implemented a wide range of economic reforms in the framework of stabilization and Structural Adjustment Programmes (SAP) and after the devaluation of the CFA (Communauté Financière d'Afrique) franc in January 1994, real GDP per capita began to rise and growth averaged at 2 per cent per year between 1994 and 2003 (Figure 6.1).

At the micro-economic level our estimates suggest that national poverty decreased, but with a low elasticity of only 0.8 per cent poverty reduction for each per cent growth of GDP per capita during this period. However, this (weak) pro-poor growth performance varied significantly over time

---

* We would like to thank Rolf Meier and Bakary Kindé for the very pleasant reception and their assistance during our stay in Burkina Faso. We also thank Lionel Demery, Francisco Ferreira, Hartmut Janus, Stephan Klasen, Andrew McKay, Marc Raffinot and Martin Ravallion for very useful comments and suggestions. Finally, we are very grateful to the GTZ and the BMZ for having supported and financed this case study. Nevertheless, any errors remain our own responsibility.

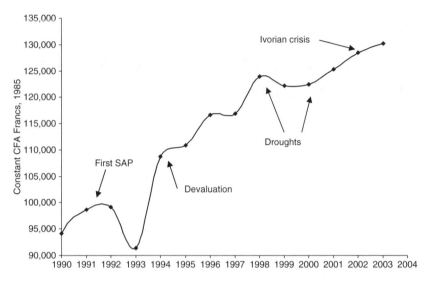

Figure 6.1 Real GDP per capita, Burkina Faso (constant CFA francs 1985)
Source: IAP (2004).

and space. Not only did poverty increase despite macro-economic growth between 1994 and 1998 in both urban and rural areas and only decreased afterwards, but also urban poverty in 2003 was still higher than in 1994. This uneven development and the weak link between growth and poverty reduction were mainly due to three macro-economic shocks: the CFA franc devaluation in 1994, the price liberalization between 1993 and 1996 and severe droughts in 1997/98 and 2000/01, which all led to significant price fluctuations with rather adverse effects on poverty reduction.

The effect of the devaluation of the CFA franc in 1994 on aggregate growth was without doubt positive; in particular, exports of cotton increased significantly after the devaluation. However, (poorer) agricultural households not involved in cotton production suffered under the increasing prices of imported fertilizer. Also urban wage-earners experienced a substantial reduction in real earnings, as their earnings were not indexed to inflation after the devaluation. Furthermore, the prize liberalization, which suppressed to a large extent existing price policies for traditional cereals and livestock, led to higher price fluctuations, which only benefited some but might have had a negative impact on poorer households. Moreover, the severe droughts led to substantial increases in the prices of food crops substantially reducing the purchasing power of the poor for whom food crops constitute on average more than 40 per cent of their total budget.

In this chapter we emphasize the adverse effects of price shocks on poverty reduction. Analytically, we show that the correct treatment of price shocks is important to correctly gauge the growth–poverty relationship. In particular, we demonstrate that if the consumption structure varies over the expenditure distribution and if relative prices shift the deflation of household expenditure over time, simply using the general consumer price index can lead to a biased assessment of pro-poor growth. Economically, we highlight that such shocks might have strong adverse effects on the poor in a context of a highly segmented economy with low market integration and no access to any formal insurance mechanisms. Moreover, we show that in such environments not only is the poverty effect of growth reduced, but many potentially profitable investments do not take place and, hence, growth itself might be lowered.

The reminder of the chapter is organized as follows. In the next section we provide a brief overview of the economic development since 1990, emphasizing the main policy reforms and macro-economic shocks Burkina Faso faced during that period. We then present an assessment of the growth, poverty and inequality trends emphasizing the role of prices in such an assessment, before moving from pro-poor growth statistics to an analysis of the impact of price shocks on pro-poor growth. Based on these results and with regard to the objective of possible higher pro-poor growth, we draw some policy implications in the final section.

Historical and economic context

After Burkina Faso gained independence from France in 1960, real GDP per capita declined on average by almost 4 per cent per year. The economy started to recover in 1966, but not before 1980 did GDP per capita reach its level of 1960 (Summers-Heston Penn World Tables Release 6.1, 'PWT 6.1' hereafter). During this period the economic policy pursued by the Burkinabè authorities was based, as in most Sub-Saharan African countries, on the development of a large public sector. Public monopolistic companies exported few raw materials, especially cotton, the country imported some goods of first necessity and put otherwise high tariffs on trade. The economy suffered from these distortions as well as from a producer cotton price disconnected from the world market price, and high salaries in the public sector.

In 1981, after frequent changes in government, the military took power and set a first end to the democratic experience of Burkina Faso. In 1983 an insurrection brought Thomas Sankara to the top of the state. He represented a rather populist policy, putting forward social justice and national independence.[1] Prices for agricultural products were fixed to guarantee a more equitable payment to producers. The government invested heavily in education and health, started labour-intensive infrastructure projects and implemented a land reform, which mainly aimed to tackle the problem of internal migration. The development strategy was based on central planning and pervasive controls that resulted in large macroeconomic imbalances and a continuing accumulation of arrears in foreign and later also internal debt service. During this period, real GDP per capita grew by approximately 3 per cent per year (PWT 6.1), but was characterized by strong fluctuations.

In 1987 the current president Blaise Campaoré took power, turned away from the Sankaraian policy and started to undertake reforms in accord with the IMF and the World Bank. The first Structural Adjustment Programme (SAP) was signed in 1991. Due to its participation in the CFA franc zone, Burkina Faso already had relatively modest public expenditure and monetary stability. The most important element of the SAP was therefore the liberalization and privatization of the economy. But despite the SAP, real GDP per capita declined between 1991 and 1993 by approximately 4 per cent per year (see Figure 6.1).

The failure of the internal adjustment strategy in several countries of the CFA franc zone and especially in one of the most important ones–Côte d'Ivoire–led to a 50 per cent devaluation of the CFA franc parity in relation to the French franc in January 1994. After the devaluation, given the gain in competitiveness, GDP per capita growth began to rise and averaged at approximately 3.3 per cent per year between 1994 and 1998 (IAP, 2004). This growth was furthermore supported by a favourable development of the world market price for cotton and a multiplication of the land used for cotton production (through deforestation and substitution). However, the country also knew a very severe drought during the cropping season 1997/98 which, as will be shown below, had a significant impact on the consumption of rural households.

During recent years Burkina Faso has pursued efforts for structural reforms, in particular concerning price and trade liberalization. The country established its first Poverty Reduction Strategy Papers (PRSP) in May 2000 (Ministère de l'Economie et des Finances, 2000), and reached its completion point in the Heavily Indebted Poor Countries (HIPC) II Initiative in April 2002. However, in 2000/01 the economy was again affected by a drought and since December 2001 Burkina Faso has been confronted with the adverse effects of the Ivorian crisis. But, recent estimations show that GDP per capita growth in 2003 and 2004 was still higher than 2 per cent (IAP, 2004), due to, among other things, a very good harvest and a relatively quick adjustment of the country's import and export channels. The most serious negative effects from the Ivorian crisis seem to be the decrease in private workers' remittances and the migration back to Burkina Faso from Burkinabè workers in Côte d'Ivoire. It is estimated that in 2003 migration added roughly 3 percentage points to the projected demographic growth rate of 2.4 per cent. Over the whole period 1998 to 2003, GDP per capita rose by roughly 1.8 per cent per year.

Growth, poverty and inequality, 1994–2004

The first representative household survey on the national level measuring household expenditure and income in Burkina Faso was undertaken in 1994 and was repeated in 1998 and 2003.[2] These surveys served the Burkinabè authorities and international development agencies to compute poverty and inequality indicators for that period. Those indicators were then related to the evolution of real GDP per capita and real expenditure per capita of the private household sector as indicated by National Accounts to evaluate efforts to promote growth and to alleviate poverty.

It is very likely that computed aggregates from household survey data will not exactly match National Accounts data, because of conceptual differences as well as measurement errors in both data-sets. However, for the case of Burkina Faso, one has to consider several additional measurement problems, which had a substantial impact on both previous poverty indicators as well as growth rates computed from household expenditures. More precisely, previous poverty assessments including those of the Burkinabè Statistics Office, the World Bank and UNDP[3] were seriously affected by three types of bias: changes in the methodology used to compute household expenditure aggregates, changes in the household survey design, and high relative price variations over time, which were only imperfectly taken into account for the computation of the official national poverty line. We therefore recomputed time consistent consumption aggregates and poverty lines and only those are presented in what follows. A detailed description of how we proceeded can be found in Grimm and Günther (2006a). In particular, we ensured that the poverty line appropriately reflects the development of the purchasing power of the poor, an issue which is particularly important in an environment of rapidly changing relative prices (see Grimm and Günther, 2006b).

The issue of changes in relative prices

Table 6.1 below shows that our poverty line strongly increased between 1994 and 1998. This reflects that the prices of the goods of first necessity consumed by the poor increased much more than the prices of the goods consumed by the 'representative urban household', which is used for the computation of the CPI. More precisely, the poverty line increases by 55.7 per cent between 1994 and 1998 and by 55.3 per cent between 1994 and 2003, whereas the national CPI only increases by 22.7 per cent between 1994 and 1998 and by 31.4 per cent between 1994 and 2003. This sharp inflation of the poverty line, especially between 1994 and 1998, is due to the massive price increase of cereals during this period. This is illustrated in Figure 6.2.

The massive price increase of cereals was mainly caused by a very severe drought–even by Burkinabè standards–which hit the country during the

Table 6.1 Development of poverty and inequality, Burkina Faso

Indicator	Urban			Rural			National		
	1994	1998	2003	1994	1998	2003	1994	1998	2003
NPL revised (current CFA francs)	53,219 (100)				82,885 (155.7)				82,672 (155.3)
P0 (%)	14.7 (12.8; 16.7)	27.3 (25.9; 29.8)	20.3 (18.2; 22.4)	63.4 (61.4; 65.4)	68.7 (67.3; 70.1)	53.3 (1.6; 54.7)	55.5 (53.7; 57.2)	61.8 (60.5; 63.1)	47.2 (45.8; 48.6)
P1 (%)	3.9 (3.2 4.6)	8.3 (7.4;9.2)	5.7 (4.9;6.4)	24.1 (23.2;25.1)	25.8 (25.1;26.6)	18.3 (17.5;19.0)	20.9 (22.2;23.6)	22.9 (20.0; 21.7)	16.0 (15.3;16.6)
P2 (%)	1.5 (1.1; 1.9)	3.5 (3.0; 4.0)	2.3 (1.9; 2.6)	11.7 (11.1;12.3)	12.5 (12.0; 13.1)	8.3 (7.9;8.8)	10.0 (9.5;10.5)	11.0 (10.6;11.5)	7.3 (6.9;7.7)
Gini-index (nominal expend.and pop. weight.)	0.45 (0.44; 0.47)	0.50 (0.47; 0.52)	0.48 (0.47; 0.50)	0.39 (0.38; 0.41)	0.35 (0.34; 0.36)	0.39 (0.37; 0.40)	0.47 (0.46; 0.48)	0.45 (0.43; 0.46)	0.45 (0.44; 0.46)

Notes: In brackets: 95 per cent confidence intervals (bootstrapped using 100 replications).
Sources: EPI (1994), EPII (1998), EPIII (2003).

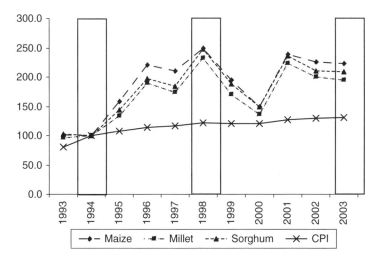

Figure 6.2 Annual cereal price variations, Burkina Faso
Note: Annual average cereal consumer prices; 1994 = 100. CPI: national consumer price index.
Sources: CPI: IAP (2004). Cereal prices: Grain Market Price Surveillance System, Burkina Faso, Ministère du Commerce (2003).

harvest period 1997/98. This drought led to a decline of food-crop production by about 20 per cent. That decline was only partly compensated by a doubling of the imports of food products (from 41.4 to 83.7 billions CFA francs, i.e. from 10 per cent to 18 per cent in relation to primary sector GDP, see IMF, 2000). Also, in 2003 cereal prices were again almost as high as in 1998 despite rather good agriculturel production in 2002/3. This can be explained, first, by a temporary strong demand for imported cereals from neighbouring countries suffering under bad harvests and, second, by a higher demand of the *'offices céréaliers'* and traders still in the remembrance of the second drought which hit the country in 2000/01.

Cereals, mainly millet, sorghum and maize, constituted on average and in nominal terms (that is, in current prices) between 29 per cent (1994), 47 per cent (1998) and 37 per cent (2003) of households' budget in the two lowest quintiles of the expenditure distribution and still between 13 per cent (1994), 24 per cent (1998) and 16 per cent (2003) in the highest quintile of the expenditure distribution. In contrast, the CPI has only a cereal share of 10 per cent. Hence, given the massive price increase of goods of first necessity and the consumption pattern of the poor, simply using the general CPI to inflate the poverty line over time would have been clearly incorrect.

Such a high differential of the inflation rate for the poor and the non-poor is not specific to the Burkinabè case. Pritchett *et al.* (2000) for instance, identified a similar problem when assessing changes in poverty in Indonesia after the 1997 crisis. Given the devaluation and the *El Nino* drought, food prices in Indonesia increased from 1997 to 1999 by more than 160 per cent, while non-food items of the CPI increased by 'only' 81 per cent. Similar to our case, not accounting properly for the weight of food consumption in the budget of the poor would clearly have led to an underestimation of poverty.

Recent development of poverty and inequality

Table 6.1 presents our poverty and inequality assessment for Burkina Faso between 1994 and 2003. On the national level the poverty headcount index, $P0$, that is the percentage of persons below the poverty line, increased strongly between 1994 and 1998 from 55.5 per cent to 61.8 per cent but then decreased also substantively between 1998 and 2003 to 47.2 per cent, that is, to a level lower than in 1994. We find the same trend whether we look at $P1$, the poverty gap, which is the average distance of the poor to the poverty line in relation to the poverty line multiplied by $P0$, or at $P2$, the severity of poverty, which is the average squared poverty gap and thus also takes into account aversion against inequality among the poor by giving more weight to the poorest of the poor. Regarding the potential of growth to reduce poverty, it should be noted that our results for $P1$ imply that the average distance of the poor to the poverty line was roughly 37 per cent in 1994 and 1998 and 34 per cent in 2003.

In rural areas we find approximately the same poverty dynamics, but at a higher level (63.4 per cent to 68.7 per cent to 53.3 per cent). Although throughout all three survey years poverty in urban areas always remained significantly lower than in rural areas, we find that urban poverty jumped from 14.7 per cent in 1994 to 27.3 per cent in 1998 and then decreased to 20.3 per cent in 2003. Therefore, and in contrast to rural areas and despite the fact that it decreased between 1998 and 2003, in 2003 urban poverty was still substantially higher than in 1994.

As shown in Grimm and Günther (2006a) our new assessment of monetary poverty is entirely in line with the development of various social indicators, which can be computed using the same household surveys. For instance, enrollment rates in urban as well as in rural areas decreased between 1994 and 1998 and increased between 1998 and 2003. The share of persons living in a household where the household head suffers some serious physical handicap increased between 1994 and 1998 and decreased afterwards. Whereas living conditions, for example electricity connection or a comfortable access to (proper) water or toilet facilities, did not improve much between 1994 and 1998 (or even deteriorated), they improved substantially between 1998 and 2003.

Between 1994 and 1998, inequality as measured by the Gini index of nominal household expenditures per capita increased from 0.45 to 0.50 in urban areas, but decreased significantly in rural areas from 0.39 to 0.35 and on a national level from 0.47 to 0.45. Thereafter between 1998 and 2003, inequality stagnated more or less in urban areas, increased again to 0.39 in rural areas, but remained constant on a national level. This indicates that between group (urban/rural) inequality decreased during that time, leading to constant national inequality rates despite increasing or constant within group inequality.

Linking poverty and inequality to growth

Table 6.2 allows a comparison of the evolution of poverty and inequality documented in Table 6.1 with the evolution of GDP, GDP per capita and private consumption from National Accounts as well as household per capita expenditure observed in the household surveys. According to the official estimates, real GDP grew by 5.3 per cent per year between 1994 and 1998, by 4.8 per cent between 1998 and 2003 and by 5.1 per cent over the whole observation period 1994 to 2003. Taking into account population growth leads to per capita growth rates of 2.9 per cent, 1.8 per cent and 2.3 per cent for the respective periods (see also Figure 6.1).

National accounts indicate an even higher growth rate for real private consumption per capita for the period 1994 to 1998 (4.6%), but a lower growth rate for the period 1998 to 2003 (2.3%). If we applied a similar price deflator to the one used to compare GDP per capita over time – that is the general CPI – to per capita household expenditure observed in the

Table 6.2 Development of GDP, private consumption and population, Burkina Faso (prices in 1994, Ouagadougou)

	1994	1998	2003
Real GDP (billion CFA francs)	1,189	1,464	1,853
Population (000 s)	9,839	10,809	12,506
Real GDP per capita (NA based, in CFA francs)	120,821	135,434	148,195
Real private consumption per capita (NA based, in CFA francs)	68,004	81,598	90,381
Real household expenditure per capita (HH survey-based, in CFA francs, HPI)[a] (for comparison)	78,772	64,952	85,428
Real household expenditure per capita (HH survey-based, in CFA francs, CPI)[b]	78,772	85,540	99,153

Notes: [a] deflated with household-specific price deflators (HPI), [b] deflated with the official CPI (IAP, 2004)

Sources: Real GDP, population estimates, real GDP per capita and real private consumption per capita: IAP (2004). Real household expenditure per capita: computations by the authors using EPI (1994), EPII (1998) and EPIII (2003). CPI deflator: IAP (2004). HPI deflator: computations by the authors.

household surveys, we would find a more or less similar trend and almost the same growth rate over the whole period 1994 to 2003. But as discussed above, the use of the general CPI is – as it was for the inflation of the poverty line over time – completely inappropriate to compute growth rates in real household expenditures over time, because it does not account for the observed consumption pattern of poorer households and therefore does not reflect correctly the development of their purchasing power.

To overcome this problem, we construct decile specific price deflators separately for urban and rural areas (HPI hereafter, for 'Household Specific Price Index'). More precisely, we computed for both areas the average budget shares at each decile of the expenditure distribution and used these shares to weigh average prices of each expenditure category to construct decile-specific price deflators. These deflators were then used to deflate household expenditure over time. Hence, we explicitly account for the consumption baskets consumed by households and thus account for the impact of relative price shifts on real expenditures.[4] Applying this procedure, we state that real household expenditures per capita decreased by 4.7 per cent per year between 1994 and 1998 and increased by 5.6 per cent per year between 1998 and 2003. Over the whole period this yields an annual growth rate of 0.9 per cent. The substantial decline of the purchasing power of households between 1994 and 1998, and therefore the rise in poverty, was (as discussed) first of all caused by the strong rise in cereal prices.

The pro-poorness of growth

The growth elasticity of poverty, which describes the relationship between growth of GDP per capita and relative changes in poverty, was positive in the period 1994 to 1998 and negative between 1998 and 2003. Table 6.3 shows that between 1994 and 1998, a 1 per cent growth of GDP per capita on the national level was accompanied by an increase of 0.9 per cent in the poverty headcount index. In rural areas this elasticity is slightly lower (0.7%) and in urban areas it is much higher (5.8%). In contrast, between 1998 and 2003 the respective elasticities are −2.9 per cent, −2.7 per cent and −3.2 per cent, illustrating that during this later period macro-economic growth clearly led to poverty reduction.

Over the whole period 1994–2003 the growth elasticity of poverty is slightly negative in rural areas, that is macro-economic growth led to poverty reduction, and slightly positive in urban areas, that is macro-economic growth was not sufficiently strong to reduce poverty. This shows that the relationship between growth and poverty can enormously vary over time and space even within a single country and that average elasticities derived from cross-country regressions as done by Dollar and Kraay (2002) are of only limited use.

To analyse the pro-poorness of growth over the whole distribution, we construct 'growth incidence curves' (GIC) (Ravallion and Chen, 2003) separately for rural and urban areas and for the country as a whole between 1994

Table 6.3 Growth elasticity of poverty, Burkina Faso (growth of GDP per capita)

	1994–98			1998–2003			1994–2003		
	Urban	*Rural*	*National*	*Urban*	*Rural*	*National*	*Urban*	*Rural*	*National*
*P*0 NPL rev.	5.8	0.7	0.9	−3.2	−2.7	−2.9	1.6	−0.8	−0.8
*P*1 NPL rev.	7.2	−4.0	1.9	0.6	−3.7	−1.3	0.8	−3.8	−1.3
*P*2 NPL rev.	8.1	−4.5	2.1	0.6	−4.4	−1.6	0.8	−4.4	−1.5

Sources: Poverty estimates: EPI (1994), EPII (1998) and EPIII (2003). GDP per capita growth rates: IAP (2004).

and 2003. These curves (Figure 6.3) draw for each percentile of the distribution of household expenditure per capita the corresponding growth rate for a given period of time. We again use decile and urban/rural household-specific price deflators (HPIs) instead of the general CPI to compare per capita household expenditures over time.

On the national level the GIC is positive over the whole expenditure distribution and relatively flat. This relatively flat line is, however, the aggregate

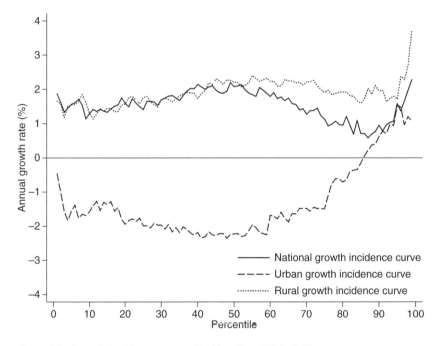

Figure 6.3 Growth incidence curves, Burkina Faso 1994–2003
Sources: EPI (1994), EPII (1998), EPIII (2003).

result of the two countervailing shaped GICs for the two sub-periods 1994–98 and 1998–2003: negative growth rates over the whole distribution between 1994 and 1998 and positive growth rates over the whole distribution between 1998 and 2003 (both curves not presented here).

In rural areas the shape of the GIC is similar to the national GIC up to the 50th percentile, but shows higher growth rates between the 50th and the 100th percentile. This implies that growth was pro-poor in absolute terms, that is poverty decreased, but not in relative terms, i.e. inequality did not decrease. In urban areas the GIC is U-shaped with negative growth rates from the first to the 85th percentile and positive growth rates thereafter. Together these curves illustrate very well the moderate decrease of poverty in rural areas and on the national level as well as the increase of poverty and inequality in urban areas.

Finally, using a methodology suggested by Datt and Ravallion (1992) we decompose changes in poverty into a growth and a redistribution component (reflecting the fact that growth rates usually vary along the expenditure distribution). To obtain a consistent decomposition, we here deflate household expenditure with the implicit inflation rate of the poverty line. This implies that the poverty impact of the shift of relative prices discussed above is included in the growth component of the decomposition. We find that the increase of the poverty headcount index by 6.3 percentage points on the national level between 1994 and 1998 is the result of a growth effect of 7.5 percentage points and of a redistribution effect of −3.4 percentage points (it remains a residual of 2.2 percentage points) (tables not presented here). In other words, the distributional neutral growth rate, that is applying the average (negative) growth rate of household expenditures per capita to all households, would have led to an increase of poverty of 7.5 percentage points. Redistribution between households, that is differences in growth rates known by households, was in favour of poorer households and reduced the potential negative effect of the average growth rate alone by 3.4 percentage points in terms of the headcount index.

For the period 1998 to 2003 the growth component as well as the redistribution component had a poverty-reducing effect. Growth alone would have led to a poverty reduction by 13.7 percentage points. Redistribution, that is on average higher growth rates for poorer households, resulted in a further poverty reduction of 1.7 percentage points. Over the whole period 1994 to 2003 and on the national level, the growth component was −3.2 percentage points and the redistribution component was −4.5 percentage points, that is the effect of growth was slightly lower than the effect of heterogeneity in growth rates over households. Looking at rural and urban areas separately, we can state for both an important growth component – poverty reducing for rural areas and poverty increasing for urban areas – and a very low redistribution component. The low redistribution component within rural as well as in urban areas, combined with the high redistribution component at the national level, shows that the poverty-reducing redistribution effect on the national level stemmed mainly from a decrease of inequality between rural and urban areas.

To illustrate again the impact of relative price shifts on poverty, the above decomposition can be reformulated by asking, what was the impact of the change in relative prices measured by the difference between the inflation of the poverty line and the inflation of the CPI holding constant the mean and the Lorenz curve of the initial distribution? To do this we compute a hypothetical poverty line by inflating the initial poverty line with the inflation rate of the consumption basket underlying the poverty line relative to the inflation rate of the CPI. The growth component represents then the change in poverty that would have occurred with the observed growth rate given that the poor had experienced the same increase in cost of living than the CPI. The 'poverty line' component represents the change in poverty that can be explained by the relative price shifts between the goods consumed by the poor and the goods consumed by the non-poor. That decomposition shows that the relative price shift alone was responsible for an increase of poverty by 11.3 percentage points in rural areas and 7.4 percentage points in urban areas between 1994 and 1998.[5]

Price shocks and their effect on pro-poor growth

As argued in the introduction, a high volatility in basic food prices (caused by severe droughts and amplified by the price liberalization) and changes in the Burkinabè terms of trade due to the devaluation determined to a large extent the development of poverty during the last 10 years. The previous sections have described this development statistically using poverty and pro-poor growth measures. We can now relate these findings to the general economic characteristics and policies of the Burkinabè economy.

First, we discuss the very different impact the devaluation and prize liberalization had on the cotton and subsistence agriculture sector, and how both sectors were related to poverty reduction. Second, we provide various arguments why price volatility especially hurt the rural poor, not only in the short term but also in the medium and long term. Third, we turn to urban households and show how they were affected by the devaluation and how this translated into the massive increase in urban poverty in the mid-1990s.

Distinct dynamics for cotton and subsistence farmers

After the devaluation of the CFA franc in 1994 and a very favourable development of the world market price for cotton between 1994 and 1998, Burkina Faso experienced, as can be seen in Table 6.4, a massive increase of export-driven cotton production while food crop production increased only slightly. Hence, in the last ten years the motor of agricultural growth has clearly been cotton production. The growth in cotton production has led to a high

Table 6.4   Cereal and cotton production, Burkina Faso 1995–2002

	Cereal production				Cotton production		
	ha	*ton*	*kg/ha*	*kg/pc*	*ha*	*ton*	*kg/ha*
1995/96	2,712	2,308	851	228	145	150	1,035
1996/97	2,700	2,448	907	236	201	199	993
1997/98	2,851	1,980	694	186	277	343	1,239
1998/99	2,981	2,620	879	239	340	325	956
1999/00	3,517	2,318	659	206	214	257	1,200
2000/01	3,517	1,593	453	138	210	213	1,012
2001/02	3,694	2,643	716	223	356	395	1,107
2002/03	3,672	2,618	713	215	414	438	1,058
Annual growth	4.4%	1.82%	−2.50%	−0.86%	16.1%	16.5%	0.3%

Notes: Cereal production includes millet, sorghum, fonio, maize and rice. ha: cultivated area. ton: tonnes produced. kg/ha: yield. pop: population. kg/pc: kg produced per capita (with an assumed population increase of 2.7 per cent per year). ha, ton and pop are in 000s.
Source: Economic accounts for the agricultural sector, based on the Enquête Permanente Agricole (1995–2002).

decrease of poverty among cotton farmers from 62.1 per cent in 1994 to 46.8 per cent in 2003.[6] However, between 1994 and 1998, the impact on poverty could have been even greater, given the fact that price gains right after the devaluation in 1994 mainly went to the benefit of the state-owned cotton marketing company Sofitex, which acts as a price stabilizor.[7] Moreover, due to the devaluation of the CFA franc, prices of imported fertilizers increased by roughly 100 per cent between 1990 and 2000 (Ouedraogo, Sanou and Sissao, 2003) reducing actual profit margins of cotton producers. On the other hand the guaranteed fixed price of Sofitex sheltered cotton producers relatively well against the falling world cotton prices between 1998 and 2002.

Poverty reduction among cotton farmers did not massively decrease total rural poverty rates, since in 1994 only 10.3 per cent of households derived part of their income from cotton production. Moreover, it seems that the increasing average income of cotton producers did not have significant demand linkages to the food-crop sector, since in most cotton regions (except 'Cascades') no substantial regional poverty decrease could be observed. However, an indirect positive effect on total rural poverty induced by the growth of the cotton production was certainly the increasing share of population involved in cotton production. This share increased from 10.3 per cent in 1994 to 18.2 per cent in 2003. This increase contributed significantly to the observed poverty reduction in rural areas between 1998 and 2003. Hence the cotton sector can in general be seen as a 'success story' for Burkina Faso.

But it is important to note that the increase of cotton production was mainly due to an expansion of land used for the cultivation of cotton and not to a substantive improvement in productivity (Table 6.4). This suggests that the growth of cotton production during recent years may not be sustainable in this form given the limited land resources in Burkina Faso suitable for cotton production. In addition, too intensive use of land for cotton production has already led to environmental degradation and will later on also limit the production of alternative crops.

Given that in 2003 food crops such as millet, sorghum and maize still accounted on average for 33 per cent of total rural household expenditure, and were produced by 95 per cent of rural households (see Table 6.5), rural living standards still seem to depend heavily on cereal production and cereal prices. The production of food crops only increased slightly between 1994 and 2003, but the growth was just high enough to keep up with population growth (see Table 6.4). Yields have remained constant at very low levels of about 0.8 tonnes per hectare and any subsistence crop agricultural growth stemmed from land and unskilled labour accumulation and neither from an increase in productivity nor from capital accumulation.

During the last decade rural literacy rates did not improve significantly and remained at a low 15 per cent for rural household heads. Also, the use of modern agricultural equipment remained, at least until 1998, rather low. This resulted partly from the significant price increase of the mainly imported agricultural inputs after the CFA franc devaluation. Having recognized this, within the last two years, the government has started to distribute free factors of production (e.g. improved seeds and fertilizer) to the poorest provinces, with some positive impacts already evident in the 2003 household survey.

In addition, whereas cotton farmers are integrated into (international) markets, producers of food crops are rarely integrated neither into international nor into national trade, which has further limited their ability to participate in growth. In 1999, only 15 per cent of cereal production was commercialized (Sirima and Savadogo, 1999) and in 1998 still only 15 per cent of rural households derived income from the sale of food crops (see Table 6.5). The problem of low market integration of the rural poor is not only due to high transportation costs and a lack of infrastructure, but also due to information asymmetries, that is a lack of education and negotiation power of farmers. The importance of the rural road system as well as farmer organizations in overcoming market isolation was for a long time overlooked. However, since the year 2000 it has attracted more attention and higher market participation can already be observed in 2003 (see Table 6.5).

Impact of price volatility on the rural poor

In addition to low productivity and low factor endowments, the unfavourable and annually changing climatic conditions also heavily determine rural

Table 6.5   Rural and urban cereal production, sale and consumption, Burkina Faso

	1994			1998			2003		
	Urban	Rural	Nat.	Urban	Rural	Nat.	Urban	Rural	Nat.
Cereal production	0.26	0.90	0.78	0.25	0.94	0.79	0.24	0.95	0.80
Cereal sold	0.02	0.16	0.13	0.01	0.15	0.12	0.04	0.30	0.25
Cereal consumption	0.12	0.27	0.24	0.23	0.46	0.42	0.17	0.33	0.30
Cereal purchased	0.83	0.15	0.26	0.91	0.49	0.56	0.86	0.33	0.42

Notes: Cereal production: share of households producing mil, sorghum or maize. Cereal sale: share of households selling mil, sorghum or maize on the market. Cereal consumption: share of cereal consumption in total consumption (expenditure). Cereal purchased: share of purchased cereal in total cereal consumption.
Sources: EPI (1994), EPII (1998), EPIII (2003).

poverty rates. In fact among the rural population, income volatility might be just as severe as the low level of income. For instance, during the droughts in 1997/98 and 2000/01 cereal production dropped by 23.5 per cent and 31.3 per cent respectively, leading to a much higher rural poverty rate at least in the year 1998. It is also interesting to note, that even a good harvest might not be particularly beneficial for food-crop farmers since an increase of agricultural production is often followed by a dramatic decrease of prices, which might offset some of the positive effects from an increase in quantity. This phenomenon is also known as King's Law. It arises because cereals are only marginally traded outside of local areas and, hence, they share some common characteristics with locally non-traded commodities. Similar evidence has been found for Mali (Marouani and Raffinot, 2004).

It is difficult to assess the overall effect of good (or bad) harvests on the income of rural households since it depends on whether they are net sellers or buyers of food. For net sellers a bad harvest may result in increasing monetary income (via higher cereal prices) whereas a good harvest may lead to decreasing monetary income (as described above). In contrast for net buyers the impact is vice versa. Hence, price effects might be more important than quantity effects. The statistics presented in Table 6.5 suggest that many rural households are net buyers in particular in bad harvest years and hence are negatively affected by high agricultural prices. For instance the share of purchased cereals in total cereal consumption of rural households increased from 1994 to 1998 by 34 percentage points.

Growth and poverty rates in the rural sector are thus very volatile, which can lead to misleading conclusions about long-term growth–poverty dynamics. The high volatility of agricultural output has, however, not only led to lower income and higher monetary poverty in the years of drought. The related income fluctuations of households might also have negative long-term effects. More precisely, income uncertainty has probably also hindered economic growth in agriculture by constraining investments in the food-crop sector. Whereas price controls on food crops were eliminated leading to high price and income variability, cotton farmers still receive a fixed producer price from Sofitex, which helps to stabilize their revenues. Their stable income in connection with the good organization of the sector allows a much higher credit use (76.8% vs. 5.2%), fertilizer use (92.2% vs. 19.2%) and plough use (57.5% vs. 30.7%) in relation to food-crop farmers. Obviously, this also leads to higher cereal yields among cotton farmers.

Since rainfall in Burkina Faso is not only irregular, but also seasonal, seasonal price fluctuations between the harvest (production surplus) and lean season (production deficit) (see Figure 6.4) further contribute to a high consumption volatility of rural households. Poor farmers are often forced – due to lack of storage facilities and the need for cash income – to sell their products when domestic terms of trade for agricultural products are low (harvest season) and to re-buy the same food items when domestic terms of trade for agricultural products are high (lean season). Hence, prize liberalization, which has certainly lead to an increase of price volatility, has probably increased the vulnerability of poor farmers, given their inability

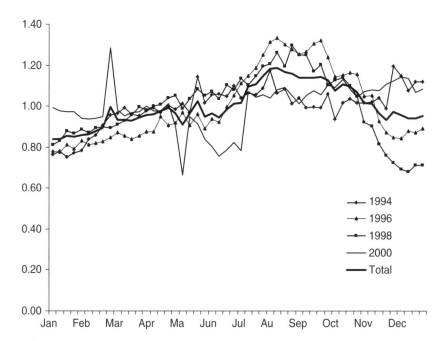

Figure 6.4 Seasonal cereal price variations, Burkina Faso

Notes: Computations for 1994, 1996, 1998 and 2000, annual mean = 1.0. 'Total' is the average 1994–2000.

Source: Grain Market Price Surveillance System, Burkina Faso, Ministère du Commerce (2003).

to cope with fluctuating prices, whereas wealthier farmers might actually have benefited from higher seasonal price variability selling their agricultural output when cereal prices are highest. Especially traders seem to have profited from prize liberalization. This is also reflected by the substantial gap between producer and consumer prices, which is in Burkina Faso twice as high as in other West African countries (Sirima and Savadogo, 1999). The problem of intra-annual fluctuations of cereal prices for poor farmers and the importance of the appropriate institutions such as access to storage or credit to mitigate this phenomenon are now frequently emphasized in the literature (see e.g. Winters, McCulloch and McKay, 2004; Marouani and Raffinot 2004).

The impact of the devaluation on urban employment, earnings and poverty

The devaluation of the CFA franc in 1994 and the resulting increase in prices of imported goods together with the increase of cereal prices in 1997/98 led to a substantial decrease of real incomes in urban areas, given that wages for formal private and public employees were not indexed to inflation. A labour code reform, which started in 1993, eliminated the indexation of wages and a new income policy changed real wage formation.

Table 6.6 shows the median as well as the average monthly earnings for the first (poorest) and second quintile of the earning distribution, separately for three types of workers – public, formal private and informal – for the years 1994, 1998 and 2003.[8] The corresponding distribution of these workers across these three sectors is shown in Table 6.7. In both the public and the private formal sector real wages declined between 1994 and 1998, and increased thereafter, without however reaching their initial level of 1994. It is interesting to note that the decline of earnings between 1994 and 1998 was less pronounced for the workers in the informal sector, showing that the devaluation had most likely positive as well as negative repercussions on the informal economy. On the one hand households of the formal sector had to reduce their total demand for informal goods given their lower real wages, but on the other hand they substituted imported goods with informal goods to certain extent.

The decline of real earnings in the formal private sector after the devaluation may surprise. Indeed in many sectors in which formal wage earners are employed value-added increased between 1994 and 1998 (e.g. manufacturing +22.8%, electricity, gas and water +106.2%, transport and telecommunication +76.8%, trade 31.7%, banks and insurance 45.6%, other commercial services +40.6%) (see Grimm and Günther, 2004), but the earnings and consumption data reported in the household surveys suggest that these benefits were not passed on to workers in form of higher earnings. However, employment in this segment of the labour market increased a bit (see below), but remained very low in absolute terms.

Table 6.6 Average urban real monthly earnings, Burkina Faso (thousands of CFA francs 1994 prices and Ouagadougou, decile-specific deflator used, HPI)

	1994	1998	2003
Public wage earner			
Median	65	57	62
(1994 = 100)	(100)	(87.6)	(95.4)
Average first quintile	32	24	25
Average second quintile	51	43	49
Private formal wage earner			
Median	27	20	24
(1994 = 100)	(100)	(74.0)	(88.9)
Average first quintile	7	7	9
Average second quintile	17	13	18
Independent (informal)			
Median	10	12	15
(1994 = 100)	(100)	(120)	(150)
Average first quintile	2	2	3
Average second quintile	5	6	7
Percentage of workers living in a poor HH			
Public wage earner	1.0	4.0	2.5
Private formal wage earner	6.6	13.3	12.8
Independent (informal)	14.3	26.4	20.3

Note: The monthly minimum wage was 25,000 CFA francs in 2004 (≈ 19,000 CFA francs in 1994 prices). In 1994, 1998 and 2003, 18.8 per cent, 13.7 per cent and 9.3 per cent of all public, private formal and informal workers declared no earnings. Those who declared no earnings are almost all workers in the informal sector; older than the average, often head of a household (except in 2003) and less educated than the average. Another bias is due to the fact that the recall period for wages in 1994 was seven days, whereas in 1998 and 2003 the interviewed person was allowed to choose the recall period. Most declarations were then made per month (25%–30%) or per year (60%). In general, declarations of individual incomes in the Burkinabè household surveys are judged as largely underestimated (for details see Somda, Koné and Sawadogo, 1999). Furthermore, it is not possible to control for the hours worked per month.
Sources: EPI (1994), EPII (1998), EPIII (2003).

As indicated in Table 6.7, the decline of real earnings in the urban labour market obviously pushed formerly inactive household members into the formal and informal labour market in order to maintain initial household income levels. Between 1994 and 1998 the inactivity rate decreased from 23.7 per cent to 17.4 per cent. This resulted in a slight increase of 'open declared' unemployment and a significant increase in the employment rate. Between 1998 and 2003 one can observe a further reduction in the inactivity rate, but this 'only' seems to have led to higher unemployment. In line with this development, the dependency ratio – non-occupied (including unemployed) household members divided by household size – decreased from 63 per cent in 1994 to 57 per cent in 1998 and remained at this level in 2003.

Table 6.7 Occupation and employment of the urban adult population, Burkina Faso (15 years and older, in %)

	1994	1998	2003
Occupied	53.2	58.7	58.2
of whom:			
Public wage earner	12.8	12.3	12.7
Private formal wage earner	13.6	16.8	17.0
Independent (informal)	41.3	(37.5)	40.6
Family help	25.6	(29.0)	21.7
Non-remunerated (outside family)	6.8	4.4	8.1
of whom (only cat. 1–3):			
Permanent contract	85.9	91.2	75.5
Seasonal	6.3	3.5	13.8
Daily	1.8	0.9	8.8
Other temporary	6.0	4.5	1.9
Unemployed (open)	8.9	9.4	12.8
Enrolled in school/univ.	14.3	14.5	13.5
Inactive	23.7	17.4	15.5
Dependency ratio (over households)	63.1	57.4	57.4

Note: Occupation and activity concerns those carried out during the seven days before the survey. However, we computed the same statistics for the main activity over the last 12 months; the results were not significantly different. Numbers in parentheses signify that we presume strong measurement error. The dependency ratio is computed over households, it is defined as the number of inactive and unemployed persons divided by the household size.
Sources: EPI (1994), EPII (1998), EPIII (2003).

A comparison of the employment structure in 1994 and 1998 shows that entries into the labour market were more or less equally distributed across all activities. The only sector which knew a small boost in employment was the formal wage-earner sector. Paid employment in the informal sector (independent and family help)[9] and employment in the public sector remained constant between 1994 and 1998. After 1998 the share of public and private formal wage earners did not change. The share of informal workers plus family helpers decreased whereas the share of non-remunerated workers increased.

Finally one can state that working conditions for those involved in the public or private formal sector or as an independent worker in the informal sector worsened. This is indicated by an increasing share of workers having agreements only on a seasonal, daily or other temporary basis (see Table 6.7). Moreover, migration from rural areas to urban areas put additional substantial pressure on the urban economy. Population census data indicates that the urbanization rate increased between 1975, 1985 and 1996 from 6.4 per cent to 12.7 per cent to 15.5 per cent (INSD, 2000). This is especially the case for Ouagadougou, even if the boom in the cotton sector temporarily reduced migration to urban areas. Recently, the crisis in Côte d'Ivoire has again accelerated urban population growth.

If we compute the poverty headcount ratios for households classified by the principal occupation of the household head, we find for the period 1994 to 1998 that poverty increased from 3.2 per cent to 9.9 per cent among households where the household head was employed in the public sector, from 7.8 per cent to 18.5 per cent among households where the household head was employed in the formal private sector, and from 16.2 per cent to 20.2 per cent among households where the household head worked in the informal sector. This latter increase might be a little surprising, given that the earnings of informal workers slightly increased (Table 6.6); but as the median wage of the informal sector is only half of the private formal sector wage and less than a fourth of the earnings in the public sector huge increases of earnings are necessary to lift an 'average' informal household out of poverty. Second, household heads working in the informal sector, that is persons who have in general to care for the main part of household income faced in fact more or less stagnating earnings, suggesting that mostly secondary household members, in general receiving rather low earnings, experienced a rise in earnings. Third, the dependency ratio in 'informal' households decreased less than in other households.

After 1998, and in line with the development of urban labour earnings, urban poverty rates for all socio-economic groups decreased without, however, reaching the levels of 1994. In this context it is interesting to note that a rise of urban poverty following the devaluation and the implementation of structural reforms was observed in other WAEMU-member countries as well (see for example Haddad, Ruel and Garrett, 1999; Grimm, Guénard and Mesplé-Somps, 2002; Azam, 2004). Moreover the rise and fall of poverty suggests that there is, in absence of any formal safety nets, a short-term trade-off between structural imbalances and poverty. In the medium and long term this trade-off may disappear (see for example the chapter on Senegal by Azam in this book).

To sum up, the main price shocks (and related reforms) in Burkina Faso during the 1990s, namely the devaluation of the CFA franc and the price liberalization, benefited the sectors connected to international as well as domestic trade (in particular cotton), but had some adverse effects on the rural and urban population not directly linked to trade. As the difference between mean income and the poverty line is rather small, the devaluation and decreasing real earnings, especially in the middle part of the urban income distribution, pushed many urban households below the poverty line. The rural poor, mainly food-crop farmers dependent on domestic production and consumption, were mainly affected by the price liberalization, in general leading to higher and more volatile prices for production inputs as well as consumption goods. Hence, since price reforms were not accompanied by technical progress and improvements of markets, they did little to increase household income of food-crop farmers to push them above the poverty line.

Policy recommendations

The analysis above suggests that growth over the last 10 years in Burkina Faso was less pro-poor than it could have been. We have argued that in particular price fluctuations prevented growth being translated into poverty reduction. In addition we have showed that only a small part of the population was directly connected to the sectors where growth arose and that spillover effects from those sectors to other sectors, especially subsistence agriculture, were generally very weak. In what follows we make some recommendations about how poor households could be better protected from price fluctuations and how growth could be fostered in the rural economy where more than 90 per cent of the poor live. The routes we indicate aim to reduce poverty as fast as possible such that the country approaches as much as possible the aim fixed in the Millennium Development Goal 1, that is to halve poverty between 1990 and 2015. In the longer run it is evident that Burkina Faso needs substantial structural change and cannot only rely on agriculture.

Rural growth to foster poverty reduction

We think Burkina Faso's development in the next ten years should be based on broad rural growth. Several other studies (including the Burkinabè PRSP) have already emphasized that rural development is the key to fast substantial poverty reduction in Burkina Faso because it is the sector where most of the poor are situated. We add three equally important issues for why pro-poor growth has to be achieved through further rural development although in the last years rural poverty has already decreased whereas urban poverty has increased.

First, growth in order to be pro-poor does not necessarily have to occur in the sectors where the poor are employed, as the poor can also participate in the growth of sectors to which they are not directly connected if positive linkages between sectors or movements between sectors exist. However, in Burkina Faso the current low market integration hinders many spillover effects between the secondary and primary sectors. Moreover, the very low human capital base of the rural population often hinders them in moving to the formal urban sector at least in the short run. Second, rural growth is also more pro-poor than growth in other sectors, as growth in the agricultural sector seems to be translated best into increasing household incomes,[10] and as the agricultural sector shows lower inequality which allows a higher growth-elasticity of poverty. Third, agricultural development might also have positive effects on the urban (informal) poor, since it decreases prices of food staples mainly consumed by the poor. Hence, we think policies should (i) further support agricultural production but with a higher emphasis on food crop farmers, (ii) reduce farmers' risk to external shocks (including diversification into non-farm incomes), (iii) integrate markets, and (iv) ensure moderate prices of goods of first necessity.

Agricultural production

To achieve a higher and a more sustained rate of pro-poor growth an intensification of agricultural production is necessary. Food-crop farmers have a much lower productivity than cotton farmers and in the past the slight increases in productivity were completely offset by population growth. An increase in productivity could be achieved through the construction of irrigation systems, the higher use of fertilizers,[11] modern equipment, investment in human capital and the expansion of cultivable land. Since land expansion has already reached its limits, increasing productivity should be the policy to choose. A policy, which aims to increase productivity through increased human capital, must however, at least in the medium run, heavily invest in adult education to see any results. Hence, investments into irrigation systems, modern equipment and subsidies for fertilizers should, at least in the short run, yield higher returns.

However, one should keep in mind that, given the irregular rainfall in Burkina Faso, a pure focus on agricultural production would increase the volatility of household incomes. Moreover, a promotion of higher productivity without at the same time ensuring better storing, processing and market integration, including export of those products, will lead to decreasing prices. This would certainly have a very positive effect on the poverty line because of the decreasing basic food prices, but this might not lead to substantial higher average household incomes as the terms of trade for farm products would decrease. This trade-off, of whether increasing agricultural productivity is good for the poor, has been intensively discussed in the literature (see for example Kydd and Dorward, 2004; Timmer, 2003). However, among others, Datt and Ravallion (1998) showed recently for the case of India that productivity increases should generally have a positive impact on poverty.

Besides agricultural intensification, another strategy might be to diversify into cash crops with higher yields and prices. An export-led agricultural growth strategy has actually been the driver of agricultural growth within the last years and has also resulted in decreasing poverty rates among cotton farmers. This trend might lead to the misleading conclusion that one should only focus on cotton (or other export crops) for rural poverty reduction. It is however important to keep in mind that, first, export oriented cash crops have much less spill-over effects than domestically traded food crops, second, external price volatility is added to the climatic risk, and third cultivatable land for cotton is limited.

Risk reduction

Output uncertainty and risk is another major barrier for rural growth and poverty reduction in Burkina Faso. Hence, there might be some benefits from temporary state interventions to reduce transitory poverty by securing more stable revenues and consumption prices for the rural poor. Moreover, such interventions could have positive effects on productivity through enhanced investments. Hence, any policy reducing the risk of farmers should not only be pro-poor but also 'pro-growth'. However, such state interventions can also heavily distort markets, leading to the question to what extent a trade-off between distorted (but stable) and free (but efficient) rural markets exists.

Policies could consider directly stabilizing prices of certain products the poor produce and consume, which would also have a very positive effect on poverty. But because this might endanger market efficiency, one would prefer to think of, first, establishing 'drought insurances' or countercyclical fiscal policies to ensure food security and moderate prices of basic food items; second, subsidizing agricultural investments and inputs (Dorward *et al.*, 2004); and, third, delivering storages, such that farmers can better stock their production throughout the year. The very well-organized cotton sector, although sometimes said to be not sufficiently liberalized, might in this case stand as an example of how moderate risk-reducing interventionist policies can lead to higher efficiency.

Since some climatic vulnerability will always remain, more important as an 'anti-risk strategy' for rural households seems to be diversification into non-farm sectors. Income diversification is indeed already present in Burkina Faso. Whereas agricultural production is most of all used for auto-consumption, most of rural household monetary earnings originate from non-farm sources (30%–40%). Another 'special feature' of Burkinabè rural household income is the high percentage of transfers either from urban or external zones. This shows that rural development policies are not well designed if they purely focus on agricultural output neglecting rural non-farm income opportunities.

Market integration

Besides increasing and diversifying agricultural output and decreasing rural risk, market integration is the third pillar on which pro-poor growth policies should build. Whereas the former two mainly enhance poverty reduction through higher (real) growth rates, greater market integration will help to translate existing growth into higher household income. To integrate markets and to reduce transaction costs heavy investments into rural infra-structure have to take place. Farmers' organizations, improved marketing channels and better information systems should be added to ensure func-tioning markets, which would foster the commercialization of agricultural products and a better allocation of resources. This would again have a positive impact on cereal prices.

Safety nets to prevent an urbanization of poverty

An important factor behind the described increase of urban poverty was the fact that there was no safety net to protect the population from the adverse effects of the devaluation and the structural adjustment programme. Real incomes stagnated or even declined, prices for several food items increased substantially and employment conditions became less stable.

Policy implications might be temporary measures which guarantee a minimum real income to the poor (for instance through price regulation for some food items of first necessity), or an adjustment of real wages in the formal sector to inflation which would also most likely have positive effects on the informal sector. Given that government pay policies and limited competition in product markets can obviously lead to wage misalignment and real wage rigidity and finally to an overvaluation of the currency (see for example Rama, 1998), these policies have of course to be undertaken carefully and with moderation.

Given that more than 60 per cent of the total urban workforce works in the informal sector, that 20 per cent of them are among the poor and that they usually face high income volatility, poverty reduction strategies have to comprise specific measures for this sector. For workers in the informal sector the most important problem is the high volatility of the demand for informal goods. A high-risk environment reduces incentives to invest and therefore investments in the informal sector are usually relatively low.

In contrast, during the last ten years the Burkinabè economy knew relatively huge amounts of public and formal private investment. However, the several growth-accounting studies suggest that the total factor productivity stagnated (Chambas, Combes and Guillaumont *et al.*, 1999; Sirima and Savadogo, 2001); that is, that obviously the returns on these investments have been very low. Given these facts, it might be promising to exploit the growth potential of individuals acting in the informal sector, which are so far most of the time prevented from investing due to limited or no access to the credit market, but who may have investment opportunities with higher marginal returns.

Conclusion

After rising poverty in the mid-1990s, and especially in urban areas, Burkina Faso now seems to be on a poverty-reducing growth path. However, the national favourable long-term growth elasticities of poverty hide a high variability of elasticities across time and across various household groups. Moreover, we have shown that growth could be even more pro-poor than it has been in the past ten years. In other words, the structure of growth does not use the whole potential the country has to reduce poverty. In particular, we have shown that the main growth-seeking policies in Burkina Faso during the 1990s, namely the devaluation of the CFA franc and a policy of trade and price liberalization, led to considerable growth rates in the sectors connected to international as well as domestic trade, but had adverse effects, at least in the short term, on large parts of the rural and especially urban population.

The devaluation of the CFA franc and price liberalization certainly led to an expansion of cotton exports and to a lesser extent to growth in the formal secondary and tertiary sector. However, all these sectors are marked by a rather small percentage of the total Burkinabè workforce and by spatial concentration. Hence, growth in Burkina Faso bypassed a large share of the informal rural and urban population. The high regional market segmentation of the economy was furthermore a barrier to significant positive spillover effects.

The CFA franc devaluation which led to decreasing real earnings among the urban population pushed many urban households below the poverty line. In addition, in contrast to what seem to have happened in Senegal (see the chapter by Azam in this book) the freed resources stemming from the fall in the real value of the government wage bill were not productively enough invested in favour of the poor. The rural poor, mainly dependent on domestic production and consumption, were more affected by the price liberalization. In combination with seasonal and annual production fluctuations, the price liberalization led to more volatile prices for production inputs as well as outputs. This was certainly beneficial for traders and some richer rural households, but had some adverse effects on many poorer agricultural households. Hence, as price reforms and shocks did not come along with technical progress, improvements of markets and safety nets, they did little to increase rural household income.

Finally, we have highlighted, based on previous work, that price shocks also constitute an analytical challenge when assessing pro-poor growth. In an economy where consumption habits are very heterogeneous across the income distribution and where relative prices show huge fluctuations due to climatic and economic shocks, it is critical to integrate these price shifts into the measurement of pro-poor growth. Otherwise, assessments of how growth translated into poverty reduction may be biased.

Notes

1. One year after the revolution the country adopted 'Burkina Faso' as the country's name. Until August 1984 the official name was 'Upper Volta'.
2. For a detailed description of the data, see Grimm and Günther (2004).
3. See, for instance Fofack, Monga and Tuluy (2001) (for the period 1994 to 1998), INSD (2003) and Lachaud (2003).
4. The general issue of taking into account differential inflation when measuring household income growth and in particular pro-poor growth over time is discussed in Grimm and Günther (2006b).
5. A detailed presentation of the results of the various decompositions can be found in Grimm and Günther (2006a).
6. However, it is important to note that the group of cotton farmers is a very heterogeneous group. It comprises some farmers with significant land areas as well as many farmers which cultivate cotton only on small plots. Moreover, most of the cotton farmers also cultivate food crops. In what follows, cotton farmers or

cotton households stand for households where at least some cotton is cultivated, independent of other cultivated crops. This classification is quite useful, as all households which sell at least some cotton to the state owned cotton marketing company Sofitex can benefit from credits and fertilizers to which subsistence farmers have hardly any access.

7. Sofitex guarantees a fixed purchasing price to cotton producers at the beginning of the cropping year. Depending on the development of the world market price for cotton, Sofitex realizes a surplus and keeps it or realizes a loss and uses past surpluses to pay producers the guaranteed price. In case of high surpluses the purchasing price can be augmented in the following season.
8. For the limits of this data, see the *Note* to Table 6.7.
9. The number of non-agricultural enterprises increased between 1994 and 1998 from 0.63 to 0.66 per household. The average number of employed persons in these enterprises increased from 2.0 to 2.2. This suggests that misclassification between independent informal and family help is most likely the reason for the significant drop in the share of informal workers between 1994 and 1998.
10. The development of sectoral value-added as indicated by National Accounts is close to the stated increase of consumption of households connected to this sector. This is not the case for most sectors in the secondary and tertiary sector, where often value-added increased much faster than household's consumption, and hence the growth-elasticity of poverty was rather low (see Grimm and Günther, 2004).
11. However, to do this appropriately more research would be necessary to develop fertilizers which are appropriate for the soils in Burkina Faso and which limit environmental damage.

References

Azam, J.-P. (2004) 'Poverty and Growth in the WAEMU after the 1994 Devaluation', *Journal of African Economies*, 13: 536–62.

Chambas, G., Combes, J.-L., Guillaumont, P., Guillaumont, S. and Laporte, B. (1999) 'Burkina Faso: les facteurs de croissance à long terme'. Document de Stratégie de Développement Rural, à l'Horizon 2015. Report prepared for the OECD research programme on emerging Africa. Paris: OECD.

Datt, G. and Ravallion, M. (1992)'Growth and Redistribution Components of Changes in Poverty Measures. A Decomposition with Applications to Brazil and India in the 1980s', *Journal of Development Economics*, 38: 275–95.

Datt, G. and Ravallion, M. (1998) 'Farm Productivity and Rural Poverty in India', *Journal of Development Studies*, 34/4: 62–85.

Dollar, D. and Kray, A. (2002) 'Growth is Good for the Poor', *Journal of Economic Growth*, 7: 195–225.

Dorward, A., Kydd, J., Morrison, J. and Urey, I. (2004) 'A Policy Agenda for Pro-Poor Agricultural Growth', *World Development*, 32/1: 73–89.

Fofack, H., Monga, C. and Tuluy, H. (2001) 'Household Welfare and Poverty Dynamics in Burkina Faso: Empirical Evidence from Household Surveys', World Bank Policy Research Working Paper no. 2590, Washington, DC: World Bank.

Grimm, M., Guénard, C. and Mesplé-Somps, S. (2002) 'What Has Happened to the Urban Population in Côte D'Ivoire Since the Eighties? An Analysis of Monetary Poverty and Deprivation over 15 Years of Household Data', *World Development*, 30/6: 1073–95.

Grimm, M. and Günther, I. (2004) 'How to Achieve Pro-Poor Growth in a Poor Economy. The Case of Burkina Faso. Report Prepared for the Operationalizing Pro-Poor-Growth-Project', sponsored by the World Bank, DFID, AFD, and BMZ (GTZ, KFW), Eschborn: GTZ.

Grimm, M. and Günther, I. (2006a) 'Growth and Poverty in Burkina Faso. A Reassessment of the Paradox', *Journal of African Economies*, forthcoming.

Grimm, M. and Günther, I. (2006b) 'Measuring Pro-Poor Growth when Relative Prices Shift', *Journal of Development Economics*, forthcoming.

Haddad, L., Ruel, M.T. and Garrett, J.L. (1999) 'Are Urban Poverty and Undernutrition Growing? Some Newly Assembled Evidence', *World Development*, 27/11:1891–1904.

IAP (2004) 'Instrument Automatisé de Prévision, Data files', Ministère de l'Economie et des Finances, Burkina Faso.

IMF (2000) 'Burkina Faso: Recent Economic Developments', IMF Staff Country Report No. 00/103, Washington, DC: International Monetary Fund.

IMF (2005) 'Burkina Faso: Selected Issues and Statistical Appendix', IMF Staff Country Report no. 05/358 (2005), Washington, DC: International Monetary Fund.

INSD (2001) 'Analyse des résultats du Recensement Général de la Population et de l'habitation de 1996', Vol. 1. Burkina Faso: Institut National de la Statistique et de la Démographie.

INSD (2003) 'Burkina Faso: La pauvreté en 2003 (Résumé)', Preliminary version. Burkina Faso: Institut National de la Statistique et de la Démographie.

Kydd, J. and Dorward, A. (2004) 'Agricultural Development and Pro-Poor Economic Growth in Sub-Saharan Africa: Potential and Policy', *Oxford Development Studies*, 32/1:37–57.

Lachaud, J.-P. (2003) 'Pauvreté et inégalité au Burkina Faso: Profil et dynamique'. Report prepared for the United Nations Development Program. UNDP, Burkina Faso: Ouagadougou.

Marouani, M. and Raffinot, M. (2004) 'Perspectives on Growth and Poverty Reduction in Mali'. Document de travail DT 05. Paris: DIAL.

Ministère du Commerce (2003) 'Grain Market Price Surveillance System', Burkina Faso: Ministère du Commerce.

Ministère de l'Economie et des Finances, (2000) 'Burkina Faso: Poverty Reduction Strategy Paper'. Burkina Faso: Ministère de l'Economie et des Finances.

Ouedraogo, N., Sanou, A. and Sissao, C. (2003)'Etude de l'impact des variations du prix du coton sur la pauvreté rurale au Burkina Faso'. Report prepared with support of the GTZ, Ministère de l'Economie et des Finances, Burkina Faso: Ouagadougou.

Pritchett, L., Suharso, Y., Sumarto, S. and Suryahadi, A. (2000) 'The Evolution of Poverty During the Crisis in Indonesia, 1996 to 1999'. Social Monitoring and Early Response Unit, Washington, DC/Jakarta: World Bank.

Rama, M. (1998) 'Wage Misalignment in CFA Countries. Are Labour Market Policies to Blame?', Policy Research Working Paper 1873, Washington, DC: World Bank.

Ravallion, M. and Chen, S. (2003) 'Measuring Pro-Poor Growth', *Economic Letters*, 78: 93–99.

Sirima, B. and Savadogo, P. (1999) 'Burkina Faso: Compétitivité et croissance économique. Orientations, Stratégies et actions', Mimeo, Burkina Faso: Ministry of Economy and Finance and World Bank.

Sirima, B. and Savadogo, P. (2001) 'Burkina Faso: Competitiveness and Economic Growth. Policies, Strategies, Actions', Mimeo, Burkina Faso: Ministry of Economy and Finance and World Bank.

Somda, P., Kone, M. and Sawadogo, S.M. (1999) 'Analyse de la qualité des données de l'Enquête Prioritaire', Project MIMAP, Burkina Faso: Cedres.

Timmer, P.C. (2003) 'Agriculture and Pro-Poor Growth. Pro-Poor Economic Growth Research Studies', Mimeo, Boston: Development Alternatives, Inc. and Boston Institute for Developing Economies.

UNDP (2004) 'The Human Development Report 2004: Cultural Liberty in Today's Diverse World'. UNDP, New York.

Winters, L.A., McCulloch, N. and McKay, A. (2004) 'Trade Liberalization and Poverty: The Evidence so Far', *Journal of Economic Literature*, 42/1:72–115.

7
A Historical Perspective on Pro-Poor Growth in Indonesia*

C. Peter Timmer

Introduction

Indonesia's experience with 'pro-poor growth', defined here to mean rapid economic growth with no significant deterioration in income distribution, has been highly varied since the late nineteenth century. This variation alone is an important result, as Indonesia's geographical location, the cultural background of its people, and its colonial settlers did not change much over that period. Thus changes in domestic policies, the gradual development of institutions, or the external environment, including new technologies, must account for both the positive and negative experiences with pro-poor growth. The goal of this chapter is to understand the historical record itself – *what* happened; the scope for domestic policy initiatives to bring about pro-poor growth – *how* it happened; and the political economy of the growth record – *why* it happened. Because much of the positive experience occurred during the Suharto regime, the story concentrates especially on that period. The analytical approach is thus 'historical political economy' and tries to incorporate both long-run economic processes and political reaction to them.

Indonesia has been very important to the development profession, and it has been studied for a long time. Java was the original home of the 'dual economy' analysed by Boeke (1946) and formalized by Lewis (1954). The Dutch exploited the Netherland East Indies from the seventeenth to early in the twentieth century, but then experimented with an 'ethical policy' for the colony under political pressure at home, and the poor benefited significantly. During the Great Depression, the Second World War and the fight for Independence, the Indonesian economy deteriorated rapidly (not helped by abysmal management of macro-economic affairs by the Dutch during the Great Depression), and the poor suffered disproportionately. After declaring

---

* This chapter draws heavily on the Indonesia country paper for the Pro-Poor Growth project carried out by the World Bank and collaborating agencies.

Independence in 1945, Sukarno eventually put 'politics in command' in 1959 and produced a ruinous inflation that brought much of the population to near-starvation in the mid-1960s. It was with just cause that Gunnar Myrdal pronounced in *Asian Drama* in 1967 that 'no economist holds out any hope for Indonesia'.

Consequently, Indonesia's rapid, pro-poor growth for the next 30 years astonished the development profession and, along with other countries in East and Southeast Asia, Indonesia became the object of intense analysis (World Bank, 1993). Weak starting conditions influenced how Indonesian economic planners approached the task of linking growth to the poor. They designed a three-tiered strategy for pro-poor growth which linked sound macro economic policy to market activities that were facilitated by progressively lower transactions costs, which in turn were linked to household decisions about labour supply, agricultural production, and investment in the non-tradable economy. The rate of poverty reduction driven by this strategy depended on the overall rate of growth in GDP, which was a function of macro-economic policy (and the external environment), and the extent to which poor households were connected to this growth.

Why President Suharto's government carried out the pro-poor strategy as aggressively as it did remains a mystery of modern political economy, although a personal concern for the welfare of farmers seems to be at least part of the explanation. This personal engagement may also have inhibited more flexible policies as the economy evolved and matured. Hull (2004) notes the continued tendency of the elite to think of peasants as illiterate, which matched President Suharto's memories of growing up among peasants in rural Central Java. The personal influence of the President played a major role in the evolution of policy, and this role probably became counterproductive as the society became more affluent and sophisticated and as the economy became more complex.

The tension created by role of a strong leader in a non-democratic system has brought the failure of political and institutional development during the Suharto era to the fore, but it also raises obvious questions about causality. Can rapid, pro-poor growth be implemented by authoritarian regimes? Indonesia's record, along with that of most of East and Southeast Asia, says yes. Can it be sustained? For three decades perhaps, but the strains on corporate and political governance were visibly showing early in the 1990s, and the Asian Financial Crisis in 1997 merely served as the catalyst to bring down a regime that was clearly not sustainable in short-run political terms or in long-run institutional terms. But which comes first? Can rapid, pro-poor economic growth build the groundwork for the political and institutional framework that will ultimately support it, or does this framework have to be put in place first? Current development strategies hang on how this question is answered.

The historical setting for Indonesia's growth experience

Under Dutch colonial rule, which started in the fifteenth century and ended with Indonesia's declaration of Independence in 1945, the trade and tax regime favoured Dutch extraction of income, except for a brief period at the beginning of the twentieth century when Dutch public opinion supported a more developmental approach to the colony, known as the 'ethical policy'. However, this policy collapsed with world prices for export commodities in the 1920s, and Indonesia experienced especially poor economic management during the Great Depression. The Dutch forced the Netherland East Indies to stay on the Gold Standard well after their regional competitors, including the Japanese, devalued.

The colonial authorities did build a significant network of irrigation canals, roads, ports and shipping facilities, and railroads. There was, however, very little investment in education of the local population. Only 3.5 per cent of the population was attending school of any kind in 1939 compared with 13.3 per cent in 1995. The historical record suggests there was severe poverty in the mid-nineteenth century, which fell gradually until the 1920s. Poverty increased rapidly until the end of the Second World War.

After Independence, the Sukarno government put 'politics in command' after 1958. It severely neglected agriculture, adopted an 'inward looking' development policy, and the result was economic and political chaos by the mid-1960s. Incomes fell and the hyper-inflation in 1965/66 had an impact on virtually everyone. The postwar recovery had helped reduce poverty, but the poverty rate increased rapidly as inflation soared and the economy collapsed. Probably 70 per cent of the population was 'absolutely poor' by 1966. Average food energy intake was about 1,600 kilocalories per day. Hunger was widespread.

Pro-poor growth in historical perspective

Thanks to the painstaking historical research of Pierre van der Eng (1993a, 1993b, 2000, 2002), it is possible to construct a long-run indicator of how well the poor have fared since 1880. Van der Eng's time-series data from 1880 to 1990 can be divided into five main epochs: Dutch colonial exploitation of the Indonesian economy (1880–1905); the 'ethical policy' era when efforts were made by the Dutch to improve living standards of native Indonesians (1905–25); the tumultuous period during the Great Depression, Pacific War and fight for Independence (1925–50); the Sukarno era (1950–65), whose 'guided economy' after 1958 created economic turmoil; and President Suharto's 'New Order' regime in the 1965–90 period, which is the main focus of this chapter. The original van der Eng data end in 1990. In view of the growing consensus in the development profession that long-run institutional development is the key to sustained economic growth and structural transformation, this historical perspective is essential to understanding the starting point for development efforts in the modern era, as well as the path-dependency of institutional evolution (North, 1990).

Three sets of calculations are made for each epoch (see Table 7.1). The first column in Table 7.1 shows the trend growth rate of incomes per capita (YPC), as estimated from a semi-logarithmic time trend for the respective time period. These growth rates vary widely. There was a sharp deterioration over the quarter century of economic chaos from 1925 to 1950, which contrasts equally sharply with strong growth in both the 'ethical policy' era under the Dutch and, strikingly, in the Suharto era. Over the entire time period for which van der Eng reports these data, per capita incomes rose 0.89 per cent per year.

Table 7.1 Long-run patterns of pro-poor growth in Indonesia[a]

(1) Time period	(2) Growth rates (%) YPC	KCAL	(3) Income elasticity for KCAL	(4) Rate of pro-poor growth (RPPG)[b]
Dutch colonial exploitation 1880–1905	0.33	−0.34	0.051 0.165	0.05
'Ethical policy' under the Dutch 1905–25	1.63	1.39	0.878 2.805	4.57
Depression, the Pacific War and the Fight for Independence 1925–50	−2.42	−0.78	0.333 1.064	−2.57
The Sukarno era, including the 'guided economy' Period 1950–65	1.46	0.68	0.509 1.626	2.37
The 'new order' Regime of Suharto 1965–90	3.45	2.10	0.595 1.901	6.56
The long-run averages, 1880–1990	0.89	0.22	0.313 1.000	0.89

Notes: [a] Details of the regressions are available from the author.
[b] The rate of pro-poor growth (RPPG) is calculated as the product of the growth rate in per capita income times the 'standardized' income elasticity of demand for food energy (KCAL), where the base income elasticity is the value for the entire time period from 1880 to 1990 (0.313). Growth rates are calculated as least-squares time trends of logarithmic values of incomes per capita (YPC) and average daily per capita food energy intake per capita (KCAL). The 'top' value for the income elasticity of demand for food energy for each epoch is estimated as a constant elasticity value from a double logarithmic function. The 'bottom' value re-scales this estimated value, with the 1880–1990 average of 0.313 equal to 1.000. As an example, the RPPG value of 6.56 for the Suharto era from 1965 to 1990 results from the OLS-estimated rate of growth in per capita income of 3.45 per cent, times the 'standardized' income elasticity of 1.901. This standardized value is computed by scaling up the OLS-estimated income elasticity for the period of 0.595 from the historical base income elasticity of 0.313. Thus 0.595/0.313 = 1.901, and 3.45 × 1.901 = 6.56.

The second column in Table 7.1 shows the similarly estimated time trend for intake of food energy, as measured from food-balance-sheet data on kilocalories (KCAL) consumed per capita per day, on average for each year from 1880 to 1990. During two epochs this time trend was negative, which indicates a decline in nutritional status on average for the whole society and the strong likelihood of significant increases in hunger among the poor. During such episodes, poverty was rising. A sharply positive trend in food energy intake, however, as during the 'ethical policy' era and the early Suharto era, suggests that income growth was reaching the poor and improving their access to food. Over the entire time period, the trend in food energy intake was just 0.2 per cent per year.

The relationship between the variables underlying these two trends is also reported in Table 7.1. The third column reports the average income elasticity of demand for food energy (KCAL), which is estimated from the annual data for each epoch. Importantly, the pattern of coefficients is similar for the income elasticities and the rate of change in food energy intake. The logic connecting the two is straightforward. Engel's Law suggests that the income elasticity of demand for food (of which energy is an important component for the poor) is a declining function of income level. When income growth includes the poor, their higher income elasticities for food energy raise the income elasticity observed on average. It is thus possible to infer what is happening to the poor during long-run periods of economic growth (or decline) by analysing these changes in food energy intake (Timmer, 1996b).

This approach works, of course, only for those societies in which the poor wish to increase their food energy intake when their incomes increase – that is, when they are still on the rising part of the Engel curve. This is the case for Indonesia. Even in 2002 when the last SUSENAS results were reported, at least the bottom half of the income distribution had significantly positive Engel elasticities for food energy. This half of the population subsists on less than $2 per day (World Bank, 2003).

Finally, Table 7.1 carries this inference process to its logical conclusion, by constructing a measure of the 'rate of pro-poor growth' in column 4. The calculation is based on an analytical relationship between the overall incidence of poverty and the observed, average income elasticity of demand. The relationship can be demonstrated formally (see the Appendix).

The income elasticity of food energy for the entire period from 1880 to 1990, estimated to be 0.313, is used as the long-run base, scaled to one. It is multiplied by the long-run growth rate in per capita incomes, 0.89 per cent per year, to generate the long-run average rate of pro-poor growth (RPPG) of 0.89. The income elasticity for each separate epoch is then scaled relative to the long-run average, and multiplied by the growth rate in per capita incomes, to generate the RPPG for each epoch.[1]

As shown in Table 7.1, the RPPG has varied dramatically over time, from −2.53 during the 1925–50 epoch, to 4.57 during the 'ethical policy' era, 1905–25. The rate is surprisingly high during the Sukarno era, when economic policy is widely regarded to have been a disaster. But a combination of a modest recovery from the quarter century of depression and wars, with average per capita incomes rising 1.5 per cent per year, and a large average income elasticity for food energy, suggest that what growth there was actually reached the poor.

The strongest pro-poor growth has been since 1965. The data analysed in Table 7.1 carry the story to 1990 (the *starting point* for many of the country studies in this project), which is well-before the Asian financial crisis in 1997/98. The quarter century from 1965 to 1990 has an IPPG of 6.56, which is more than seven times the long-run average and nearly half again as large as during the next best epoch, from 1905 to 1925. Clearly, something quite outside earlier historical experience was going on during the first two and a half decades of the Suharto era. It is important to understand what made this era so pro-poor.

Recent experience with pro-poor growth

This remarkable record came to an abrupt end with the Asian financial crisis that began late in 1997. A particularly dramatic way to see the impact of the crisis on the entire income distribution is to see how the distribution of food consumption from starchy staples changes. The starchy staple ratio – an indicator of food quality that measures the share of food energy intake derived from such starches as rice, wheat, corn, potatoes, cassava and yams – is a sensitive indicator of welfare status. Better-off households consume higher quality foods, including animal products, fruits and vegetables. Changes in the starchy staple ratio (SSR), especially in relation to the percentile of household expenditures or income, can illuminate changes in income distribution – hence pointing to changes in levels of poverty.

These distributions are available for 1996, just before the financial crisis; 1999, in the middle of the crisis; and 2002, as the recovery slowly gained momentum. The potential to see changes in the distribution of income is clearly evident in the SSR plots for these three years. These plots are based on individual household records from SUSENAS and reported in Molyneaux (2003) (see Figure 7.1).

The impact of the financial crisis on well-being for the entire Indonesian society is readily seen in the shift upward in the SSR curve between 1996 and 1999. A 'flattening' of the curve in 1999 reveals a more equal income distribution. This shift is also apparent in summary measures of income distribution: the Gini coefficient fell significantly between the two years, from 36.5 to 31.5 (Papanek, 2004).

What is startling is the dramatic improvement in nutritional welfare of the poor between 1999 and 2002. Except for the top decile of expenditures, the levels surpassed even those of 1996. The evidence points to substantial gains in dietary quality, especially a rapid increase in consumption of

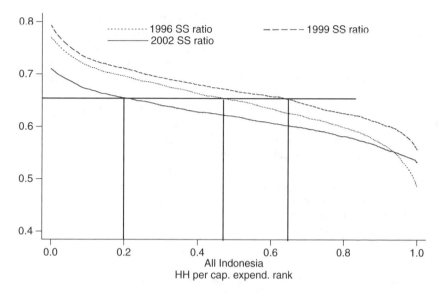

Figure 7.1   Starchy staple ratios by income percentile and year, Indonesia
Source: Molyneaux (2003).

foods rich in micronutrients. The notable improvement in the quality of the average Indonesian's diet since the mid-1990s, with greater quantities of fruits, vegetables and livestock products, has significant implications for agricultural development strategy, especially for Java's very small farmers (see Molyneaux and Rosner, 2004).

The strategic approach to pro-poor growth: connecting the poor

The Mellor model of poverty reduction shows why growth in production of non-tradables is the main mechanism pulling the rural underemployed out of poverty (Mellor, 2000). In Mellor's interpretation, the non-tradables sector is demand-constrained. Only rapid growth in incomes in households that *purchase* the goods and services produced by this sector can stimulate rapid reductions in poverty. These purchasing households might not necessarily be poor by the standards of the country.

Historically, the sources of such growth were rapid increases in the incomes of commercial agricultural households and, somewhat later, in the incomes from wage labour in the manufactured export sector. When both commercial agriculture and the manufactured export sector are booming, demand for non-tradable goods and services also booms, leading to accelerated impact on poverty reduction.

In the real world of policy-making, there is a major distinction between knowing 'what to do', as suggested by the Mellor model, and knowing 'how to do it' (Pardey and Smith, 2004). The writings, statements and memoirs of officials who served in the Suharto government offer a gold-mine of information to address both the 'how' and the 'why' (see also below) (Thee, 2003; Prawiro, 1998; Afiff, 2004).

The pro-poor growth strategy articulated by these officials emphasized rapid increases in the demand for unskilled labour. A macro-economic policy that stressed stability to lower risks to investors, a competitive exchange rate to keep tradable goods production profitable, and a monetary and fiscal policy that did not subsidize the use of capital, was the growth engine for the market economy. Markets were the arena for participation by the poor in economic activities that improved their productivity and house-hold incomes. The household economy served as the foundation of the pro-poor strategy, with *public* investments made to improve their human capital and capabilities. The local market economy then served as the bridge to the growth-oriented macro policy. This market economy was accessible to the poor because transactions costs of engagement were manageable and the risks low.

Even a casual reading of the memoirs of the technocrats who were respons-ible for designing economic policy in the early years of the Suharto regime reveals their emphasis on the importance of economic growth as the only way to reduce poverty.[2] Their assessment of the economic situation in late 1965 was stark; nearly the entire population was poor by absolute standards. Indonesians had one-half the per capita income of India at the same time, for example. In the short term there was simply no choice but to stress economic growth over poverty reduction – there was nothing to 'redistribute'. The first steps were straightforward: government activities that were repressing economic growth had to stop.[3]

In the medium and longer run, policy-makers had an array of stra-tegic choices. Since the disastrous experience of 'politics in command' of the 'guided economy' under Sukarno was vivid in everyone's mind, the early strategy had a clear focus: stabilize macro-economic policy through a balanced budget and a realistic exchange rate; stabilize the food economy by controlling rice prices (using market-compatible interventions); and rehab-ilitate infrastructure using the proceeds from foreign aid. Trade and invest-ment policy was opened, and in 1971 the capital account was dramatically liberalized.[4]

Note how unorthodox this early experiment with liberalization and struc-tural adjustment was, and yet how effective. There was much more govern-ment intervention in maintaining a stable exchange rate, and in overall trade policy than is now fashionable. The opening of the capital market preceded (by decades) efforts to provide sound regulation of the banking sector. It is now argued that the seeds of economic collapse during the Asian financial crisis were planted during this early reform era (Cole and Slade, 1998). But three decades of rapid, pro-poor growth intervened.

Paradoxical as it seems now, it was Suharto himself who stressed to the technocrats the importance of connecting the poor to economic growth, and political scientists continue to debate why he was so concerned about this connection. Much of the emphasis on improving the welfare of the rural population was, in fact, initiated by the President.[5] He knew that most of the poor lived in rural areas and that they could be helped through agricultural development, schools, clinics and family-planning centres, and investments in rural infrastructure (Rock, 2002, 2003). Out of this concern, the technocrats evolved a development strategy that consciously tried to merge the ingredients of rapid economic growth with powerful connections to the livelihoods of the poor. The rural economy was the key element in these connections.

Expenditures on the education and health sectors were the most important way Indonesia attempted to influence returns to the portfolio of assets held by the poor. These kinds of human development expenditures, as emphasized by Hull (2004), had a transforming effect on Indonesian society. Beyond these sectors, however, there was little effort to address poverty *directly*. At least during the Suharto regime, when the pro-poor strategy was most effectively implemented, there were few efforts to influence wage rates directly, and organized labour was actively suppressed. The technocrats closely monitored Indonesia's wages relative to such competitors as Malaysia and Thailand in the early years, and China, Vietnam and India in later years. The concern was always on job-creation and the profitability of labour-intensive activities, not on transfer programmes to the poor.

An active price policy for rice attempted to stabilize the returns to small-holders producing the commodity. At least until the 1990s there was no long-run effort to raise these returns above trends in the world market, converted at the open-market exchange rate. The impact of this price stabilization policy on farm productivity, consumer welfare and national food security was highly positive (Timmer, 1996a). According to finance theory, both farmers and consumers gain if the average prices they receive and pay are stabilized at their long-run mean. Reduced variance for the same mean improves the performance of a diversified asset portfolio (for a risk-averse investor). Until the 1990s, the costs of this price policy, as implemented by the market-oriented operations of BULOG, were modest (Pearson, 1990). By the mid-1990s, with Suharto's reign nearing an end simply because of his age, corruption expanded so rapidly that the agency no longer carried out its mandate.

The pro-poor strategy worked extremely well, as poverty rates fell rapidly between the late 1960s and the mid-1990s, and economic growth averaged more than 5 per cent per capita per year. But how well the strategy works obviously depends on the efficiency of transmission mechanisms that connect the poor, through factor and product markets, to the overall growth process. The efficiency of these mechanisms depends on demand and supply pressures in the markets for unskilled labour and how well-integrated these markets are across skill classes and regions. Initial conditions for income and asset inequalities play an important role in the connection process, possibly because of failures in credit markets that make it hard for the poor to invest in their own human capital (Gugerty and Timmer, 1999). Thus *public* investments in education and rural public health are likely to be necessary for the transmission mechanisms to work effectively for the poor. Further, migration, job mobility and flexibility in the face of shocks all help maintain upward mobility during the growth process, and cushion the irreversibility of suddenly falling into poverty seen in so many countries. The flexible response of the rural economy to the sudden shock from the Asian financial crisis in 1998 shows that these mechanisms were in fact operating reasonably efficiently in the Indonesian economy.

Making policy choices in the face of tradeoffs

Economics is often defined as the science of opportunity costs, or tradeoffs. Because the chief economic policy-makers in the Suharto government were well-trained economists, they were acutely aware of the tradeoffs they faced in the design of basic development strategy and the implementation of economic policies. Many of the tradeoffs that were dealt with during the Suharto era remain as issues for the new democratic government.

In academic and policy circles in Indonesia, much nonsense has been bandied about with respect to targeting industrial policies on behalf of the poor. The arguments always involve industrial protection and inevitably raise the costs of inputs to labour-intensive industries. Agricultural protection (for sugar, especially) leads to high costs for food processors. Protection of rice producers raises the cost of labour, inducing an anti-labour bias in the choice of rural technologies in small- and medium-sized enterprises. Growth in agricultural *productivity* has, in fact, been pro-poor: such growth requires substantial public investments – perhaps even active price policy and support. Possibly, a significant tradeoff exists between enhancing agricultural growth and keeping the economy fully open to trade, which stimulates faster overall economic growth.

Understanding tradeoffs analytically

The analytics needed to understand these kinds of tradeoffs are extremely complicated, with very heavy data requirements to build even roughly realistic models. Various approaches to evaluating policy tradeoffs can only be reviewed briefly, as there is a substantial literature on the topic, even when restricting the discussion to Indonesia. There is a note of caution on the use of computable general equilibrium (CGE) models to provide guidance on such broad issues as which economic sectors lead the reduction in poverty.

Because Indonesia is rich in data and has attracted some of the best modellers to address its policy issues, several models 'duel' with each other in the literature, each with conflicting structures, assumptions and conclusions. A review of these issues is in order.

To ask 'what if' questions about the impact of alternative policies in a given setting, it is necessary to find similar experiments in similar settings for other time periods, mostly the province of economic historians and comparative economists, or to build economy-wide models that replicate the issues under debate (Pardey and Smith, 2004). A particularly relevant example to be reviewed here is the model by Fane and Warr (2003). Based on a substantial literature on computable general equilibrium models for Indonesia, the authors construct a specific CGE model to ask how economic growth reduces poverty in Indonesia.

The model disaggregates GDP into agriculture (18 sectors), agricultural processing (9 sectors), resources (5 sectors), services (15 sectors) and manufacturing (18 sectors). There are seven rural household 'types' and 3 urban types. The 1993 Social Accounting Matrix prepared by the Central Bureau of Statistics is used to link household types to ownership of factors, and these are disaggregated to the individual household level using plausible statistical distributions to generate estimates of poverty and inequality. The model assumes perfectly competitive factor and product markets, and international trade is modelled with standard Armington elasticities. Not all factors are fully mobile, especially from agriculture to other sectors.

Two 'shocks' to the model – Hicks-neutral increases in total factor productivity (TFP) by each broad sector, or increases in factor supply – are used to calculate the impact of a given increase in GDP on poverty, that is to calculate the extent to which growth from a particular sector or factor is 'pro-poor'. The results are radically different by source of growth. When TFP increases equally across all sectors, the elasticity of poverty reduction is −4.33. When the shock is in a specific sector, however, the elasticities vary from −5.91 in services to only −1.46 in agriculture. This apparently perverse result stems directly from the structure of the model. Demand for agricultural output is inelastic and factors cannot leave quickly. Increasing agricultural productivity *lowers* returns to these immobile factors, which include poor rural workers.

Similarly, an increase in skilled labour has a poverty elasticity of −7.65, but an increase in land has an elasticity of just −1.46, mobile agricultural capital of −1.61, and of unskilled labour of −2.51. Thus Fane and Warr conclude:

> The results and methodology reported here suggest that large over-simplifications are involved in relating poverty reduction directly to GDP growth without distinguishing among different possible sources of growth. Contrary to the assumptions of many commentators, the poor do much better if a given amount of GDP growth is produced by technical

progress in services or in manufacturing than if it is owing to technical progress in agriculture. Although more work needs to be done to improve on the parameter values assumed in this study, these qualitative results are robust with respect to wide variations in assumptions about elasticities of substitution among goods and factors.

The results also imply that growth in broad sectors – agriculture, manufacturing, services and so on – will be associated with very different effects on poverty and inequality depending on whether the exogenous shocks affect demand or supply. For example, an increase in the supply of factors used intensively in agriculture depresses the real returns to these factors while raising agricultural output; whereas an increase in demand for agricultural products, perhaps owing to policy changes, would raise both agricultural output and the real returns to the factors used intensively in agriculture (Fane and Warr, 2000, pp. 232–3).

A further issue is whether 'empirical' or 'analytical' models are more forward-looking. By their nature, empirical studies of the impact of growth in agricultural productivity on poverty reduction, for example, are backward-looking, relying on lengthy time-series data to produce significant results. Unless these analyses are truly dynamic, and thus model the changing degree of impact over time in order to capture the evolving economic structure, their lessons are naturally time-bound. In contrast, CGE parameters can be forward-looking (although, to the extent that they too are econometrically estimated, they suffer the same backward-looking orientation as simpler empirical models). Hence, as McCulloch (2004a) argues, part of the divergence between the CGE models and empirical models on the sources of poverty reduction in Indonesia might stem from the *direction* of the time horizon.

Although CGE models do have the potential to help analysts understand general tradeoffs in the Indonesian economy, they do not have the clarity and focus to reveal these tradeoffs at the specific level of different parts of the income distribution. They do not speak directly to costs and benefits of different approaches to poverty reduction, especially to the tradeoffs between speeding economic growth as one strategy and spending more money on anti-poverty programmes as a second. Unfortunately, these are the types of tradeoffs being faced by policy-makers in Indonesia, as the following examples indicate.

Human capital investments versus investments in infrastructure

There are very different time horizons for payoffs to human capital investments versus infrastructure investments: 15 to 20 years for education and child health, for example, and just three to five years for roads, ports, communications, market facilities, and so on.[6] What rate of time discount should be used for these decisions? What opportunity cost of capital? Does the government have to pay for all of these investments, or will partial subsidies and incentives work? The key tradeoff is short-run versus long-run growth, and whether the poor can 'wait' for payoff to their human capital. A 'win–win' strategy might be for the poor to be actively engaged in building the infrastructure, thus earning income in the short run and being able to afford to keep their children in school, with its long-run payoff.

An important counterfactual question is the role of oil revenues in funding Indonesia's massive investments in rural schools and infrastructure after 1974. How 'pro-poor' would Indonesia's economic growth have been if these investments had been scaled back significantly for budgetary reasons? Such a question can be answered only in the context of a detailed and dynamic general equilibrium model, as less oil revenue would have meant a more competitive Rupiah and more stimulus to the tradables sector. No models currently available can address this specificity of budget allocations and impact on both growth and distribution.

Cushioning transition costs

General tradeoffs may exist between 'payoffs' to ensure political stability (to individuals, industrial groups, students, military, and/or labour unions) and efficient resource allocation, leading to faster economic growth. Protection of farmers in East Asia during their rapid structural transformation is a key case in point. Historically, the three fastest episodes of pro-poor growth occurred in Japan, Korea and Taiwan. These three countries also had the fastest growth in agricultural protection, and reached the highest levels of protection at the end of their period of rapid growth. Malaysia utilizes similar protection for its rice farmers, despite remaining an important exporter of other agricultural commodities. Indonesia is now significantly protecting its rice farmers, despite the immediate impact on the poor.

The debate over rice prices and poverty goes to the core of current political realities and the prospects for a return to pro-poor growth. In particular, the debate over the full impact of the tariff on imported rice has been heated and voluminous. Extensive data and analysis show that higher rice prices increase the level of poverty fairly immediately. Alternatively, the induced employment effects from higher rural incomes might actually reduce poverty within a reasonably short period of time. This debate is reviewed carefully in McCulloch (2004b).

One major reason for the continuing controversy is the rapidly changing structure of Indonesia's food demand and supply. As noted in the discussion of the starchy staple ratio, and the detailed analysis by Molyneaux and Rosner (2004), food consumption patterns, even among the poor, have moved away from heavy reliance on rice, cassava and maize, and towards higher-value foods (both nutritionally and economically) such as fruits, vegetables, fish and livestock products – especially eggs and chicken. The patterns of Indonesian agricultural output have been slow to diversify in the face of changing demand patterns, although the share of farmers describing themselves as fruit and vegetable producers in 2003 (38 per cent) was double the level in the previous Agricultural Census in 1993.

Now, the rapid emergence of supermarkets is offering Indonesian farmers an opportunity to participate in these new supply chains for higher-value commodities, but procurement officers are ruthless in looking for the lowest-cost products. Understanding the competitiveness of Indonesia's farmers is thus an important research task, but it is already apparent that artificially supporting the price of rice has direct consequences for the cost of production of other commodities, especially on the tiny farms characteristic of Java.

The rice tariff thus not only has an impact on Indonesia's poor consumers immediately and directly, with a micro-based estimate suggesting that every 10 per centage points of import tariff on rice pushes an additional one million Indonesians below the poverty line (Buehrer, 1999). If higher rice prices also have net costs to Indonesian farmers, an outcome that now seems likely in view of the evolving production structure, they have an unambiguous and unmitigated negative impact on poverty. The analysis in McCulloch (2004b) comes to the same conclusion.

Reaching the absolute poor versus the near-poor and vulnerable

Despite the impressive record in reducing the numbers of absolute poor over the past three decades, two large problems remain. First, there are many poor just above the official poverty line. For example, the Asian Development Bank reports that 53 per cent of the Indonesian population subsists on $2 per day or less, whereas only 7 per cent subsists on less than $1 per day (ADB, 2004). That is, more than two-fifths of the population is 'near poor' in monetary terms, with significantly diminished levels of welfare in other dimensions as well. Second, this large proportion of the population near the poverty line is vulnerable: even modest shocks to the economy or to basic food prices can drive large numbers of people into absolute poverty.

The appropriate government response to these two problems presents another trade-off. Should most resources be devoted to continuing the attack on the small share of the population below the official poverty line (or below the $1 per day standard)? Or should policies now be re-focused on the much broader share of the population, nearly half, whose households have risen above those poverty lines but who remain highly vulnerable to economic shocks? Is pro-poor growth the best strategy for dealing with 'poverty', or are targeted programmes now the main hope for reaching the absolutely poor?

Some policy approaches will be complementary, of course, as efforts to stabilize the economic environment of most Indonesian households would also benefit the remaining households that are absolutely poor. But tradeoffs will remain, as many of these poor households will be helped only gradually by a return to pro-poor growth and a more stable economy. Speedier assistance will be needed in the form of serious budget commitments to improving rural health and education programmes to reach these households. These resources will have significant opportunity costs in terms of broader investments in supporting infrastructure, improvements in the quality of secondary and tertiary education, and improving the quality of governance at both national and local levels.

The political economy of pro-poor growth in Indonesia

The standard story to explain the political economy of the Suharto regime's emphasis on agriculture (and pro-poor growth) relies on conflict between traditional political forces – communist-inspired peasants and workers faced opposition from an authoritarian military. Buying off the peasants was cheaper than repression. Rural development was seen as the least-cost approach to political stability. Large-scale ethnic (Chinese) businesses bought protection from Suharto and his military allies and received lucrative import and operating licenses in return. When these highly protected businesses, and their closely associated banks, collapsed in the Asian financial crisis, the entire regime unravelled. The vacuum of political institutions, deliberately created by Suharto to remove any challenge to his authority, exposed the country to years of political chaos and weak leadership.

As with most stories based on conventional wisdom, there are substantial elements of truth in this one. But it misses what distinguishes the Suharto regime from otherwise similar military dictatorships around the world: its focus on *development* and the effort to improve the welfare of the poor by connecting the rural economy to rapid economic growth. Fear of radical peasants wielding scythes simply does not explain this passion, or the massive budgetary resources devoted to it. Oil revenues in the mid-1970s helped, to be sure, but the basic strategy was already laid down before the OPEC price shock. A much more nuanced story is needed, one that includes the complexities of the structure of political power and the role of leadership.

The story begins with two concerns of the emerging Suharto government in the late 1960s (he was not assured of full power until 1968). The first was the misery and discontent of the rural masses, which had supported Sukarno's communist leanings and populist rhetoric. After a decade of active discrimination against their livelihoods, they were near starvation and an obvious source of opposition unless the new government could incorporate them in its development plans. Second, the hyperinflation of the mid-1960s, total disintegration of the market economy, and political chaos meant the entire population was ready for a more stable life. A strategy that promised stability and rural recovery would win wide support (as it would throughout densely settled East and Southeast Asia).

This is the message that Suharto delivered to his technocrats. This economic team, many trained at Berkeley (and hence the term the 'Berkeley

Mafia'), had engaged Suharto and other senior military officials in economic training exercises at the Military College. They were handed the macro-economic portfolio and told to deliver on what became known in Indonesia as the 'development trilogy', growth, equity and stability. To many in the political arena, stability meant repressive measures to stifle dissent, but to the technocrats it meant restraining inflation (which they did in spectacular fashion in just three years) and stabilizing the rice economy, which was still a quarter of GDP and which provided half the average Indonesian's calories.

The most debated political economy aspect of the New Order government was the near schizophrenia between macro and sectoral policies. What is so puzzling is why macro-economic policy was left largely in the hands of very talented, but highly apolitical, technocrats. Persuasive arguments are made that they provided access to the donor community, which has been a strong, almost lavish, supporter of Indonesia since the late 1960s. But another argument is simply that the technocrats delivered the economic growth the country so desperately needed. In a comparison of the political economy of growth in the Philippines and Indonesia, Thorbecke (1995) came to the following conclusion:

> In the final analysis, the most fundamental difference between the development environments in the two countries relates to the macroeconomic policy management and the role of the technocrats. In Indonesia, the latter followed a consistent, far-sighted, credible, and enlightened macroeconomic policy that was outward-oriented and provided a framework within which both economic growth and poverty alleviation could occur. In particular, the key policy instrument that the technocrats relied on was an appropriate exchange rate. Even at the height of the oil boom, when Indonesia was swimming in petro-dollars and was generating large balance-of-payments surpluses, and when the natural inclination would have been to let the Rupiah appreciate, instead the technocrats devalued the currency to protect the traditional tradable sectors – foremost among them agriculture – and recycled large parts of these windfall profits back into agriculture. This policy contributed substantially to the phenomenal poverty alleviation process in the rural areas that characterized Indonesia in the seventies and eighties. (Thorbecke, 1995, pp. 34–5)

The technocrats had no political base of their own. They depended entirely on their patron, Suharto, to implement their plans and policies. The President was an active participant in every major macroeconomic decision, especially the timing and magnitude of changes in the exchange rate. Despite the control of the economic team over macro economic policy, with the President's equally clear support and blessing, Suharto used trade policy to protect special interests in his circle and even beyond, sometimes with no more apparent rationale than a nationalist interest to develop a modern industrial capacity. The role of good *economic* governance and political commitment to poverty reduction is a key lesson from this experience, but the paradox is why the autocratic Suharto regime provided both ingredients for so long, and why the new democratic governments have not.

Part of Suharto's commitment to the rural economy seems to have come from the highly visible politics, and power, of food security. The drive for higher agricultural productivity – a key ingredient in pro-poor growth – was fuelled at least in part by the desire for households, and the country, to have more reliable supplies of rice than what was available, at least historically, from world markets. When the world rice market quite literally disappeared for several months during the World Food Crisis in 1973, Indonesia's dependence on imported rice to stabilize domestic prices highlighted its vulnerability to external markets beyond its control – the opposite of food security in the minds of most Indonesians – and showed how important it was to increase rice production (Timmer, 2000). A ratcheting up of policy attention to agriculture and budget support for rural infrastructure followed the traumatic loss of control of rice prices in 1972–73.

Behind the Suharto regime's commitment to pro-poor growth were two important constituencies: one that backed economic growth itself; and the other that expressed concern for the poor. The growth coalition was made up of the modernizing elements of the military, the business elite not already comfortably protected by anti-growth protectionist measures, and most of the rural sector, which was near starvation in the mid-1960s.

The voices for the poor included many of this same coalition, but for somewhat different reasons. The military was concerned about rural unrest. It did not have the coercive resources to suppress it by force alone. The Jakarta political elite, led by President Suharto, increasingly staked its credibility on political stability. Both the urban and rural poor could pose a threat to that, as the 1974 Malari riots demonstrated. One of the major grievances of the student rioters was the loss of control over rice prices in the previous year, and the continuing high rice prices. Increasingly, the donor community came to stress the importance of poverty reduction. The World Bank made a major commitment in the late-1980s to the analytical work that surfaced in its 1990 report on poverty.

The fortuitous intersection of the growth and poverty coalitions thus offered the Suharto regime a political opportunity to do well by doing good. In the context of widespread opportunities to stimulate rapid growth in rural areas through high-payoff investments in rehabilitating irrigation systems and rural infrastructure and the importation of new rice technologies, a cumulative process started that built both rapid growth and poverty reduction into the basic dynamics of the Indonesian economy. But the process started in the agricultural sector.

This cumulative process appeared to have ended in the early 1980s, as prices for agricultural commodities collapsed in world markets, oil prices declined, and the whole growth process seemed threatened. Fortuitously, again, but under the determined guidance of the technocrats, and with the full support of the President, the economy was restructured to make it more open to foreign trade and investment, just as Japan and Korea came looking for opportunities to invest in labour-intensive manufacturing facilities. Only with the economic and political collapse in 1998 did this source of pro-poor growth disappear (and with it the patron of the technocrats).

What next? The strategy of the new democratic governments for dealing with poverty – direct fiscal transfers to the poor – has obvious political appeal. In principle, these transfers have immediate and visible impact on the recipients, and the political 'pitch' for the programmes makes it sound as though the government is actively committed to poverty reduction. Although democracy has probably *increased* the size and influence of the political coalition concerned about poverty, it has greatly *undermined* the coalition supporting economic growth as the main mechanism for dealing with it.

In the current political rhetoric, poverty reduction is no longer linked to economic growth. In fact, as the agency distributing subsidized rice to the poor, Bulog seems to have built an 'anti-poverty' political coalition similar to the one supporting Food Stamps in the US Congress. Support in the USA comes from conservative rural legislators eager to have additional markets for the food that is produced in surplus by their farm constituents and from urban liberals who have in their constituency many poor people who use food stamps as a major source of income.

Similarly, Bulog is the agency that procures rice domestically with budget support from Parliament, and distributes this rice to the poor at low prices that are, again, subsidized by the budget. Bulog has mobilized political support from two constituencies concerned with poverty: first, for its rice procurement programme, on the grounds that it helps rice farmers; and second, for its implementation of the 'special market operations' (OPK) programme that delivers subsidized rice to the poor. As Stephen Mink (2004) of the World Bank has observed, no parliamentarians have been willing to take on both dimensions of the rice programme simultaneously. As a result, the huge budget subsidies that accrue to Bulog to run these programmes, and the corruption that accompanies them, go unchallenged.

Rebuilding the economic growth coalition is likely to take a long time. It will depend on the underlying conditions of economic governance – political stability, rule of law, control of corruption, and so on – that have been difficult to improve. Probably the best that can be done in the short run – the next three to five years – is to minimize policy damage to the interests *of the poor* while trying to improve the effectiveness of the programmes transferring resources directly *to the poor.*

Summary and conclusions

Thirty years of rapid economic growth, with equally rapid rates of poverty reduction, was politically popular, even if there was no direct test of the hypothesis at the polls. Few observers doubted that Suharto would have won the elections held every five years in a fair poll, but all the results were contaminated by heavy guidance and local pressures. An important outcome of this voting process, however, was that people *expected* to vote every five years, and they expected that their ballots would be counted. Individual provinces, even Jakarta on a regular basis, did not vote for Golkar, the party of the government. Every five years, the polling results were gleaned for signs of disappointment with the development programme. Despite the heavy hand, real information was flowing from villages up to the centre, and that is one of the major tasks of representative government, whether it meets the standards of Western democratic rules or not.

Thus political institutions were taking root, almost despite the intentions of the Suharto regime, and these institutions provided feedback to the policy approach of the government. After the 1974 Malari riots, ostensibly in response to a visit by the Japanese Prime Minister but in fact a reaction to the visibly widening income distribution, especially in urban areas, the government responded. First, it brutally put down the riots and imprisoned the student leaders. Then it mounted a serious effort to figure out how to make the economy more equitable. The result, stimulated as well by the World Food Crisis in 1973/74, was a major shift in priorities toward rural development and a push toward increasing domestic rice production. Behind this push was the stabilization objective as well as the equity objective. To lose control of the rice economy was to lose control of what mattered to Indonesian society.

The restructuring of Indonesia's development approach after 1974, and especially the pre-emptive devaluation of the rupiah in 1978, signalled the government's determination to include the poor in the development process. The stability of the Gini coefficient seen from the late 1960s to the present should not be taken as the result of market-driven forces in the face of given technology, but rather as a conscious government effort, led from the macroeconomic arena by the technocrats but blessed by the President, to stimulate what is now called 'pro-poor growth' (Timmer, 2004). This effort succeeded in spectacular fashion until the mid-1990s, when cronyism and the growing influence of Suharto's children on economic decision-making caused the approach to unravel. Part of the problem of post-Suharto governments has been the need to distance themselves from this record of repression and cronyism, despite the results of three decades of pro-poor growth.

Despite all these problems, the Indonesian economy is growing 4–5 per cent per year. The poor seem to be participating in this growth, but it is not rapid enough to reduce the structural unemployment and heavy reliance on jobs in the informal sector that make the poor so vulnerable. To raise the quality of employment and reduce the vulnerability of the poor to economic shocks is the next 'pro-poor' task for the government.

The analytical approach used here – historical political economy – runs contrary to much of modern development economics, concerned as it is with micro data-sets, experimental design and identification strategies. But what the approach lacks in methodological rigour it makes up for with insights into long-run processes of structural transformation and how politics and policies influence those processes. Alexander Gerschenkron used to tell his seminar students at Harvard that 'for example is no proof'. But he also reminded us that a good historical example could undermine the cleverest theoretical proof. There is room for both approaches, of course, and the intent here is not to undermine more rigorous methodologies but to enrich them. By example.

Appendix: derivation of the analytical relationship between changes in per capita income, food energy intake, and the poverty headcount index

Known:

Long-run average Engel curve,

$$C = a + b \, \text{Log} Y_t$$

where C = daily per capita food energy intake in kilocalories; $\log Y_t$ = logarithm of average per capita income at some point in time t; and a, b = parameters that are constant for a given income distribution, set of food prices, etc.

Income distribution,

$$D(Y) = c + d \, \text{Log} Y_i$$

where $D(Y)$ = cumulative income distribution in percent; c, d = parameters for a given distribution, and the i refers to income percentiles. With this distributional form, 'neutral' economic growth is reflected by a progressive reduction in the intercept term c (that is, the entire income distribution shifts evenly to the right). If income distribution becomes more equal, d becomes larger, and vice versa.

Let C^* = the 'nutritional poverty line', and $\text{Log} Y^*$ = the equivalent income poverty line.

At time t_0, we observe per capita income Y_0 and the associated average food energy intake C_0. From Figure 7A.1 we can see that the initial incidence of poverty, HCI^*, is determined by the intersection of D with $\text{Log} Y^*$. Note that D is drawn on the basis of $\text{Log} Y_0$, C_0 as the averages observed at time=0, and is consistent with the Engel curve relationship.

At time=1, all we observe is Y_1 and C_1, with no additional information on any changes in D. What can we say about changes in HCI?

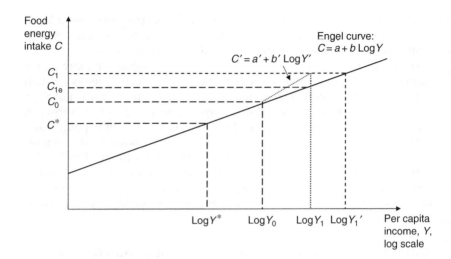

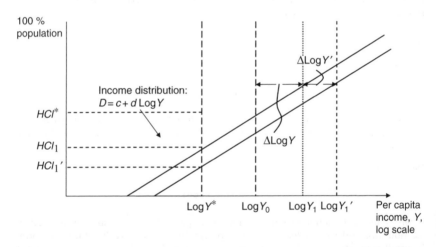

Figure 7A.1 The relationship between the Engel curve for food energy (C) and the poverty headcount index (HCI), in Indonesia.

Answer: Within this poverty framework, HCI at $t = 1$ is completely identified with knowledge of the income elasticity of demand for food energy between $t = 0$ and $t = 1$. This (arc) elasticity can be estimated from (Y_0, C_0) and (Y_1, C_1), both of which are observed data points.

Proof: Note that when D is constant, the change in HCI is simply $\Delta HCI = -d \cdot \Delta \text{Log} Y$, where $\Delta \text{Log} Y = \text{Log} Y_1 - \text{Log} Y_0$.

In such cases, the *observed* C_1 lies on the average estimated Engel curve, at C_{1e}.

However, when C_1 is above (or below) C_{1e}, income distribution has improved (or worsened). This distributional change can be quantified as the additional (or reduced) income, if neutrally distributed, that would be needed to induce the consumption of the *observed* food energy, C_1. In the log-linear model of Figure 7A.1, the additional food energy consumed $(C_1 - C_{1e})$ is proportional to the additional income needed to generate it $(\text{Log}Y_1' - \text{Log}Y_1 = \Delta\text{Log}Y')$.

By the rule of similar triangles, this proportion is equal to b'/b, where b' is the slope of the new Engel curve reflecting the relationship between (Y_1, C_1). But $b'/b = E'/E$, where E = long-run average income elasticity of demand for C. Note $E = b/C$.
E' = period-specific income elasticity of demand for C, between $t = 0$ and $t = 1$.
Thus $[\Delta\text{Log}Y + \Delta\text{Log}Y'] = [E'/E]\Delta\text{Log}Y$
and $\Delta HCI = -d[E'/E]\Delta\text{Log}Y$.

Notes

1. Note that the RPPG incorporates both the growth and distributional dimensions of pro-poor growth, and this rate is thus a country-specific version of equation 1 in 'Concept Paper on Operationalizing Pro-Poor Growth' (World Bank, 2004).

2. Some commentators have taken this to mean that the Suharto government was not *interested* in poverty reduction by more direct means (Booth and McCawley, 1981; Fox, 2002). The themes developed in this chapter argue, to the contrary, that the government had a *conscious* strategy for reducing poverty, but it concentrated in the early years on economic growth that reached the poor.

3. A review of the notes from the planning sessions held in 1968, as the first five-year plan (REPELITA I, 1969–74) was being drafted, shows that both government planners and their foreign advisors had a clear picture of steps needed to re-start growth. There was much less agreement about a medium-term growth strategy (World Bank, 1968; Harvard Development Advisory Service, 1968). For a historical perspective on economic growth as the 'natural course of things', once governments stop repressing it, see Jones (1988).

4. The best references on these issues are Hill (2000), and Hofman, Rodrick-Jones and Thee (2004).

5. In his 'balance sheet' on successes and failures of the Suharto regime, McCawley places growth and development, and poverty reduction, at the top of his list of successes. 'Perhaps the single most notable characteristic of economic policy-making during the Soeharto era was the central commitment to growth and development (Soeharto, 1989; Elson, 2001). This was reflected in President Soeharto's unwavering support for *pembangunan* (development). The President made it clear that this broad stance of policy was non-negotiable. For many years, this policy received strong support across the nation. It led, amongst other things, to sharp reductions in the measured levels of mass poverty in Indonesia' (McCawley, 2002, p. 261).

6. The different time horizon for impact of investments significantly affects the payoff to different types of foreign assistance. Clemens, Radelet and Bhanvani (2004) show that the 45 per cent of development assistance that might reasonably have an impact within four years of the investment has a large and statistically significant impact on economic growth. The 45 per cent of development assistance with a longer time horizon, especially education and health projects, has no measurable impact on growth within the four-year horizon of the growth panels. The remaining 10 per cent of foreign assistance is for humanitarian assistance and emergency relief. Not surprisingly, this component has a small negative association with economic growth.

References

Afiff, S. (2004) 'Scaling Up Poverty Reduction in Indonesia', Presented at the World Bank Conference on Scaling Up Poverty Reduction, Shanghai, China, 27 May.

Asian Development Bank (ADB) (2004) 'Poverty in Asia: Measurement, Estimates and Prospects', Special Chapter in *Key Indicators*, Manila.

Boeke, J.H. (1946) *The Evolution of the Netherlands Indies Economy*. New York: Institute of Pacific Relations.

Booth, A. and McCawley, P. (eds) (1981) *The Indonesian Economy During the Soeharto Era*. Petaling Jaya: Oxford University Press.

Buehrer, T.S. (1999) 'Rice Prices, Tariffs, and Poverty', Memorandum 136/99/525. 19 November, Indonesia: Harvard Advisory Group.

Clemens, M., Radelet, S. and Bhavnani, R. (2004) 'Counting Chickens When They Hatch: The Short-term Effect of Aid on Growth', Working Paper no. 44, Washington, DC: Center for Global Development.

Cole, D.C. and Slade, B.F. (1998) 'Why Has Indonesia's Financial Crisis been so Bad?', *Bulletin of Indonesian Economic Studies*, 34/ 2: 61–6.

Elson, R.E. (2001) *Soeharto: A Political Biography*. Cambridge: Cambridge University Press.

Fane, G. and Warr, P. (2003) 'How Economic Growth Reduces Poverty: A General Equilibrium Analysis for Indonesia', in R. van der Hoeven and A. Shorrocks (eds), *Perspectives on Growth and Poverty*. WIDER: United Nations University Press, pp. 217–34.

Fox, J.W. (2002) 'Poverty Reduction in Indonesia, 1967 to 1997: A Country Case Study', Technical Report submitted by Nathan Associates, Inc. to USAID, Washington under Contract no. PCE-I-00-00-00013-00, 29 November.

Gugerty, M.K. and Timmer, C.P. (1999) 'Growth, Inequality and Poverty Alleviation: Implications for Development Assistance', Prepared for CAER II, USAID, Washington DC, November.

Harvard Development Advisory Service (1968) 'An Appropriate Tactic for the Five Year Plan: Notes on the "Bull Session" held 16–17 March to prepare for REPELITA I', 20 March, mimeo Jakarta.

Hill, H. (2000) *The Indonesian Economy since 1966*, 2nd edn. Cambridge: Cambridge University Press.

Hofman, B., Jones, R. and Wie, T. Kian (2004) 'Indonesia: Rapid Growth; Weak Institutions', Paper prepared for the Shanghai Conference on Scaling up Poverty Reduction, 28–29 May. Jakarta: The World Bank.

Hull, T.H. (2004) 'Indonesia's Demographic Turning Point', August, Working Paper, Australian National University, Canberra.

Jones, E.L. (1998) *Growth Recurring: Economic Change in World History*. Oxford: Clarendon Press.

Lewis, W.A. (1954) 'Economic Development with Unlimited Supplies of Labour', *The Manchester School*, 22: 3–42.

McCawley, P. (2002) 'Economic Policy During the Soeharto Era: A Balance Sheet', in M. Ikhsan, Ch. Manning and H. Soesastro (eds), *Ekonomi Indonesia di Era Politik Baru: 80 Tahun Mohammad Sadli* [The Indonesian Economy in the New Political Era: Mohammad Sadli's 80 Years], Penerbit Buku Kompas Jakarta, June: 259–270.

McCulloch, N. (2004a) 'Some Comments on the Indonesia Country Study by Peter Timmer', 8 July, Jakarta: World Bank.

McCulloch, N. (2004b) 'Trade and Poverty in Indonesia—Assessing the Links', 5 May, Working Paper, Jakarta: World Bank.

Mellor, J.W. (2000) 'Agricultural Growth, Rural Employment, and Poverty Reduction: Non-Tradables, Public Expenditure, and Balanced Growth', Prepared for the World Bank Rural Week March.

Mink, S. (2004) 'Comments on Presentation by Jorge Garcia-Garcia on the Costs and Benefits of Bulog's commodity Interventions from 1993 to 1998', 7 July, Washington, DC: World Bank.

Molyneaux, J. (2003) 'Starchy Staple Consumption and Household Nutrition: A Fresh Look at Indonesian Welfare', Indonesian Food Policy Program (www.macrofoodpolicy.com), February, Jakarta.

Molyneaux, J.W. and Rosner, L.P. (2004) 'Changing Patterns of Indonesian Food Consumption and their Welfare Implications', Food Policy Support Activity (FPSA) Working Paper, DAI/USAID/BAPPENAS. May, Jakarta.

Myrdal, G. (1968) 'Asian Drama: An Inquiry into the Poverty of Countries', New Delhi: Kalyani Publishers.

North, D. (1990) *Institutions, Institutional Change and Economic Performance*, Cambridge: Cambridge University Press.

Papanek, G. (2004) 'The Poor During Economic Decline, Rapid Growth and Crisis: The Case of Indonesia', Prepared for the USAID Project on Pro-Poor Growth conducted by DAI and BIDE, Bethesda, MD.

Pardey, P.G. and Smith Vincent H. (eds) (2004) *What's Economics Worth? Valuing Policy Research*, Baltimore, MD: Johns Hopkins University Press for IFPRI.

Pearson, S.R. (1990) 'Financing Rice Price Stabilization in Indonesia', *Indonesian Food Journal*, 4/ 7: 63–83.

Prawiro, R. (1998) *Indonesia's Struggle for Economic Development: Pragmatism in Action*, Kuala Lumpur: Oxford University Press.

Rock, M.T. (2002) 'Exploring the Impact of Selective Interventions in Agriculture on the Growth of Manufactures in Indonesia, Malaysia, and Thailand', *Journal of International Development*, 14/4: 485–510.

Rock, M.T. (2003) 'The Politics of Development Policy and Development Policy Reform in New Order Indonesia', William Davidson Institute Working Paper no. 632, November, Processed.

Soeharto (1989) *Pemikiran, Ucuapan dab Tindakan Saya: Otobiografi*, Jakarta: PT Citra Lamtoro Gung Persada.

Wie Thee K. (ed) (2003) *Recollections: The Indonesian Economy, 1950s–1990s*, Singapore: Institute of Southeast Asian Studies, and Canberra: Research School of Pacific and Asian Studies, Australian National University.

Thorbecke, E. (1995) 'The Political Economy of Development: Indonesia and the Philippines', The F.H. Golay Memorial Lecture, Ithaca, NY: Cornell Southeast Asia Program.

Timmer, C.P. (1996a) 'Does BULOG Stabilise Rice Prices in Indonesia? Should it Try?', *Bulletin of Indonesian Economic Studies*, 32/2: 45–74.

Timmer, C.P. (1996b) 'Economic Growth and Poverty Alleviation in Indonesia', *Research in Domestic and International Agribusiness Management*, 12: Greenwich, CT: JAI Press, 205–234.

Timmer, C.P. (2000) 'The Macro Dimensions of Food Security: Economic Growth, Equitable Distribution, and Food Price Stability', *Food Policy,* 25: 283–295.

Timmer, C.P. (2004) 'The Road to Pro-Poor Growth: The Indonesian Experience in Regional Perspective', *Bulletin of Indonesian Economic Studies*, 40/2: 173–203.

Timmer, C.P. (2005) 'Operationalizing Pro-Poor Growth: The Indonesian Experience', Prepared for the World Bank, Washington, DC.

van der Eng, P. (1993a) 'Agricultural Growth in Indonesia Since 1880: Productivity Change and the Impact of Government Policy', Rijksuniversiteit Groningen.

van der Eng, P. (1993b) 'Food Consumption and the Standard of Living in Indonesia, 1880-1990', *Economics Division Working Papers: Southeast Asia*, 1, Canberra: Research School of Pacific and Asian Studies, Australian National University.

van der Eng, P. (2000) 'Food for Thought: Trends in Indonesia's Food Supply, 1880–1995', *Journal of Interdisciplinary History*, 30/4: 591–616.

van der Eng, P. (2002) 'Indonesia's Growth Performance in the Twentieth Century', in Angus Maddison, D.S. Prasada Rao, and William F. Shepherd (eds), *The Asian Economies in the Twentieth Century*, Edward Elgar.

World Bank (1968) 'Economic Development in Indonesia', Vol. 1 Main Report. Report: AS-132a, 12 February. (Then known as the International Bank for Reconstruction and Development, or IBRD.)

World Bank (1993) *The East Asian Miracle*, Oxford University Press for the World Bank. Washington, DC.

World Bank (2003) 'Indonesia: Country Assistance Strategy, FY *2004-2007*', (Advance Copy), Jakarta.

World Bank, (2004) 'Concept Paper on Operationalizing Pro-Poor Growth', A Research Project sponsored by AFD, DFID, GTZ, KfW and PREM. 11 May, Washington, DC.

Part III

Modelling and Simulating Pro-Poor Growth Strategies

8
Analysing Pro-Poor Growth in Bolivia: Addressing Data Gaps and Modelling Policy Choices[*]

*Stephan Klasen, Melanie Grosse, Jann Lay, Julius Spatz,
Rainer Thiele and Manfred Wiebelt*

Introduction

As one of Latin America's poorest countries with high inequality, high ethnic polarization, and great political and social instability over the past decades, Bolivia urgently needs to achieve high rates of pro-poor growth. In order to understand the linkages between policies, growth and poverty, it is first necessary to have a clear understanding of trends and determinants of poverty and its linkages to policies and growth in the past. This is already a significant challenge in Bolivia as nationally representative and (roughly) comparable household surveys are only available since 1997 while surveys from urban areas are available starting in 1989. There are nationally representative Demographic and Health Surveys (DHS) which also date back to 1989, but they do not contain any income information and cannot therefore be used directly for poverty analysis. Second, to guide policy-makers, it would be particularly useful to model the linkages between policies, growth, and inequality to both understand the record of pro-poor growth in the past as well as simulate the impact of policies in the future.

This chapter will focus on these two issues.[1] It will first present a method and results from an exercise linking the urban household surveys starting in 1989 with the Demographic and Health Surveys to generate a consistent nationally representative time series of poverty and inequality. In order to address the second challenge, a dynamic computable general equilibrium

[*] This chapter is based on a larger study that was funded by the sector project 'Pro-Poor Growth' of German Development Policy (BMZ, GTZ and KfW Entwicklungsbank) available at www.oppg.de. We gratefully acknowledge the financial support as well as the advice and suggestions we received from members of the three institutions. We also thank two World Bank-appointed referees as well as participants in several workshops for helpful comments and suggestions. Nevertheless, any errors remain our own responsibility.

191

(CGE) model linked to micro data on poverty and inequality is presented and applied to explicitly study the linkages between shocks and policies on the one hand, and growth, poverty and inequality on the other.

The chapter is organised as follows. The next section provides a short overview of Bolivia, followed by a presentation of methods and results from the cross-survey simulation, comparing them to those obtained from competing methods to study poverty trends. We then present and apply the dynamic CGE model, while a final section concludes, highlighting methodological and analytical challenges.

Background on Bolivia

Bolivia is a large land-locked country with low population density, difficult terrain, and consequently a poorly developed transport and communications infrastructure. It is characterized by great economic and social inequalities with deep historical roots. Bolivia is one of the most ethnically diverse countries in Latin America with an economic and political elite dominated, until the recent election of a President of indigenous origins, by people of Spanish and mixed descent and a large, and largely marginalized, indigenous population. It is a country experiencing great political and social instability, including recently frequent changes of governments and a large and vocal extra-parliamentary opposition engaging frequently in various forms of mass protest.

Economically, Bolivia is a highly dualistic economy. Its export base depends mostly on natural resources (minerals, oil, and gas) and agricultural commodities produced on large capital-intensive commercial farms in the lowlands, while the majority of its indigenous population is concentrated in a smallholder subsistence agricultural sector in the highlands of the country.[2] The manufacturing sector and the formal urban economy are very small, while there is a large urban informal economy mostly consisting of recent migrants from the poor rural areas in the highlands.

Bolivia had pursued a state-led import-substitution regime until the 1980s. After decades of military rule the first democratic government (1982–5) faced a very difficult internal and external environment (debt crisis, global recession and collapse in tin prices in 1985) and was unable to stabilize the economy but instead allowed a hyperinflation to develop, which led to the collapse of the government in 1985. The subsequent government first undertook a strict stabilization plan that ended hyperinflation. In addition, the government began implementing a wide range of structural reforms. These reforms were continued by most of the successive governments so that Bolivia stands out as a country having undertaken more structural reforms in line with the so-called 'Washington Consensus' than most developing countries (Lora, 2001). They included: (i) product market deregulation (e.g. freeing of prices); (ii) capital market deregulation (e.g. freeing of interest rates, liberalization of the external capital market); (iii) fiscal reforms (e.g. a simplification of the tax structure); (iv) trade liberalization (e.g. sharp reduction of import tariffs, elimination of non-tariff barriers); (v) liberalization of the FDI regime (e.g. equal treatment of domestic and foreign investors); (vi) restructuring, closing and 'capitalisation' of the large state-owned companies. The one area where there were only few reforms was the labour market.

Bolivia's structural reforms produced many positive outcomes. Macroeconomic stability was achieved and maintained throughout the period. Economic growth also improved and Bolivia grew at around 4 per cent per year from 1990–98, but only about 1.5 per cent in per capita terms. A favourable external environment, most notably a surge in foreign direct investment that accompanied the capitalisation process, aided this relatively positive performance. From 1998 to 2003, economic growth decelerated to an average of only about 1.5 per cent per year and became negative in per capita terms, despite rising revenues from gas exports. The main causes for this slowdown were a series of external economic shocks, including a dramatic fall in foreign capital inflows and an appreciating real exchange rate associated with the strong devaluations and recessions in Brazil and Argentina in 1999 and 2002. The economy has recently been recovering from this slowdown, aided by a favourable external environment (including high commodity prices).

Set against this background, the analytical challenge for pro-poor policymaking is to first understand poverty trends and determinants since the economic reforms of the 1980s, and second to determine the effects of policies and shocks on these poverty and inequality outcomes.

Creating a time series of poverty and inequality: methodology and findings

Regarding poverty and inequality trends, nationally representative household surveys with income or expenditure information are only available from 1997 onwards.[3] Before, there are income surveys for the nine departmental capitals (plus El Alto, the city adjacent to the capital La Paz) going back to 1989, and there is some spotty survey information from non-urban areas. Thus rural areas (comprising about 40 per cent of the population in 1994, with the share falling over time) and towns (comprising 12 per cent of the population in 1994 with the share rising over time) were excluded from these surveys. In addition, there are three nationally representative Demographic and Health Surveys (1989, 1994 and 1998), none of which contains income information. As a result there is great uncertainty and considerable disagreement about actual poverty trends in Bolivia in the 1990s.[4]

Methodology

For the purpose of analysing pro-poor growth in the era of structural reforms, it was critical to generate nationally representative poverty data going as far back as 1989. In order to achieve this, we extend the static cross-survey microsimulation methodology of Hentschel *et al.* (2000) and Elbers *et al.* (2002), who create micro-level poverty maps by combining contemporaneous information from a household survey and a national census. Our approach extends their static model of poverty mapping to two periods and proceeds in three steps, which we refer to as estimation, validation and simulation which is shown in simplified form in Table 8.1.[5] In the estimation step, we choose a base period in which we have a nationally representative household income survey as well as a nationally representative DHS, and estimate a regression model of income/consumption[6] using the household survey data. In doing so, the set of covariates is restricted to those that are also available in the corresponding DHS. In this regression model, the emphasis is not to create a causal model of incomes but simply to determine correlations with variables that are available in the DHS. In the validation step, we check the consistency of our estimates which involves two sub-steps. First we simulate incomes for each household in the household income surveys using the regression coefficients and including a random error term[7] to see whether we are able to adequately replicate incomes in the household income surveys. Second, we simulate incomes based on the DHS, using the same regression coefficients and the same random error term to study our ability to predict incomes using the DHS.

Lastly, in the simulation step we choose an earlier period in which the household survey covers only departmental capitals, but we have a nationally representative DHS at our disposal. This step again consists of three sub-steps. First, we re-run our regression model using that income survey to obtain coefficient estimates for the departmental capitals in that period. Second, we make another validation, this time only for the departmental capitals, for which we compare predicted with observed incomes. Third, we then assume that the absolute difference in regression coefficients between departmental capitals on the one hand, and towns and rural areas on the other hand, did not change between the two periods (that is that the coefficients on the interaction terms, i.e. γ and δ in Table 8.1, stayed constant over time). This allows us to simulate incomes for towns and rural areas in the period that is not covered by household survey data using the DHS. We then simulate incomes for towns and rural areas by applying the regression coefficients from the regression model of the departmental capitals augmented by the interaction terms for towns and rural areas (and including an area-specific random error term again). In this way we can use the simulated incomes from the DHS to construct intertemporally comparable poverty profiles of national coverage for Bolivia.

To investigate the robustness of our procedure, we conduct two kinds of sensitivity analysis. First, the assumption of unchanged differences over time in regression coefficients between departmental capitals and other areas

Table 8.1 Overview of cross-survey simulation methods

Step	Sub-step	Data source	Year	Method	Equation
Step 1: Estimation		National Income Survey (LSMS)	1999	Income regression	$Y = \alpha + \beta X + \gamma rX + \delta tX + \varepsilon$
Step 2: Validation	Predicting incomes in income survey	National Income Survey (LSMS)	1999	Prediction drawing area-specific random error term	$\hat{Y} = \hat{\alpha} + \hat{\beta}X + \hat{\gamma}rX + \hat{\delta}tX + \hat{\varepsilon}$
	Simulating incomes in DHS	DHS	1998	Prediction drawing area-specific random error term	$\hat{Y} = \hat{\alpha} + \hat{\beta}X + \hat{\gamma}rX + \hat{\delta}tX + \hat{\varepsilon}$
Step 3: Simulation	Estimation	Urban Income Survey (LSMS)	1989, 1994	Income regression	$Y = \varphi + \pi X + \vartheta$
	Validation	Urban Income Survey (LSMS)	1989, 1994	Prediction drawing random error term	$\hat{Y} = \hat{\varphi} + \hat{\pi}X + \hat{\vartheta}$
	Simulation	DHS	1989, 1994	Prediction using interaction term from step 1 plus drawing area-specific random error term	$\hat{Y} = \hat{\varphi} + \hat{\pi}X + \hat{\gamma}rX + \hat{\delta}tX + \hat{\vartheta}$

Notes: Explanation of the symbols: $Y(\hat{Y})$ = observed (predicted or simulated) income. X = covariates available in both the LSMS and the DHS. r = dummy for rural areas. t = dummy for other urban areas (towns). $\varepsilon(\hat{\varepsilon})$ = observed (simulated or predicted) area-specific random error term. Subscripts are suppressed for ease of presentation. For details refer to Grosse *et al.* (2004).

might lead to an overestimate of the decline of poverty in rural areas.[8] In our sensitivity analysis we replace the fixed difference assumption with the assumption that the difference in overall incomes (the constant term in the regression) in the three areas developed according to the overall growth rates for rural areas, departmental capitals and towns, respectively.[9] Second, we contrast our results with the asset-index approach developed by Sahn and Stifel (2003) and Filmer and Pritchett (2001). To proxy welfare in the absence of income or expenditure data, this approach assumes that the asset ownership of households closely reflects their living standards. Using DHS data, we define a set of assets and construct an asset index, where the asset weights are determined by means of a principal components analysis as in Pritchett and Filmer (2001). Due to limitations in the data, we can construct the asset index only for 1994 and 1998 which will still allow us to compare the results from our method with an asset index approach for these two years.

Results

The most important results regarding poverty (headcount and poverty gap) and inequality (Gini coefficient), based on the cross-survey simulation methodology, are summarised in Table 8.2. We use the moderate poverty line which is based on the costs of a basic food basket, which is updated using prices of the items in the basket, and makes allowance for non-food basic needs.[10] We present the observed poverty and inequality measure, if available from the income survey, the predicted indicator using the income survey, and the simulated indicator using the DHS. For the simulated incomes we present our main estimates but also include (in brackets) the results based on the alternative assumption regarding the dynamics of the simulation (see above).

The results in Table 8.2 suggest that with our methodology we are able to reproduce actual poverty trends in departmental capitals (where we have actual data for comparison) fairly well, particularly for the poverty gap measure, which is quite reassuring. The predictions and simulations work particularly well for 1989 and 1999 where they are mostly not significantly different (at the 95 per cent level) from the observations, while they appear to be slightly less accurate for 1994. We tend to slightly under-predict the headcount ratio (poverty rate) most of the time, but the most important trends (in capital cities where we can make a comparison) are accurately reflected.[11] Inequality levels and trends are also quite accurately reflected in the predictions and simulations. It is also reassuring to note that our sensitivity analysis, which assumes declining returns to assets in rural areas, only has a minor impact on poverty trends and differentials and, as expected, slightly lowers poverty in rural areas in 1989 and 1994, and thus lowers poverty reduction since then (see figures in brackets). Thus our

Table 8.2 Estimated poverty and inequality trends using moderate poverty line, Bolivia[a]

| | 1989 | | | 1994 | | | 1999 | | | 2002 |
| | Income survey | | DHS | Income survey | | DHS | Income survey | | DHS | Income survey |
	Observation	Prediction	Simulation	Observation	Prediction	Simulation	Observation	Prediction	Simulation	Observation
Headcount										
Departmental capitals[b]	67.2	65.4*	64.8	59.5	58.1	57.4	51.1	50.5*	48.1	55.1
Towns			81.1 (80.7)[c]			75.1 (15.1)	69.1	67.6*	64.2	67.7
Rural			89.7 (87.8)			89.6 (87.8)	83.4	84.3*	79.1	83.8
Total			76.9 (76.0)			72.4 (71.6)	65.2	65.0*	60.3	67.2
Poverty gap										
Departmental capitals	32.9	33.1*	32.9*	25.7	25.9*	25.3*	21.0	22.5*	21.3*	24.4
Towns			51.3 (50.7)			44.7 (44.0)	34.7	35.3*	33.6*	32.9
Rural			58.3 (55.2)			60.9 (58.2)	47.7	48.7*	43.1	44.9
Total			45.5 (44.1)			41.9 (40.7)	32.5	33.7	30.1	32.9

Table 8.2 (Continued)

	1989 Income survey Observation	1989 Income survey Prediction	1989 DHS Simulation	1994 Income survey Observation	1994 Income survey Prediction	1994 DHS Simulation	1999 Income survey Observation	1999 Income survey Prediction	1999 DHS Simulation	2002 Income survey Observation
Gini										
Departmental capitals	0.505	0.492*	0.497*	0.481	0.470	0.455	0.480	0.491*	0.488*	0.540
Towns			0.547			0.537	0.455	0.482*	0.500	0.452
Rural			0.475			0.497	0.423	0.444*	0.443*	0.421
Total			0.555			0.550	0.525	0.538*	0.531*	0.551

Notes: [a] The moderate poverty line is, in line with standard practice in Bolivia, applied to income in urban areas, and consumption in rural areas (as income data are considered not to be reliable there and consumption data are not available for the urban household surveys prior to 1997). While the extreme poverty line in Bolivia is only based on ensuring adequate nutrition, the moderate poverty line also makes allowance for some non-food expenditures. The moderate poverty line stood at about US$40 per capita and month, the extreme poverty line at about US$20. For details on the poverty lines and the results for the extreme poverty line, refer to Grosse *et al.* (2004).
[b] Departmental capitals refer to the 9 departmental capitals and El Alto (the city adjacent to La Paz). Towns refer to other urban areas.
[c] The figures in parentheses refer to the sensitivity analysis which no longer assumes that the impact of endowments on growth did not change between urban and rural areas between 1989 and 1998 but that it changed in proportion with the differential in aggregate growth performance in the three areas. For details and full results, see Klasen *et al.* (2004).
* denotes that the 95% confidence interval includes the actually observed index value (i.e. prediction or simulation do not differ significantly from the actual observation, where such an observation is available).

methods appear accurate enough to be used for assessments of poverty and inequality trends across space and time in Bolivia.

Regarding the substantive findings, Table 8.2 shows that there is a steep gradient in poverty levels between capital cities, towns and rural areas, with poverty being much higher in the last. As far as the poverty rate is concerned, this differential between capital cities and rural areas gets larger over time (from about 25 percentage points in 1989 to nearly 29 percentage points in 2002). This is not true, however, when we consider the poverty gap, for which the differential has somewhat narrowed. This suggests that the very poor have been able to make some gains in the 1990s while rural dwellers close to the poverty line did not benefit as much. There is a clear poverty trend in capital cities, which closely mirrors macroeconomic conditions. Thus poverty (using the headcount or the poverty gap measure) declines considerably between 1989 and 1999 and then increases again between 1999 and 2002. In towns and rural areas, by contrast, the dynamics of poverty are not as closely aligned to macroeconomic developments. In particular, there is no poverty reduction at all in rural areas between 1989 and 1994, then considerable poverty reduction between 1994 and 1999, and stagnation (headcount) or slight further reductions (poverty gap) between 1999 and 2002. In towns, poverty reduction has been faster than in capital cities and has continued even after 1999, although at a much slower pace.

Turning to inequality, the trends closely follow the poverty discussion, but with some additional features. In particular, the sharp increase in inequality in capital cities between 1999 and 2002 is noteworthy. Measures that are more sensitive to the bottom of the distribution, show even more dramatic deteriorations, suggesting that the urban poor have fared particularly badly in the last few years (see Grosse *et al.*, 2004). In other areas, inequality seems to have fallen, thereby somewhat offsetting the dramatic worsening of inequality in departmental capitals. Overall, the Gini in 2002 is similar to 1989. It thus appears that the fate of the urban population, including the urban poor, has been closely linked to macro developments and has recently led to a significant deterioration in poverty and inequality. In contrast, the much poorer rural poor have been more detached from improvements and deteriorations in the overall economic environment and their poverty trends have followed another logic.

Using the asset-based approach to generate poverty data largely confirms the findings discussed above regarding trends and differentials in poverty, but with some nuances.[12] First, the gradient in poverty between capital cities and rural areas is much larger using the asset index than using our approach. Second, poverty reduction appears much faster using the asset index than our approach, particularly in capital cities and towns while the asset index shows hardly any poverty reduction in rural areas. We suspect that the differences between urban and rural areas are much more driven by differences in preferences for assets, their relative prices or accessibility in rural and urban areas rather than differences in income poverty which the asset index is meant to proxy. Also, it is likely that the faster decline in poverty measured using the asset index is largely due to changes in preferences for assets over time (e.g. televisions and radios), declines in relative prices for some assets (e.g. telephones, televisions), and public investments in human assets (e.g. expansion of education). As a result, we suggest that our approach to measuring income poverty is more suitable for poverty comparisons across space and time than the asset index often used in applied work.

Having constructed a time series of poverty and inequality, we now take a closer look at the links between poverty, inequality and growth, using two different methodologies: first, we carry out a decomposition of the observed poverty reduction; and, second, we provide estimates of growth incidence curves and the associated rates of pro-poor growth.

The decomposition of the observed poverty reduction into a growth and an inequality contribution uses the methods proposed by Datt and Ravallion (1992).[13] The results of the decomposition analysis for the entire period (Table 8.3) reveal that about two-thirds of the 10 percentage point decline in poverty for total Bolivia is attributable to growth, and about one-third to a distributional shift favouring the poor. As the income

Table 8.3   Growth-inequality decomposition of poverty changes (moderate poverty), Bolivia

	1989–99	*1999–2002*	*1989–2002*
Total Bolivia			
Change in poverty	−0.118	0.020	−0.099
Growth component	−0.080	0.018	−0.064
Redistribution component	−0.038	0.002	−0.035
Departmental capitals			
Change in poverty	−0.163	0.040	−0.123
Growth component	−0.105	0.025	−0.080
Redistribution component	−0.057	0.015	−0.043
Towns			
Change in poverty	−0.117	−0.015	−0.132
Growth component	−0.067	0.017	−0.074
Redistribution component	−0.050	−0.032	−0.058
Rural areas			
Change in poverty	−0.068	0.005	−0.064
Growth component	−0.041	−0.005	−0.039
Redistribution component	−0.028	0.010	−0.025

Notes: Calculated using the Datt–Ravallion (1992) method of growth-inequality decomposition. Mean of growth rates for poorest tracks the Ravallion–Chen rate of pro-poor growth for all possible initial poverty headcounts.
Source: For the extreme poverty line, see Klasen *et al.* (2004).

distribution hardly shifted between the two periods (see Table 8.2), most of this distributional shift is actually due to the decline in the relative price of food which increased the real purchasing power of the poor. Considering sub-periods and different parts of the country shows a more differentiated picture. In the period 1989–99 both the growth and redistribution[14] effect served to reduce poverty in all parts of the country. In the latter three years, the picture changed drastically. Poverty increased nationally, and particularly in departmental capital cities where 60 per cent was due to falling incomes and 40 per cent due to adverse distributional shifts.

A second way to examine the linkages between growth, inequality and poverty is the Ravallion–Chen measure of pro-poor growth, which takes the average of growth rates of the quantiles of the population that were poor in the initial period (see Ravallion and Chen, 2003). The growth incidence curves underlying this measure are shown below (Figures 8.1–8.4) for the entire period (1989–2002). For Bolivia as a whole, the growth incidence curve is above 0 for all groups, and moderately downward-sloping from the 10th to the 90th percentile, suggesting that overall the poor gained proportionately more from growth than the rich. This is not true below the 10th percentile and above the 90th percentile, suggesting that the extremely poor were not benefiting as much and that the very rich were benefiting more from growth. A more differentiated picture emerges when one considers the different parts of the country. In the departmental capitals (and El Alto), growth over the period was anti-poor, with the poor gaining less than the rich (particularly due to the influence of the period after 1999), while it was strongly pro-poor in towns, and moderately pro-poor in rural areas.

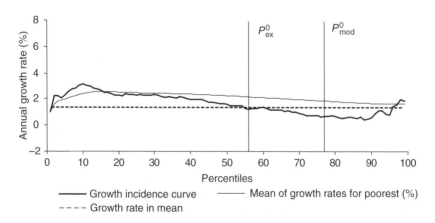

Figure 8.1 Growth incidence curve for total Bolivia, 1989–2002

Note: Mean of growth rates for poorest tracks the Ravallion–Chen rate of pro-poor growth for all possible initial poverty headcounts.

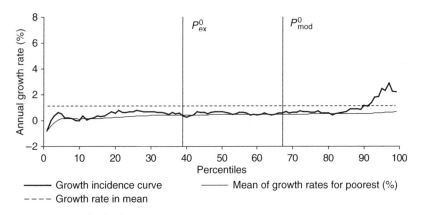

Figure 8.2 Growth incidence curve for the departmental capitals, Bolivia 1989–2002
Note: Mean of growth rates for poorest tracks the Ravallion–Chen rate of pro-poor growth for all possible initial poverty headcounts.

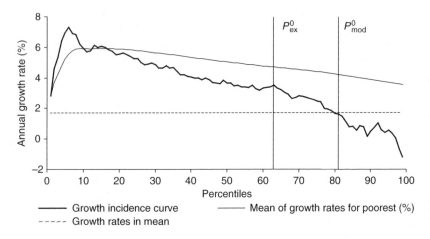

Figure 8.3 Growth incidence curve for towns, Bolivia 1989–2002
Note: Mean of growth rates for poorest tracks the Ravallion–Chen rate of pro-poor growth for all possible initial poverty headcounts.

The annual rate of pro-poor growth, shown in Table 8.4, summarizes the information provided in the growth incidence curves by averaging the growth rates of the initially poor centiles of the income distribution.[15] Between 1989 and 1999, economic growth in Bolivia can clearly be classified as pro-poor. For both poverty lines and for all three regions, the rates of pro-poor growth exceeded the growth rate of mean income, which suggests that growth was accompanied by falling inequality. The particularly high growth rate in total Bolivia (2.23 per cent) is due to growth in the three areas plus a shift in the composition of the population from the

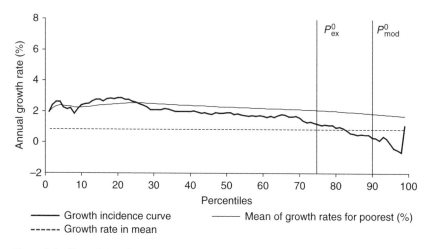

Figure 8.4 Growth incidence curve for rural areas, Bolivia 1989–2002

Note: Mean of growth rates for poorest tracks the Ravallion–Chen rate of pro-poor growth for all possible initial poverty headcounts.

poorer rural areas to the richer urban areas. Between 1999 and 2002, growth performance differed substantially between the three regions. The departmental capitals experienced a strongly anti-poor contraction, which wiped out a substantial part of the gains the poor had made in the previous ten years. In towns, this contraction was pro-poor so that, despite negative growth rates in mean income, the poor could more or less keep their living standard. In rural areas, consumption even continued to rise, albeit very slowly, and consumption growth continued to be somewhat higher for the poor than for the non-poor. Given that most income is generated in urban areas, but most of the poor live in rural areas, economic growth in total Bolivia was negative during the period 1999–2002, but only slightly anti-poor or even pro-poor depending on the choice of the poverty line.

The finding that growth was at least moderately pro-poor in rural areas seems to be at odds with the results in Table 8.1, which show only slowly falling rural poverty rates since 1989. However, this puzzle is resolved when taking into account that the depth of poverty in rural areas is so large that even considerable pro-poor growth did not lift many of the poor above the poverty line although it did reduce the depth of poverty measured by the poverty gap substantially (particularly between 1994 and 1999, see Table 8.1). Hence, the prime concern for Bolivian policy-makers should not be that growth in the 1990s was anti-poor, but that growth was so low and that initial inequality was so high that the poor remained poor during these nearly ten years of growth in the 1990s. It would have taken another decade of such growth to make serious inroads into poverty, particularly in rural areas. Unfortunately, the future prospects are even bleaker. If the meagre

Table 8.4 Annual pro-poor growth rates (per capita), Bolivia

	1989–2002	*1989–1999*	*1999–2002*
Total Bolivia			
Growth rate in the mean	1.41 (1.25)	2.23 (2.02)	−1.29
Mean of growth rates for			
extremely poor	2.16 (1.74)	3.39 (2.81)	−0.88
moderately poor	1.85 (1.49)	3.21 (2.74)	−2.22
all	1.67 (1.34)	2.98 (2.56)	−2.56
Departmental capitals			
Growth rate in the mean	1.19	2.01	−1.51
Mean of growth rates for			
extremely poor	0.44	2.56	−6.30
moderately poor	0.48	2.58	−6.44
all	0.69	2.50	−5.01
Other urban areas			
Growth rate in the mean	1.76 (1.58)	2.89 (2.64)	−1.90
Mean of growth rates for			
extremely poor	4.70 (4.53)	6.23 (6.01)	0.48
moderately poor	4.22 (4.03)	5.80 (5.55)	−0.22
all	3.75 (3.56)	5.25 (5.00)	−1.03
Rural areas			
Growth rate in the mean	0.87 (0.17)	0.94 (0.02)	0.59
Mean of growth rates for			
extremely poor	2.07 (1.40)	2.31 (1.39)	1.86
moderately poor	1.86 (1.18)	2.18 (1.28)	0.99
all	1.73 (1.02)	1.99 (1.06)	0.86

Source: Own calculations based on the method of Ravallion and Chen (2003). Growth rates use the actually observed levels of income/expenditure where available (in capital cities throughout and elsewhere from 1999 onwards). Figures in parentheses are based on a sensitivity analysis as discussed in the text.

growth performance since 1999 continues, rural poverty will decline even less and urban poverty will rise. This makes it all the more important to understand the linkages between policy, growth, and poverty, a subject to which we now turn.

Analysing past and future policy options for pro-poor growth using a CGE model

In this section, we use a dynamic CGE model to assess the impact of shocks and policies on pro-poor growth. While the general approach is to simulate forward-looking policies, it may also be used to explore how the role of shocks and policies affected the past evolution of growth, inequality, and poverty reduction.

Methodology

A technical description of the CGE model can be found in Wiebelt (2004). Here, we only briefly sketch some key elements: first, the model distinguishes 12 sectors (see Table 8.5). A peculiarity is the explicit treatment of traditional agriculture and (urban) informal services as informal production sectors, where most of Bolivia's poor earn their living. Workers in these sectors are considered self-employed; they for the most part rely on their own labour inputs and use only small amounts of capital. This implies that, over one year, supply is almost constant for a given number of workers; if demand slackens, adjustment will mainly run through a fall in prices and incomes of those employed in these sectors. By contrast, formal sectors tend to produce with capital-intensive techniques, giving them greater flexibility on the supply side.

Second, supply-side adjustment and earning possibilities are constrained by a high degree of factor market segmentation. As regards labour markets, beside the self-employed smallholders and urban informals, we distinguish between two types of unskilled labour (agricultural and non-agricultural), employers, as well as skilled labour (employees, see Table 8.5). Labour markets are linked via rural-rural and rural-urban migration. While the former involves smallholders becoming hired workers in modern agriculture, the latter involves the absorption of smallholders by the urban informal sector. The decision to migrate depends on wage differentials. For all labour markets, full employment is assumed. Capital markets are also segmented, with a distinction made between formal capital and informal capital owned by smallholders, urban informals, and employers. In addition, we separate public infrastructure capital, which is assumed to have a crowding-in effect on sectoral production (Agenor *et al.*, 2003).

Table 8.5   Classification of the CGE model, Bolivia

Production sectors	*Production factors*	*Economic agents*
Traditional agriculture	Skilled labour	Households
Modern agriculture	Agricultural unskilled labour	smallholders
Oil& gas	Non-agricultural unskilled	agricultural workers
Mining	labour	non-agricultural
Consumer goods	Smallholder labour	workers
Intermediate goods	Urban informal labour	employees
Capital goods	Corporate (formal) capital	urban informals
Utilities	Employers' capital	employers
Construction	Urban informals' capital	Public enterprises
Informal services	Smallholders' capital	Private enterprises
Formal services	Public (infrastructure)	Government
Public services	capital	Rest of the world

Third, the model identifies six representative private households groups, which are basically characterized by their distinct factor endowments. This is justified because factor income is the single-most important income source in Bolivia given the low degree of redistribution. In addition, workers and the self-employed are disaggregated regionally as their earning possibilities and consumption patterns tend to vary between regions. Four of the six household groups (smallholders, urban informals, and agricultural and non-agricultural workers) predominate among the poor, while the other two groups (employees and employers) are mostly non-poor.

Fourth, the model is recursive-dynamic, which means that the model is solved for a sequence of static equilibria. The dynamics of the model are based on assumptions concerning exogenous growth rates for different variables such as labour supply and government expenditures, as well as the endogenous savings and investment behaviour of economic agents. A general advantage of the dynamic specification is the possibility to generate a medium to long run growth path.

Fifth, the model is calibrated to a Social Accounting Matrix for 1997. This is because crucial data, in particular an Input–Output table and a household survey are available for that year, and because 1997 appears to be a fairly 'normal' year for the Bolivian economy in the sense that no major shocks occurred.

Sixth, the distributional results of the CGE model are linked to information of the 1999 household income survey (mainly on factor incomes), which we already used for the poverty analysis above, to obtain detailed results on the poverty and distributional impact of the simulated policies. The link between CGE and the survey is simply sequential: each individual factor or household income component in the household survey is scaled up or down according to the CGE results.

Results

Table 8.6 shows the results of the simulations of the different scenarios. We show the estimated growth rate, as well as national, urban and rural poverty headcounts at the end of a 10-year simulation period. For rural areas, we also show the poverty gap as the poverty headcount is extremely high and thus not greatly affected by the economic situation of the average poor.

Baseline scenario

A scenario that describes how the Bolivian economy might evolve in the absence of shocks and policy changes serves as a benchmark against which all alternative developments will be evaluated. In this scenario, the economy exhibits smooth economic growth of about 4.7 per cent on average over a ten-year period (Table 8.6),[16] where economic growth is driven by capital accumulation, (exogenous) growth of the labour force, and (exogenous) technical progress (2 per cent TFP growth). This not only describes an optimistic

Table 8.6 The impact of shocks and policies on growth and poverty, Bolivia

	Average growth (%)	National[a] headcount	Urban[a] headcount	Rural[a] headcount (gap)
Baseline scenario	4.7	55.3	38.9	82.8 (59.2)
El Niño	4.4	56.3	39.7	84.1 (60.8)
Declining capital inflows	4.4	56.3	40.3	83.3 (59.5)
Labour market reform	5.0	54.4	37.4	82.8 (58.7)
Tax reform (revenue-neutral)	5.0	53.9	37.0	82.4 (58.7)
Gas projects (higher government consumption)	5.1	54.9	37.8	83.8 (61.3)
Gas projects (constant government consumption)	5.3	53.8	36.1	83.7 (60.9)
Gas projects (constant government consumption) plus labour market reform plus tax reform	5.8	52.0	33.5	83.0 (61.5)
Improved access to credit for smallholders	4.7	55.2	38.8	82.8 (58.9)
Investment in rural infrastructure	4.8	55.0	38.6	82.4 (58.2)
Transfer programme (lower government consumption)	4.7	53.8	37.9	80.5 (56.6)
Transfer programme (lower public investment)	4.5	54.6	38.9	81.1 (57.2)
Gas projects plus transfer programme	5.1	53.5	37.1	81.0 (58.6)

Note: [a] Ratio at the end of the 10-year simulation period. Please note that the initial poverty headcounts are: 63.6% national, 49.7% urban (including departmental capitals and towns), and 86.9% rural, with the poverty gap in rural areas at 63.7%.
Source: Own calculations based on the CGE model.

forward-looking scenario, but is also a fairly good description of the record of Bolivia up to 1998.

From a distributional point of view, the baseline scenario suggests that without further policy reforms and without external shocks the rural–urban gap in income levels will widen as urban areas will benefit disproportionately from growth. In both urban and rural areas inequality is already at very high levels, which is why aggregate growth in Bolivia barely translates into poverty reduction. This holds in particular for rural areas. Over the simulated 10-year period, the national headcount moderately declines from 63.6 per cent to 55.3 per cent. The reduction is a result of a decrease in the urban headcount from 49.7 per cent to 38.9 per cent, and a reduction in rural poverty (headcount as well as gap) of only about 4 percentage points from 86.9 per cent to 82.8 per cent (gap from 63.7 to 59.2 per cent).

External shocks

The assumption made in the baseline scenario that no external shocks occur during the simulation period is highly unrealistic in the Bolivian context. Most predictably, the agricultural sector is recurrently hit by the El Niño phenomenon. Furthermore, the experience of the Brazilian crisis suggests that the high level of foreign capital inflows realized in the mid-1990s should not be taken for granted. Doubts about the sustainability of these inflows are reinforced by the fact that most foreign direct investment was related to the capitalization process, which was more or less completed at the end of the 1990s.

An El Niño shock of average size causes considerable short-run agricultural output losses. It may lower GDP growth by about one percentage point in the year of its occurrence. Since this is only partly compensated by higher growth in subsequent periods, and since El Niño tends to occur every three years, the losses add up to significantly lower average growth rates (Table 8.6). In addition, the fall in agricultural exports during El Niño years leads to a real depreciation of the boliviano, which in turn gives rise to a reallocation of resources from inward-oriented sectors such as construction and informal services to more outward-oriented sectors.

The direct distributional consequence of El Niño is that smallholders and agricultural workers suffer income losses. The same is true for employers, who obtain a significant share of their capital income from investments undertaken in modern agriculture. In urban areas, the only major effect of El Niño on household incomes runs via the real devaluation, which makes the providers of non-traded informal services worse off. By contrast, the overall income position of non-agricultural workers and employees is hardly affected, as their gains in tradable sectors tend to offset their losses in non-tradable sectors. The decline of urban informal income results in a quite considerable increase in the urban poverty incidence.

If foreign direct investment (FDI) falls by almost one-third, as has been the case in the year 2000, this causes only about half the immediate output losses of El Niño, but the impact turns out to be much more persistent. Even after ten years, growth has not fully recovered. Due to the heavy dependence of domestic investment on foreign capital (a result of the low domestic savings rate), the fall in FDI lowers the domestic investment ratio by about 2.5 percentage points. The ensuing losses at the macro level are spread over all sectors using formal capital, and over those producing capital goods. Since traditional agriculture and informal services lack access to formal capital, smallholders and urban informals are the only households not immediately suffering from the shock. The real devaluation brought about by this shock, however, indirectly hurts the urban informals, while it benefits modern agriculture to such an extent that the sector's loss of FDI is overcompensated. Temporarily, smallholders and agricultural workers gain slightly from the shock, but lose somewhat in the medium run as a result of lower economic growth. This drives the evolution of the rural poverty incidence, which decreases slightly in the shock period, but increases afterwards. Over the entire simulation period, the rural income distribution improves quite considerably. By contrast, all urban households are negatively affected by the decrease in FDI in the short and long run.

A similar drop in portfolio investment, which was the main consequence of the Brazilian crisis, strongly reinforces the negative short-run impact of the fall in FDI. During the initial year, both shocks combined drive the growth rate down by about 1.5 percentage points. Since lower portfolio investment reduces growth only temporarily, the medium-run impact is dominated by the reduction of FDI. Average growth over the whole simulation period is about 0.3 percentage points lower than in the baseline scenario. The medium-run poverty outcome for the combined shocks is very similar to the FDI shock alone. In the short run, however, the impact on urban poverty is much stronger.

The simulations in Table 8.6 may also help explain the past evolution of the economy. The foreign investment boom triggered by the capitalization process has in all likelihood been a key factor behind the comparably high growth rates until 1998, with a poverty impact that was biased in favour of urban households, but did not completely bypass the rural economy. Compared to this effect, agricultural shocks have only played a minor role between 1990 and 1998. The only major exception is a severe El Niño, which contributed to negative per capita income growth in 1992 and thus may have worsened the overall poverty outcome for rural areas in the early 1990s (as found above). A favourable external environment for agricultural production may at least partly explain why the rural poor fared exceptionally well over the period 1994 to 1998. The recession that started in 1999 has in all likelihood hit urban households harder than rural households because the sharp decline in foreign capital inflows in the year 2000 has clearly dominated the El Niño shock that set in a year earlier.

Looking forward, a realistic scenario for Bolivia's medium-run development prospects would imply that under the current policy framework average growth rates are unlikely to exceed 4 per cent. Compared to the optimistic baseline scenario in Table 8.6, this implies worse prospects for poverty reduction. We also investigate the impact of changes of the current policy framework and discuss the most important results.

Macro policies

We investigated the impact of macro policies on pro-poor growth, particularly focusing on exchange-rate policies, the results of which are discussed in detail in Klasen (2006) and Schweickert *et al.* (2005). Due to Bolivia's high *dollarization*, a nominal devaluation (achieved via interventions in the foreign exchange markets) would do little to improve international competitiveness but cause significant foreign debt problems so that growth would decline and poverty increase as a result of such a measure. A real devaluation (achieved via restrictive monetary policies), could, after a short-term contraction, make a slight positive contribution to growth and poverty reduction. High external vulnerability, low domestic savings, high dependence on external finance, and high *dollarization* severely limit the room to manoeuvre as far as pro-poor macro policies are concerned.[17]

Structural reforms

By Latin American standards, Bolivia has made remarkable progress in the area of structural reforms (see for example Lora, 2001). The main exception is labour market reform. Among the labour market distortions that still prevail, the segmentation of the urban labour market stands out. The tax system is another area where further reforms may be warranted; in particular, the question arises of whether the income tax should become a major source of government revenues.

If the government makes it easier for urban informals to be employed as unskilled workers in the formal labour market, for example by lowering the costs of dismissal or by granting more options for temporary work, the obvious direct effect is that average real wages go down for unskilled workers and up for urban informals. Better earning opportunities in the urban informal sector, in turn, induce rural-urban migration on a significant scale, which moderately increases the incomes of those who stay in traditional agriculture. At the macro level, the efficiency gains achieved by reducing labour market segmentation – the wage differential between informal labour and unskilled labour is roughly halved – translate into average economic growth rates which are more than 0.3 percentage points higher than in the base run.

On balance, these developments cause negligible distributional shifts in urban areas because higher incomes for informals are offset by lower incomes for unskilled workers. Nonetheless, urban poverty decreases because of higher growth, but it takes some periods for the positive growth effect to materialize. The rural income distribution changes somewhat in favour of poorer groups due to the gains experienced by smallholders. This change and a slight increase in rural growth do not show up in the poverty headcount, but the rural poverty gap falls moderately.

A rise in income taxes for all household groups except smallholders and urban informals directly forces the two richest household groups, employers and employees, to consume and save less. For worker households the impact on disposable income is not strong enough to alter consumption and savings significantly.[18] The main indirect effect runs via a tax-induced fall in aggregate private consumption, which lowers the prices und thus the incomes received by smallholders and urban informals. If the government broadly retains the original structure of expenditures, the tax increase is likely to be moderately contractionary in the medium run, as the rise in public investment does not suffice to fully offset the fall in private investment. This in turn would have a negative impact on the factor incomes of all household groups.

If higher income taxes are combined with lower indirect taxes so as to arrive at a revenue-neutral tax reform, the economy-wide outcome is different. Lower indirect tax rates cause an expansion of capital-intensive industries, where the indirect tax burden is highest, and thus boost investment and growth. Overall, given the current tax structure, a revenue-neutral tax reform can be expected to improve Bolivia's growth performance. As for household incomes, the decrease in indirect taxes raises private consumption expenditures, thereby offsetting the negative demand effect that higher income taxes have on smallholders and urban informals. The main beneficiaries of the reform are non-agricultural workers, many of whom work in capital-intensive sectors, as well as in construction, which benefits from higher investment demand. The expansion of the construction sector additionally favours urban informals so that on balance their incomes also rise significantly. The gains of these two groups reduce the urban headcount ratio by up to 2 percentage points.

Perhaps more than the structural reforms, the development of the natural-gas sector might change the medium-run growth path of the Bolivian economy, and has been at the centre of economic policy-making and political discussions in recent years. If all the projects planned at around 2001 were realized, the share of oil and gas in total domestic production would roughly double, and oil and gas would finally account for as much as 50 per cent of total exports. The natural-gas boom would translate into markedly higher economic growth. In 2008 and 2009, when the planned projects are expected to reach full capacity, the growth rate could approach 6 per cent. The size of the growth effect depends on how the government uses its additional revenues. If the receipts are channelled into consumption, the average gains over the simulation period are only about two-thirds as large as if consumption growth is left constant.[19]

A real appreciation of the boliviano leads to a contraction of export-oriented sectors such as modern agriculture, and an expansion of nontradables. This is the well-known Dutch Disease effect of resource booms. By keeping consumption growth constant, the government can slightly dampen the Dutch Disease effect. A restructuring of final demand away from private consumption exerts pressure on smallholders' and urban informals' prices as they can hardly adjust supply. Together with rising rural–urban migration, this explains why urban informals are slightly worse off as a result of the gas projects even though they benefit from the real appreciation. Overall, rural areas, that is smallholders as well as agricultural workers, suffer significant income losses.

These changes in relative factor prices induce major distributional and poverty changes. Inequality increases substantially, which is mainly due to rising inequality between urban and rural areas. Despite considerably higher growth rates, the decrease in nation-wide poverty is only moderate. More remarkably, rural poverty (headcount and gap) even increases substantially. A somewhat more favourable outcome could be expected if the government refrained from raising consumption expenditures. In this case, the headcount would be significantly lower in urban areas, but rural households would hardly benefit and thus would remain markedly worse off than without the gas projects.

A fairly large medium-term boost for Bolivia's economy might be possible if the gas projects were combined with the structural reforms discussed above. The gains would, however, exclusively accrue to urban households. They would benefit from a substantial drop in the poverty rate by more than 5 percentage points compared to the base run, while the rural poverty headcount would rise a little and the poverty gap would rise substantially. Clearly, such a strategy maximizes growth, but not pro-poor growth.

Targeted interventions in favour of the poor

In rural areas in particular, many households are too poor to be lifted above the poverty line by moderate economic growth alone. Among the policies that might help the rural poor, improved access to credit for smallholders and investment in public goods such as rural infrastructure are particularly relevant. Transfer programmes constitute a more direct way of raising incomes of the poor.

Efforts to improve credit availability for smallholders, for example by making land tenure more secure, are likely to raise investment in traditional agriculture significantly, albeit from a very low base.[20] The impact tends to decelerate over time, but even after 10 years real investment could still exceed the base-run level by almost 50 per cent. However, since the contribution of capital to sectoral value-added is very small, the investment boom only raises output by about 3 per cent in the medium run. This supply response is too moderate to induce major adjustments in the rest of the economy. Aggregate investment rises slightly and average economic growth is less than 0.05 percentage points higher than in the base run. Smallholders' real income position improves somewhat as a result of the output expansion, but this does not show up in the rural headcount, and even the poverty gap falls only marginally. Hence, the loosening of smallholders' credit restrictions must be regarded as largely ineffective in the medium term, at least without further complementary measures.

Specific investments in public goods – for example the development of more productive crop varieties or the construction of rural roads – might constitute one such complementary measure. However, even if public investments are tailored to smallholders' needs, its impact is constrained by the difficult natural conditions prevailing in the Bolivian highlands. Here we consider a fairly optimistic scenario where smallholder's average output is raised by about 10 per cent compared to the base run. The expansion of smallholder agriculture comes partly at the expense of modern agriculture so that smallholders realize income gains, whereas agricultural workers experience a less pronounced decline in wages. Due to a small real appreciation, urban informals can slightly improve their income position. Despite considerably higher income gains in rural areas, reductions in the urban and rural headcount are small and roughly equal. The difference between the two regions manifests itself in a significantly higher fall of the rural poverty gap, which goes down by one percentage point.

With respect to transfers we assume that the government expands existing programmes so that gross incomes of the four poor household groups are raised every year by roughly 5 per cent compared to the base run. We thus assume no improvements in the targeting performance of transfer programmes which is a realistic but conservative assumption given the currently poor targeting of some of the transfer programmes (including particularly public pensions, see Klasen *et al.*, 2004). Whether the impact of such programmes goes beyond the direct beneficiaries largely depends on how the government finances the outlays. If it substitutes transfer payments for consumption expenditures, economy-wide repercussions are negligible and average growth is not affected. Since the transfers mainly benefit smallholders and urban informals, both urban and rural poverty fall markedly. Inequality, by contrast, rises in both rural and urban areas. This surprising result can be explained by the fact that the transfers currently tend to reach richer rather than poorer segments of the smallholders and urban informals. Thus if transfers were better targeted they would generate a more favourable poverty and inequality outcome (see Klasen *et al.*, 2004).

Financing transfer programmes through cuts in investment spending has a much stronger impact on the economy as it lowers aggregate investment and saving ratios by over one percentage point and thereby leads to reduced economic growth. The investment slowdown is most strongly felt in the construction sector, which implies that factor incomes of workers and urban informals decline. For urban informals, a restructuring of final demand towards private consumption cushions the decline. The shift in final demand equally raises smallholders' factor incomes so that they enjoy direct and indirect benefits. Overall, the secondary effects via the fall in investment fully offset the transfer-induced urban poverty reduction, whereas rural poverty alleviation remains sizeable.

The model results suggest, overall, that there are no magic bullets to promote rapid pro-poor growth in Bolivia. While there is a range of options to moderately improve the growth performance of the economy, it appears much harder to ensure that growth reaches the poor. To achieve this, a coordinated package of specific interventions for the poor combined with more and better-targeted transfer programmes (including, for example, demand-side cash transfer programmes) would help to improve the poverty performance moderately. To have a larger impact, the large inequalities and structural segmentations between the poor, particularly those in rural areas, and the rest of the economy would need to be tackled more directly to improve the poverty reduction performance (see Klasen *et al.*, 2004 for details).

Conclusions

It may be useful to summarize both the methodological as well as the substantive findings emanating from this analysis of pro-poor growth in Bolivia. Beginning with the latter, the analysis has shown that growth in the 1990s has been pro-poor overall, but anti-poor in capital cities due to the recent economic crisis. Overall poverty reduction was only moderate, however, due to only moderate economic growth and high initial income inequality. In particular, rural poverty has been little affected, which is a result of large initial rural–urban inequality and the highly dualistic nature of Bolivia's economy where most growth has been generated by developments benefiting the urban economy. Looking forward, it will be a challenge to maintain the moderate growth rates that were achieved in the 1990s, as the country is very vulnerable to external and climatic shocks. As the model-based simulations suggest, there is a range of options to improve the growth performance of the economy. Gas exports, combined with labour market and tax reforms, would significantly raise growth and contribute to accelerated poverty reduction in urban areas. But they would do nothing to further poverty reduction in rural areas and even specific interventions for the rural poor would only have relatively small effects. Given the dualistic nature of the economy, only transfer programmes are found to make a significant dent in rural poverty. Consequently, policy should aim to tackle the vast rural–urban inequalities (which are highly correlated with income and ethnic inequalities), if progress is to be made in accelerating pro-poor growth in Bolivia.[21]

Turning to methodological and analytical issues, this chapter has shown that two analytical tools, dynamic cross-survey simulations and dynamic CGE models, can be successfully applied to improve the analysis of pro-poor growth in Bolivia (and elsewhere). In particular, the cross-survey simulations appear to be suitable to create reliable time series of inequality and poverty when nationally representative income surveys are lacking (a common problem in many Latin American and African countries), and appear to yield more plausible estimates than the often-used asset-based approach.

At the same time, several methodological and analytical challenges remain. First, due to the lack of precise locational information in some of the surveys, it was not possible to include cluster-level information in the simulation methodology. This is something to be improved when this method were to be applied elsewhere. Second, the simulations currently are based on the average return to assets across the income distribution. If the returns are lower for poor than for rich households, this might overstate incomes of the poor. Here, the potential for quantile regressions should be explored. This is particularly important as the growth incidence curves and the associated measures of pro-poor growth are highly sensitive to income levels and changes at the bottom of the distribution. Third, different specifications of the distribution of the error term should be considered to improve the precision of the predictions and simulations in Table 8.1. Lastly, the comparison of this method with the asset-based approach should be investigated more closely and extended to other contexts to study the relative merits of both approaches.

Regarding the CGE model, it has demonstrated its utility for formally assessing the impact of shocks and policies on pro-poor growth. It shows a high ability to explain past trends in pro-poor growth and provides instructive guidance regarding the pro-poor growth impact of forward-looking policy options. Substantively, it has shown that the opportunities for achieving pro-poor growth differ markedly between urban and rural areas. This has been true for the 1990s, where until the outbreak of the recent crisis urban households have benefited disproportionately from foreign investment-led growth. And it is also true with respect to future prospects, as the available policy options could at least to some extent alleviate urban poverty, while they would largely bypass rural households.

Also, here, a few important methodological and analytical lessons can be drawn. First, there may be two reasons why the relatively small overall effects of shocks and policies are understating the true impacts. One is that the demand-side of the economy is not considered here and boosts on the demand-side in an economy that is operating below full capacity might magnify some of the effects discussed here. Another is the assumption of national market clearing and homogeneous prices in the model simulations, while for developing countries generally and the rural sector in particular, price dispersion is a pervasive characteristic and major determinant of inequality. Indeed, greater market access can be a potent catalyst for poverty alleviation on the countryside. These issues need to be considered further.[22] Second, the model simulations all assume an exogenously fixed rate of technological progress. While it is very difficult to come up with a more plausible assumption, it could well be that some of the structural reforms or targeted interventions in favour of the poor raise total factor productivity growth and thus would have a larger impact. Finally, the linking of the CGE model's distributional results with information from the household survey is based on the so-called micro-accounting approach that does not take explicitly into account the behaviour of agents at the micro level. Yet linking the core CGE model to a micro-simulation model, either by being fully integrated or through some less formal link to a micro-econometric model of the income generation at the household level would be necessary to explore in detail how household heterogeneity combines with market equilibrium mechanisms to produce changes in poverty and inequality as a consequence of shocks or policy changes.

Notes

1. See *Klasen et al.* (2004) for more details on other aspects of pro-poor growth in Bolivia.
2. Starting in the 1970s, Bolivia became a major exporter of coca leaves, the input to cocaine, which became Bolivia's most lucrative cash crop and heavily uses labour from poor rural areas. But this coca production has always been under threat from eradication initiatives and the ebb and flow of these eradication efforts have played a significant role in the income sources of poor rural households surrounding the coca growing regions.
3. The 1997 national survey is also not comparable to later surveys so that a consistent national time series only emerges in 1999.
4. See Klasen *et al.* (2004) for a literature review of poverty trends in Bolivia.
5. For more details and further results, please refer to Grosse *et al.* (2004).
6. As is standard practice in Bolivia (e.g. INE-UDAPE, 2002), we use consumption (including auto-consumption) as the welfare measure for rural areas and incomes for urban areas as rural incomes, which are on average some 25 per cent below rural consumption, are widely believed to be severely understated. Thus the regression model also uses incomes in urban and consumption in rural areas. Using incomes in rural areas would significantly increase measured inequality. It is not possible to use consumption in all areas as consumption data are not available prior to 1999. Thus this combination seems most appropriate for the setting in Bolivia although we acknowledge that using consumption in one area and income in another may lead to biases that are hard to quantify.
7. The error is drawn from a normal distribution with the area-specific variance. We generate 200 replications which also allows us to generate confidence intervals and test for statistically significant differences of our results.
8. As growth between 1989 and 1999 was slower in rural areas than in departmental capitals, our assumption of a constant difference in coefficients in those two years assumes that the widening of the urban–rural divide during that time is, thus, entirely attributed (a) to changes in the endowment of covariates in favour of urban areas, and (b) to nationwide changes in the return to covariates in favour of those covariates which are relatively abundant in urban areas. If this assumption does not hold, i.e., if additionally (c) the returns to covariates in rural areas deteriorated relative to those in urban areas, the widening of the urban–rural divide would be understated in the simulation.
9. We thus implicitly assume that the widening of the urban–rural divide is entirely due to a deterioration of the returns in rural areas, relative to departmental capitals. For details, see Grosse *et al.* (2004).

10. As the food prices have risen somewhat less than the CPI, the poor have been benefiting from this favourable shift in relative prices which helped to further reduce poverty. For details, see Klasen *et al.* (2004).
11. It is interesting to note that the prediction using the income survey always shows higher poverty rates than the simulation, but typically lower than the observation. The difference between the observation and the prediction is due to the assumptions regarding the error term, while the difference between the prediction and the simulation is largely due to differences in the level of the covariates between the income survey and the DHS.
12. See Grosse *et al.* (2004) for detailed results and discussions.
13. There is a residual which, however, cancels out if one averages the results from the forward and backward decomposition. As discussed in detail by Grimm and Günther (2006) and in Chapter 6 in this volume, the distribution component in this decomposition also implicitly includes the impact of changes in the real value of the poverty line (i.e., how prices paid by the poor have moved relative to the overall price level). As shown in Klasen *et al.* (2004), the prices paid by the poor (in particular food prices) have risen somewhat less than the overall price level (particularly in recent years) so that the purchasing power of the poor has increased by more than suggested by the change in their real incomes. This is implicitly captured in the decomposition as a distributional shift favouring the poor.
14. This again includes the effect of changes in the real purchasing power of the poor.
15. We also show the results of our sensitivity analysis for towns and rural areas (and by implication, all Bolivia) in brackets.
16. For more detailed information, see Klasen *et al.* (2004), which also includes other poverty and inequality measures. It should be pointed out that the poverty gap often shows larger results than the poverty headcount, as has been the case in the past.
17. See Klasen (2006) and Schweickert *et al.* (2005) for further discussion of these issues and potential policy implications.
18. The impact of the tax increase on aggregate poverty and income distribution cannot be calculated because the household survey on which the distributional measures are based does not contain information on income tax payments.
19. We only consider gas projects for which contracts have been signed and which are currently under implementation nor do we consider the recent renegotiations of the new government under Evo Morales. There are further plans to expand gas exports, possibly via liquefied natural gas exports to the USA. See IMF (2004) for details.
20. Improved access of smallholders to credit is modelled via two mechanisms. First, the credit constraint for smallholders is relaxed by assuming that their credit is no longer determined residually by the banking system after all other agents' demand has been satisfied, but rather according to rentability criteria. Second, substitution elasticities of portfolio selection are increased for banks, which implies that their credit allocation becomes more sensitive to differences in sectoral rentabilities.
21. See Klasen *et al.* (2004) and Klasen (2006) for more detailed policy recommendations.
22. See, for example, also Jemio and Wiebelt (2003) who consider a short-run model and study implications for changes in aggregate demand.

References

Agenor, P.-R., Izquierdo, A. and Fofack, H. (2003) 'The Integrated Macroeconomic Model for Poverty Analysis: A Quantitative Macroeconomic Framework for the Analysis of Poverty Reduction Strategies', Policy Research Working Paper no. 3092, Washington, DC: World Bank.

Datt, G. and Ravallion, M. (1992) 'Growth and Redistribution Components of Changes in Poverty Measures: A Decomposition with Applications to Brazil and India in the 1980s', *Journal of Development Economics*, 38/2: 275–95.

Elbers, Ch., Lanjouw, J.O. and Lanjouw, P. (2003) 'Micro-Level Estimation of Poverty and Inequality', *Econometrica*, 71/1: 355–64.

Filmer, D. and Prichett, L. (2001) 'Estimating Wealth Effects without Expenditure Data – or Tears: An Application to Educational Enrollments in States of India', *Demography*, 38/1: 115–32.

Grimm, M. and Günther, I. (2006) 'Measuring Pro-Poor Growth when Relative Prices Shift', *Journal of Development Economics*, (forthcoming).

Grosse, M., Klasen, S. and Spatz, J. (2004) 'Creating National Poverty Profiles and Growth Incidence Curves with Incomplete Income or Consumption Expenditure Data: An Application to Bolivia', Discussion Papers no. 129. Göttingen: Ibero-America Institute for Economic Research.

Hentschel, J., Lanjouw, J.O., Lanjouw, P. and Poggi, J. (1998) 'Combining Census and Survey Data To Trace the Spatial Dimension of Poverty', *World Bank Economic Review*, 14/1: 147–165.

IMF (2004) 'Bolivia: Second Review under the Stand-By Arrangement and Request for Waiver of Applicability and Modification of Performance Criteria', IMF Country Report 5. Washington, DC.

INE-UDAPE (2002) 'Mapa de Pobreza 2001', mimeo, La Paz: INE, UDAPE.

Jemio, L.C. and Wiebelt, M. (2003) 'Existe Espacio para Políticas Anti-Shocks en Bolivia? Lecciones de un Análisis basado en un Modelo de Equilibrio General Computable', *Revista Latino Americana de Desarollo Económico*, 1/1: 37–68.

Klasen, S., Grosse, M., Lay, J., Spatz, J., Thiele, R. and Wiebelt, M. (2004) 'Operational-izing Pro-Poor Growth – Country Case Study Bolivia. Main Report', commissioned by AfD, BMZ (GTZ and KfW), DFID and the World Bank. Frankfurt: KfW, available at http://www.oppg.de

Klasen, S. (2006) 'Macroeconomic Policy and Pro-Poor Growth in a Dualistic Economy: The Case of Bolivia', in A. Cornia, (ed), *Pro-Poor Macroeconomics*, London: Palgrave Macmillan.

Lora, E. (2001) 'Structural Reforms in Latin America: What Has Been Reformed and How to Measure it', Inter-American Development Bank, Research Department, Working Paper no. 466.

Ravallion, M. and Chen, S. (2003) 'Measuring Pro-Poor Growth', *Economics Letters*, 78/1: 93–99.

Sahn, D. and Stifel, D. (2003) 'Exploring Alternative Measures of Welfare in the Absence of Expenditure Data', *Review of Income and Wealth*, 49/4: 463–489.

Schweickert, R., Thiele, R. and Wiebelt, M. (2005) 'Macroeconomic and Distributional Effects of Devaluation in a Dollarized Economy: A CGE Analysis for Bolivia', Discussion Papers no. 120, Göttingen: Ibero-America Institute for Economic Research.

Wiebelt, M. (2004) 'GEMPIA – A Dynamic Real-Financial General Equilibrium Model for Poverty Impact Analysis', Kiel Working Papers no. 1230. Kiel: Institute for World Economics.

9
The Role of Agriculture in Pro-Poor Growth: Lessons from Zambia

*James Thurlow and Peter Wobst**

Introduction

The role of agriculture in development theory has evolved gradually over the last half century. Early theorists attributed a more passive role to the sector, essentially as a supplier of food and surplus labour to the industrialization process (Lewis, 1954; Hirschman, 1958). Subsequent theorists have suggested a more active role, emphasizing agriculture's growth linkages to the rest of the economy, both as a supplier of inputs and as a source of demand in domestic markets during the earlier stages of development (Johnson and Mellor, 1961; Hazell and Roell, 1983; Adelman, 1984). Recent theory has gone beyond sectoral and rural linkages to emphasize the efficiency gains of overcoming the urban bias in public investments, and the productivity gains from improved nutrition and food security (Timmer, 2002).

Today there is growing debate over whether traditional development theories still apply, and accordingly, whether agriculture can contribute significantly to growth in Sub-Saharan Africa (SSA).[1] Proponents focusing on agriculture suggest that only the agricultural sector has sufficient scale and growth linkages to significantly influence aggregate growth, and that the sector's past poor performance implies that there are potential gains from catching-up to the productivity levels of other developing countries. Furthermore, these 'agricultural-optimists' suggest there are few viable alternatives to agriculture, especially given Africa's small industrial base, which has performed poorly in the past and now faces increasing competition from large emerging economies like China and India. By contrast, agriculture's skeptics suggest that the large size of the agricultural sector is indicative of Africa's failure to develop, and that agriculture's strong growth linkages have been eroded by low commodity prices and greater import competition in

* This study was funded by the United Kingdom's Department for International Development (DFID) under the multi-donor project 'Operationalizing Pro-Poor Growth' (see Thurlow and Wobst, 2005).

today's global economy. More specifically, food imports have reduced the need to invest in domestic agriculture so as to ensure low urban food prices and hence industrial competitiveness. Under these emerging conditions it is difficult for agriculture to generate economy-wide growth and facilitate the economic transformation predicted by theory or witnessed in the past successes of other developing countries. These 'agricultural-pessimists' tend to be more optimistic about African industry, suggesting that manufacturing and mineral and oil resources offer more viable alternative sources of growth (Collier, 2005).

Despite contrasting opinions on the relative importance of agriculture and industry in generating overall growth, there should presumably be less contention surrounding the role of agriculture in *pro-poor* growth, especially given the importance of agricultural incomes for Africa's poorest populations. However, even amongst agriculture's proponents there are conflicting opinions over what should be the focus of an agricultural development strategy for low-income Africa. Some argue that agricultural growth can be a powerful engine for poverty reduction if it focuses on small-scale farms in the food and staples sectors. Alternatively, others suggest that high-value export agriculture has greater growth and market potential than food crops and can therefore more effectively reduce poverty. Therefore, the current debate is twofold, focusing first on the relative potential of agriculture and industry, and second within agriculture, on the ability of the food and export crop sectors to generate pro-poor growth.[2] This chapter contributes to this debate by examining how accelerating growth though the sectors emphasized by agriculture's proponents and its skeptics can influence a country's ability to significantly reduce poverty.

Zambia is an ideal case study as it has many characteristics relevant to the current debate and similar to most SSA countries. First, Zambia has potential for agricultural growth, although this is not evenly distributed within the country and has been periodically undermined by fluctuations in weather patterns and world commodity prices.[3] Secondly, Zambia has substantial mineral resources, which offer potential sources of growth other than agriculture.[4] Thirdly, Zambia has low agricultural productivity but a large rural population and agricultural sector, although the latter is smaller than the SSA average.[5] Fourthly, Zambia has a liberalized trading regime but is landlocked within central Southern Africa.[6] Finally, like many SSA countries, Zambia is politically stable but suffers from corruption and generally poor governance.[7] Zambia's initial conditions are therefore not biased in favour of either agriculture or industry, and reflect many of the opportunities and constraints facing other African countries.

The next section reviews the development of agriculture and industry in Zambia and considers how changes in the sectoral structure of growth have influenced inequality and poverty. We find that the country underwent significant changes in the structure of economic growth, with agriculture and industry playing important roles at different stages. The resulting shifts in the income distribution have had important implications for the effect-iveness of growth to reduce poverty. Furthermore, recent structural reforms have created new opportunities for both agricultural and industrial growth. The chapter then returns to the current debate by examining the implica-tions of placing either agriculture or industry at the forefront of Zambia's development strategy. This is done using an applied general equilibrium and microsimulation model, which assesses how accelerating growth in altern-ative sectors influences the rate of poverty reduction. The methodology is described and the findings presented, and the chapter concludes by drawing implications for Zambia's development strategy and for the ongoing debate on the role of agriculture in pro-poor growth.

Analysis of past growth and poverty in Zambia

Zambia is one of the poorest countries in SSA.[8] However, in the 1960s it was a middle-income country believed to have considerable growth poten-tial. The key to understanding the country's development history lies in the expansion and decline of the mining sector. By 1991 around four-fifths of foreign earnings were generated by copper exports. These revenues were used to finance an ambitious programme of state-led import-substitution indus-trialization, such that by 1991 over three-quarters of GDP was generated by state-owned enterprises (McCulloch *et al.*, 2000). Public investment was initially more diversified across urban and rural areas leading to improve-ments in most social indicators. However, as copper prices began to fall during the 1970s the government could no longer cross-subsidize its social programmes and protectionist policies, and as a result investment became more concentrated in urban areas. This created a pronounced bias against agriculture and worsening rural investment and social indicators (World Bank, 2004). Agriculture was further distorted through pan-territorial pricing and marketing support for maize, ostensibly to ensure low food prices in urban areas. By 1991, agricultural subsidies accounted for 20 per cent of government expenditure and most smallholder farmers were near mono-culturists (Saasa, 2003).

Falling copper prices and export revenues made it increasingly difficult for the government to support inefficient manufacturing and maintain a large civil service. Rather than engage in politically-difficult reforms, the govern-ment continued to borrow abroad, eventually making Zambia one of the most indebted countries in the world (Dinh *et al.*, 2002).[9] The government also increased the money supply to finance expenditures, leading to high inflation, negative real interest rates and macroeconomic instability, which together undermined investment. Economic growth during the late 1980s was modest and GDP per capita continued its steady decline that began in the 1970s (cf. Table 9.1). Much of the growth that did take place during

Table 9.1   Growth in gross domestic product, Zambia 1985–2001

	GDP share 1991	Real annual compound growth rate (%)		
		1985–91 Pre-reform period	1991–98 Structural adjustment	1998–2001 Renewed growth
GDP (factor cost)	100.0	1.6	−0.3	3.7
Agriculture	15.5	2.8	2.2	2.9
Industry	40.0	2.2	−4.0	1.7
Manufacturing	10.9	5.8	0.8	3.5
Services	44.5	0.7	1.6	5.1
GDP (market prices)	100.0	1.3	0.1	3.6
Private consumption	85.0	−4.7	−2.7	1.7
Government consumption	28.2	6.4	−9.9	−3.0
Fixed investment	9.2	−4.6	7.2	11.0
Exports	29.6	−2.4	3.8	5.0
Imports	−32.2	−4.9	3.9	1.1
Population growth		3.0	2.4	2.0

Source: Based on *World Development Indicators* (World Bank, 2004).

this 'pre-reform period' was driven by agriculture and state-subsidized manufacturing. By contrast, the rest of the industrial sector, including mining, was in sharp decline and the service sector remained stagnant. Therefore, while agriculture and industry were growing prior to reforms, this was not a sustainable position and did not accurately reflect the country's pending economic crisis.

A new government was elected in 1991 on a platform of comprehensive reforms. It inherited an unstable and contracting economy, a collapsing copper-dominated export sector, and massive foreign debt. An ambitious structural adjustment program was adopted, which included macroeconomic stabilization, external liberalization, privatization and public and agricultural-sector reforms. Most of these reforms had been implemented by 1998 during which time the economy experienced considerable adjustment costs. Agriculture and services continued to grow despite structural adjustment, but were offset by the collapse of the industrial sectors, which left overall growth stagnant. In line with falling average per capita incomes, the incidence of extreme poverty rose from 56.5 per cent in 1991 to 59.8 per cent in 1998 (cf. Table 9.2).[10] Therefore, while the pending economic crisis of the late 1980s provided a strong case for structural reforms, the envisaged effect of these reforms on growth and poverty were not felt immediately.

The rapid increase in urban poverty during structural adjustment was driven by the collapse of the industrial sector, which suffered under trade liberalization and privatization. Trade liberalization was achieved through

Table 9.2 Poverty profile, Zambia 1991 and 1998

	Population Share 1991	Poverty rate (%)					
		Incidence (P0)		Depth (P1)		Severity (P2)	
		1991	1998	1991	1998	1991	1998
National	100.0	56.5	59.8	32.4	27.6	23.2	16.2
Rural	54.6	80.1	73.3	51.1	36.4	38.4	22.1
Small-scale farm	48.0	82.6	74.4	53.5	36.9	40.4	22.3
Medium-scale farm	2.7	67.8	62.3	38.0	30.0	27.1	17.9
Non-farm	3.7	58.6	67.5	31.6	34.8	21.8	22.0
Urban	45.4	28.2	37.3	9.8	13.0	4.9	6.3
Central province	9.1	54.6	63.2	27.7	31.6	17.8	19.7
Copperbelt	15.0	35.1	48.8	12.2	19.4	6.2	10.1
Eastern	12.8	76.2	66.1	49.2	31.9	37.7	18.6
Luapula	9.5	76.2	66.1	49.2	31.9	37.7	18.6
Lusaka	16.1	18.0	35.2	6.6	12.9	3.6	6.6
Northern	12.6	74.4	72.1	45.0	34.0	31.7	20.1
North-western	5.2	67.1	62.3	38.6	26.9	27.8	14.9
Southern	11.9	68.8	65.2	42.9	31.9	33.0	19.6
Western	7.8	75.2	79.2	49.5	40.7	37.8	25.8

Note: 1998 food poverty line (Kw32,232 adult equivalent per month) deflated to 1991 using the consumer price index. Large-scale farms are also identified in the survey but are excluded from the table due to their small sample size.
Sources: 1991 Priority Survey and 1998 Living Conditions Monitoring Survey.

extensive rationalization and the lowering of trade protection. By 1996 the government had removed all quantitative restrictions and reduced the number of applied tariff rates. This made Zambia one of the more open economies in Africa and stands in stark contrast to the country's earlier strategy of import substitution. A large increase in imports was prevented by a depreciation of the exchange rate, which also encouraged real export growth. However, inefficient state-owned enterprises did not respond positively to the removal of protection and formal manufacturing employment fell rapidly (Mulikita, 2002).

The negative employment effects of trade liberalization were exacerbated by privatization, which was initially slow due to political opposition but accelerated under donor pressure. By 1997 over 80 per cent of state enterprises had either been dissolved or sold to the private sector. However, private investors remained hesitant due to macro-instability and uncertainty over the government's commitment to reforms (Rakner *et al.*, 1999). This uncertainty was partly a result of the delayed sale of the large state copper mines, whose privatization began in 1996 and was only completed in

Table 9.3   Inequality measures, Zambia 1991 and 1998

	Gini coefficient		Theil mean log deviation	
	1991	1998	1991	1998
National	0.59	0.49	0.78	0.42
Rural	0.62	0.48	0.85	0.41
Small-scale farm	0.59	0.47	0.79	0.39
Medium-scale farm	0.58	0.52	0.80	0.49
Non-farm	0.53	0.50	0.65	0.45
Urban	0.47	0.43	0.40	0.32

Sources: 1991 Priority Survey and 1998 Living Conditions Monitoring Survey.

2003. Public investment in the mines dropped dramatically during the privatization period and, together with falling world prices, led to a near collapse in mining production and employment. Therefore, trade liberalization and privatization undermined industrial production and led to higher urban unemployment and poverty, especially in the Central, Copperbelt and Lusaka provinces (cf. Table 9.2). Furthermore, higher-income urban households were more dependent on formal mining and manufacturing employment than were lower-income households, and so these households experienced the largest increases in poverty. Therefore, while the depth and severity of urban poverty worsened as all urban households experienced falling incomes, the large declines amongst higher-income households meant that urban inequality fell (cf. Table 9.3).

An unusual outcome during structural adjustment was that, while GDP growth declined and national poverty rose, the depth and severity of poverty fell alongside inequality. This can be explained by changes taking place within agriculture and rural areas. Rural poverty fell due to agricultural growth, which continued at an annual rate of over 2 per cent. As mentioned above, the pre-reform government favoured maize production through pan-territorial pricing, input and output marketing assistance, and food subsidies in urban areas. In 1991, the new government began eliminating subsidies and reducing state involvement in the maize and fertilizer sectors. Although the resulting increases in food prices were met with considerable urban opposition and were exacerbated by severe droughts, the reforms were eventually completed by 1995. The artificial profitability of maize production was revealed when many farmers reverted to non-maize food crops, especially in more remote areas where formal markets are typically underdeveloped (Zulu *et al.*, 2000).[11] Maize production continued in areas nearer to the main urban centres where input and output markets were more accessible. Many of the alternative food crops that farmers turned to were better suited to their local

agro-ecological conditions. Drought-tolerant sorghum and millet production rose in the southern provinces, while cassava production expanded
in the northern provinces.[12] So the effects of structural adjustment on the
staples and food sector were less pronounced than on the industrial sectors
because rural farmers were more able to adapt to reforms than were urban
workers. Thus while rural poverty rose during the early 1990s, it had fallen
by the end of the decade throughout most of the rural population. Furthermore, the continued growth in food staples was particularly important for
poor small-scale farmers, whose resulting decline in poverty contributed
greatly to the overall drop in the national depth and severity of poverty and
inequality.

Agricultural exports also performed well as a result of reforms, although
the participation of farmers was conditioned by market access and location. Diversification into agricultural exports was facilitated by the partial
correction of the overvalued exchange rate and new foreign investments
following macro-stabilization. Cotton, sugar and floriculture all increased
production after the mid-1990s.[13] However, despite their rapid growth, these
crops remained concentrated in specific areas of the country, such as cotton
in the Eastern province and floriculture outside of Lusaka. Therefore, while
incomes rose and poverty fell amongst medium-scale farm households, its
effect on national poverty remained small.

Agricultural growth therefore played an important role during the structural adjustment period by preventing stagnant economic growth from translating into worsening rural poverty, especially amongst the country's poorest
populations. New opportunities for agricultural exports also contributed to
falling poverty amongst medium-scale farmers. By contrast, the staples crop
and food sector contributed more to the falling depth and severity of rural
poverty, especially amongst small-scale farmers. Therefore, while the large
increases in incomes amongst the poorest rural households were insufficient to move them above their respective poverty line, it did dramatically
reduce the depth of rural poverty and inequality (cf. Tables 9.2 and 9.3).
However, poverty rose amongst non-farm rural households as they did not
benefit from the expansion of staples and export crops and had stronger
linkages to urban areas. Therefore, the weak rural–urban linkages resulting
from the long-standing bias against agriculture meant that rural households did not participate in the country's historically urban-centric growth
path. However, these weak rural–urban linkages also meant that rural households were less affected by the collapse of the urban-based industrial sectors
during the 1990s.

Decomposing changes in poverty into growth and distribution effects also
reveals the sharp disconnect between Zambia's rural and urban economies
during the structural adjustment period and provides a summary of the
growth and poverty outcomes of the 1990s (cf. Table 9.4). The national
incidence of poverty rose by 3.3 percentage points due to a drop in overall

Table 9.4   Poverty decompositions, Zambia 1991–98

	National poverty (%)			Rural poverty (%)			Urban poverty (%)		
	P0	*P1*	*P2*	*P0*	*P1*	*P2*	*P0*	*P1*	*P2*
Total change	3.3	−4.8	−7.0	−6.8	−14.7	−16.3	9.1	3.2	1.4
Growth effect	7.2	4.7	3.5	−6.7	−5.4	−4.3	13.8	5.7	3.2
Distribution effect	−3.9	−9.5	−10.5	−0.1	−9.3	−12.0	−4.7	−2.5	−1.8

Note: 1998 food poverty line (Kw32,232 adult equivalent per month) deflated using the consumer price index. P0, P1 and P2 represent the incidence, depth and severity of poverty respectively.
Sources: 1991 Priority Survey and 1998 Living Conditions Monitoring Survey.

mean income caused by the collapse of urban industry (that is, a positive or poverty-raising growth effect). This was only partially offset by falling inequality or progressive shifts in the income distribution (that is, a negative distribution effect). However, the distribution effect dominates the decline in the depth and severity of poverty under structural adjustment. This was due to continued agricultural growth, which increased incomes amongst poorer households. Therefore, changes in poverty during the 1990s were characterized by large distributional effects caused by a shift in the composition of growth towards agriculture and away from industry. Further evidence that distributional shifts were driven by agriculture can be seen in the rural poverty decomposition, where changes in the distribution outweighed growth in determining the depth and severity of rural poverty. By contrast, evidence that the collapse of the urban industrial economy dominated national growth effects can be seen in the urban decomposition, where growth effects outweighed distribution effects regardless of which poverty measure is used.

The above decomposition of poverty can be reformulated to produce poverty-growth and poverty-inequality elasticities (cf. Table 9.5). The poverty-growth elasticity for the incidence of poverty averaged 0.62 during 1991–98. This means that, holding the expenditure distribution constant, an additional 1 per cent of GDP per capita reduced the poverty headcount rate by 0.62 per cent. Conversely, holding mean income constant, a 1 per cent decline in the Gini coefficient (i.e., inequality) reduced the incidence of poverty by 0.25 per cent. Both the growth and inequality elasticities are higher for the depth and severity of poverty.

Looking forward, these elasticities can be used to estimate the effects of recent and future growth on poverty. The poverty-growth elasticity suggests that Zambia would need to have sustained an annual GDP growth rate of 7 per cent from 1998 onwards to meet the Millennium Development Goal of halving the 1991 incidence of poverty by 2015. Unfortunately, while Zambia has indeed experienced accelerated growth following structural reforms, the

Table 9.5 Poverty-growth and poverty-inequality elasticities, Zambia 1991 and 1998

	Poverty-growth elasticities			Poverty-inequality elasticities		
	1991	1998	1991–98	1991	1998	1991–98
Incidence (P0)	−0.65	−0.58	−0.62	0.31	0.19	0.25
Depth (P1)	−0.75	−0.98	−0.87	1.85	1.54	1.70
Severity (P2)	−0.79	−1.19	−0.99	3.35	2.85	3.10

Note: 1998 food poverty line (Kw32,232 adult equivalent per month) deflated using the consumer price index. Growth is based on mean expenditure from the household surveys, while inequality is based on the Gini coefficient. A simple average of 1991 and 1998 estimates is used for 1991–98.
Sources: 1991 Priority Survey and 1998 Living Conditions Monitoring Survey.

average annual growth rate has fallen short of the estimated MDG target (cf. Table 1).[14] Furthermore, the structural adjustment period of the 1990s highlighted the importance of taking both growth *and* distributional change into account. In this regard, recent growth has has been driven by a resurgence of mining following privatization and higher world copper prices, while agriculture has continued to grow steadily at around 2 per cent. These differences in agricultural and industrial growth have again led to significant structural change. This new structure of growth will have influenced the distribution of incomes and, by implication, the magnitude of the poverty-growth elasticity. Therefore, using static poverty-growth elasticities, which ignore distributional change, may be inappropriate in cases where the structure of growth is changing.

In summary, the 1990s was a period of stagnant growth and rising poverty in Zambia. However, aggregate growth hides the distributional changes taking place across sectors and regions. While industry collapsed and drove up urban poverty, there was sustained growth in the agricultural sector and a decline in the incidence of rural poverty. Furthermore, agricultural growth raised rural incomes amongst poorer households, causing a decline in the depth and severity of poverty. Therefore, changes in the composition of growth and income distribution were important in determining winners and losers from the reform process. Growth has accelerated rapidly since 1998 and poverty may have declined.[15] However, this renewed growth has been driven by industry rather than agriculture suggesting that there may have again been changes in the income distribution. Zambia's development history therefore confirms the relevance of the current debate concerning the role of agriculture or industry in pro-poor growth. However, it also suggests that assessing the effects of agricultural and industrial growth requires a methodology capable of capturing both growth *and* distributional change.

Modelling distributional change

Survey-based poverty-growth elasticities were used in the previous section to estimate the effect of increasing growth on poverty. This approach assumes that the income distribution remains constant and that growth continues to be as effective at reducing poverty. However, Zambia's past experience has shown how shifts in the structure of growth can cause significant distributional change. Therefore, in addressing the current debate on the relative importance of agriculture and industry in pro-poor growth, it is necessary to employ an analytical method that isolates the effects of agricultural and industrial growth on poverty, while also incorporating the effects of structural change on the magnitude of the poverty-growth elasticity. Accordingly, this section describes the dynamic computable general equilibrium (CGE) and microsimulation model that is used to analyse distributional change in Zambia. Since the detailed specification of the model is presented in Thurlow and Wobst (2005), the following description focuses on the key features of the model and how it addresses the various aspects of the current debate.

As mentioned earlier, an important factor determining the contribution of agriculture and industry to overall economic growth are the linkages between these sectors and the rest of the economy. Agriculture's proponents argue that agriculture has strong growth linkages. Both consumption (forward) and production (backward) linkages are captured in the CGE model, whose nested constant elasticity of substitution (CES) production functions allow producers to generate demand for both factors and intermediates when maximizing profits. To reflect the heterogeneity of Zambian producers, the model is calibrated to a highly disaggregated 2001 social accounting matrix (SAM) that distinguishes between 243 productive activities (27 sectors in nine provinces) and 27 commodities. These commodities are traded within national markets (that is, the model does not capture interregional trade). The model identifies 48 factors of production, including capital and province-specific land and labour. Labour is disaggregated across provinces, gender and education. Land and labour are fully employed, earn flexible returns under fixed supply, and are mobile across sectors. Provincial labour markets allow workers to migrate within but not across provinces. By contrast, capital is immobile across sectors earning flexible activity-specific returns. The detailed specification of production and factor markets in the model allows it to capture the changing scale and technology of production across sectors and provinces, and therefore how changes in Zambia's structure of growth influences its distribution of incomes.

The second area of the debate relates to international trade. Agricultural pessimists suggest that import competition has undermined agriculture's growth linkages and that food imports reduce the need for investment in domestic agriculture. Furthermore, the debate within agriculture concerns the greater market opportunities of export crops compared to food crops. The model captures both import competition and export opportunities by allowing producers and consumers to shift between domestic and foreign markets depending on changes in the relative prices of imports, exports and domestic goods. More specifically, the decision of producers to supply domestic or foreign markets is governed by a constant elasticity of transformation (CET) function, while substitution possibilities exist between imports and domestically supplied goods under a CES Armington specification. In this way the model captures how import competition and the changing export opportunities of agriculture and industry can strengthen or weaken the linkages between growth and poverty.

A third area in the debate concerns the relative importance of agriculture and industry in generating household livelihoods. Income and expenditure patterns vary considerably across households, especially across regions and rural and urban areas. These differences are important for distributional change, since the incomes generated by agriculture and industry will accrue to different households depending on their location and factor endowments. To capture these differences, the model distinguishes between 63 representative households, each of which is an aggregation of a group of households in the 1998 Living Conditions Monitoring Survey (LCMS). Households in the model receive monetary and non-monetary income through the employment of their factors of production, and then pay taxes, save and make transfers to other households. Each household uses its remaining income to consume commodities under a linear expenditure system (LES) of demand. In order to retain as much information on households' income and expenditure patterns as possible, the CGE model is linked to a microsimulation module based on the 1998 LCMS. Endogenous changes in commodity consumption for each aggregate household in the CGE model are used to adjust the level of commodity expenditure of the corresponding households in the survey. Real consumption levels are then recalculated in the survey and standard poverty measures (including the poverty-growth elasticity) are estimated using this updated expenditure measure.

The model makes a number of assumptions about how the Zambian economy maintains macroeconomic balance. These 'closure rules' concern the foreign or current account, the government or public sector account, and the savings-investment account. For the current account, a flexible exchange rate maintains a fixed level of foreign savings. This assumption implies that Zambia cannot increase foreign borrowing but has to generate export earnings in order to pay for food or other imports. While this assumption realistically limits the degree of import competition in the domestic market, it also underlines the importance of the agricultural and industrial export sectors. For the government account, tax rates and real consumption expenditure are exogenously determined, leaving the fiscal deficit to adjust to ensure that public expenditures equal receipts. For the savings-investment account, real investment adjusts to changes in savings (i.e., savings-driven investment). These two assumptions allow the model to capture the negative crowding-out effects of falling government revenues when the structure of growth shifts towards lower tax-paying sectors such as agriculture.

Finally, the CGE model is recursively dynamic, which means that key parameters in the model are updated each period based on intertemporal behaviour and results from previous periods. The model is run over the 14 years 2001–15 with each equilibrium period representing a single year. During this time the model captures exogenous demographic and technological change. Changes in the population, labour supply, human capital and total factor productivity (TFP) are based on AIDS-adjusted projections (World Bank, 2004). Mining production is driven by exogenous foreign investment and world copper prices (Lofgren *et al.*, 2004). By contrast, capital accumulation is endogenous, with previous-period investment generating new capital stock. Although the allocation of new capital is influenced by each sector's initial share of gross operating surplus, the final allocation depends on depreciation and sector profit-rate differentials. Sectors with above-average returns in the previous period receive a larger share of the new capital stock in the current period.

In summary, the CGE model incorporates distributional change by (i) disaggregating growth across provinces and sectors; (ii) capturing employment effects through factor markets and price effects through commodity markets; and (iii) translating these two effects onto each household in the survey according to its unique factor endowment and income and expenditure patterns. The structure of the growth–poverty relationship is therefore defined explicitly *ex ante* based on observed country-specific structures and behaviour. This allows for the model to capture the distributional change associated with growth in agriculture and industry in Zambia.

Analysis of future growth and poverty

The current debate concerning the role of agriculture is twofold, focusing first on the relative roles of agriculture and industry in African development, and, secondly, on the potential contributions of the staples and food sector and export agriculture to pro-poor growth. Evidence from Zambia suggests that shifts in the structure of growth can generate substantial distributional changes, which in turn influences the size of poverty-growth elasticities. The CGE model captures the impact of distributional change when linking sectoral growth to household incomes and poverty. The model is used in this section to examine the effectiveness of agricultural and industrial growth to reduce poverty; and the respective impact of food and export agriculture on pro-poor growth. However, a baseline growth scenario is presented first that assesses the effects of current growth on poverty reduction and provides a counterfactual for subsequent scenarios.

The baseline scenario

The baseline scenario of the model is calibrated to follow recent trends and assumes that Zambia will grow at an annual rate of 4 per cent during 2001–15 (cf. Table 9.6).[16] Both agricultural and industrial growth is higher in the baseline scenario compared to 1998–2001 (cf. Table 9.1); agriculture grows rapidly reflecting the stronger performance of both staples and export agriculture. Ten-year yields determine crop-specific productivity growth in each agricultural sector (FAOSTAT). While the mining sector has grown particularly fast over recent years, past volatility in the copper sector suggests that such high growth may not be sustainable. Accordingly, the model adopts the more conservative forecast that mining growth will average around 2 per cent until 2015.[17] Population growth rates are also conservative at 2 per cent per year, reflecting the continued effects of HIV/AIDS (World Bank, 2004). AIDS-adjusted labour supply is differentiated between lower- and higher-educated labour, which grow at 1.7 and 2 per cent respectively (World Bank, 2004).

The national incidence of poverty declines under the baseline scenario from 59.8 per cent in 2001 to 51.4 per cent in 2015. Faster agricultural growth raises rural real incomes causing the incidence of poverty to fall amongst both small-scale and medium-scale farm households. Growth in the staple crops is widespread and fosters broadbased poverty reduction. Growth in export agriculture is concentrated within provinces with better access to export markets. Agricultural growth also fosters growth linkages to the rest of the economy, favouring for example the more urban-based processing sectors. Urban households benefit from this stronger performance and urban poverty declines throughout the country. However, while the resurgence of the mining sector also raises urban incomes and lowers poverty, these gains are concentrated within certain provinces.

The results indicate that the poverty rate should fall if Zambia can maintain the renewed growth achieved during 1998–2001. However, both the observed poverty-growth elasticities (cf. Table 9.5) and the results from the dynamic model suggest that the declines in poverty will remain small and will fall short of the Millennium Development Goal of halving poverty by 2015. In fact, despite the falling poverty rate, population growth implies that the absolute number of people falling below the poverty line will increase by 808,000 during 2001–15 under the baseline scenario. Therefore, as with most African countries, economic growth must be accelerated if significant declines in poverty are to be realized. The remainder of this section considers how differences in the source of this additional growth might influence the rate of poverty reduction.

Table 9.6 Growth and poverty results from the model simulations, Zambia

	GDP share or poverty rate (%), 2001	Baseline scenario	Agriculture-led scenario	Industry-led scenario	Food and staples-led scenario	Agriculture export-led scenario
Real annual compound growth rate (%) 2001–15						
GDP (factor cost)	100.0	4.0	5.0	5.0	5.0	5.0
Agriculture	4.7	4.6	7.7	4.5	7.8	7.1
staples crops	22.6	4.1	7.3	4.2	7.9	4.0
export crops	1.4	10.2	13.2	7.7	6.9	22.8
Industry	27.3	3.6	3.5	6.1	3.5	3.3
mining	11.0	1.9	1.9	4.8	1.9	1.9
manufacturing	16.2	4.5	4.5	6.9	4.5	4.2
Services	48.0	3.9	4.2	4.5	4.1	4.7
Final year poverty rate (%) 2015						
Incidence (P0)	59.8	51.4	40.9	47.3	40.8	44.4
Rural	73.3	63.7	50.4	61.0	50.0	55.6
small-scale farms	74.4	64.2	50.1	62.0	49.6	56.1
medium-scale farms	62.3	52.8	39.7	50.5	40.6	40.5
Urban	37.3	30.9	25.2	24.4	25.5	25.6
Depth (P1)	27.6	21.8	15.5	19.7	15.5	17.7
Rural	36.4	28.7	20.0	27.0	19.9	23.5
small-scale farms	36.9	28.8	19.5	27.3	19.3	23.4
medium-scale farms	30.0	22.4	16.1	21.4	16.4	17.1
Urban	13.0	10.3	7.9	7.7	8.0	8.1
Severity (P2)	16.2	12.1	8.0	10.8	8.0	9.5
Rural	22.1	16.4	10.7	15.2	10.7	13.0
small-scale farms	22.3	16.4	10.2	15.3	10.1	12.9
medium-scale farms	17.9	12.9	8.9	12.1	9.0	9.5
Urban	6.3	4.8	3.6	3.5	3.6	3.7

Note: The model's initial poverty rates in 2001 are calibrated to those in the 1998 LCMS household survey.
Source: Zambia CGE and microsimulation model results.

Comparing agricultural growth with industrial growth

The first part of the current debate concerns the relative effectiveness of agricultural and industrial growth at reducing poverty. In the case of Zambia, this is examined by accelerating the projected average GDP growth rate from its current 4 per cent to 5 per cent per year. Two scenarios are developed in which the source of this additional growth differs, first being agriculture and food processing and then mining and manufacturing. Although both scenarios generate the same overall GDP growth rate, the required increases in sectoral growth are different due to their relative sizes and growth-linkages. Under the *agriculture-led* scenario, the growth rate of agriculture increases from 4.6 per cent under the *baseline* scenario to 7.7 per cent, while industrial growth remains unchanged. Conversely, under the *industry-led* scenario, industrial growth increases from 3.5 to 6.1 per cent per year, while agricultural growth remains unchanged.

By assumption, faster agricultural growth in the *agriculture-led* scenario is driven by staples and export crops and forestry and fishing. However, the model suggests that export crops would grow faster than other agricultural sub-sectors due to better foreign market opportunities and hence smaller declines in domestic prices after production is expanded. Agricultural production directly raises incomes amongst rural households and indirectly raises real incomes amongst urban households through reduced food prices.[18] Therefore, the incidence of both rural and urban poverty falls, although these declines are more heavily concentrated amongst rural households. Rising incomes and expenditures are particularly pronounced amongst the poorest populations, as seen in the substantial decline in both the depth and severity of rural poverty. Therefore, while all households benefit from faster agricultural growth, it is the poorer rural households that benefit the most.

By contrast, the benefits of faster mining and manufacturing growth under the *industry-led* scenario are more heavily concentrated amongst less poor households and within urban areas. Urban poverty declines only slightly more than under *agriculture-led* growth because poor urban households are less likely to be employed in the formal mining and manufacturing sectors while the informal manufacturing sector is small. Increased incomes from mining sector growth are also concentrated within the mining provinces, implying that few households are able to benefit directly from growth in this sector. Furthermore, mining growth is highly capital-intensive and so does not create substantial employment opportunities. Therefore, while urban poverty declines, there is relatively little spillover to rural households, whose poverty remains virtually unchanged compared to the declines experienced under the *baseline* scenario.

Returning to the current debate, one of the key arguments presented by the proponents of agriculture is that this sector has sufficient scale to generate significant economy-wide growth. For example, in the case of Zambia, agriculture and food processing generates 28.2 per cent of GDP, while mining and non-food manufacturing generate 23.7 per cent. Therefore, since a 1 per cent increase in agricultural GDP is larger than a 1 per cent increase in industrial GDP, it might seem trivial to suggest that agricultural growth is better at reducing poverty. However, the above two scenarios are 'scale-neutral' since the same aggregate GDP growth rate was targeted in both scenarios. Therefore, the results suggest that it is not only agriculture's large share of GDP that determines its ability to generate broadbased poverty reduction, but also its particular ability to generate employment and incomes amongst the poor population.

Proponents also emphasize agriculture's strong growth linkages to the rest of economy. However, in Zambia it appears that industry has stronger linkages to the service sectors, whose growth accelerates more rapidly in the *industry-led* scenario (cf. Table 9.6). Agriculture is better at generating employment and raising incomes of poor rural households and is almost as good as industrial growth at raising real incomes of poor *urban* households. Therefore while agriculture's economy-wide growth-linkages are less pronounced than industries, it is the former that has stronger *pro-poor* growth-linkages. This greater 'pro-poorness' of agricultural growth can be seen in Table 9.7, which presents the poverty-growth elasticities from the model simulations.

Comparing the estimated elasticity with the observed elasticity for 1991–98 suggests that although recent growth has accelerated, as reflected in the *baseline* scenario, this growth is less effective at reducing the incidence of poverty than was growth during the 1990s. For example, 1 per cent per capita GDP under the *baseline* scenario reduces the poverty rate by 0.53 per cent compared to the 0.62 per cent estimated from the 1991 and

Table 9.7 Poverty-growth elasticities from the model simulations, Zambia

	Observed elasticity, 1991–98	Simulated average annual growth-poverty elasticities, 2001–15				
		Baseline scenario	Agriculture-led scenario	Industry-led scenario	Food and staples-led scenario	Agriculture export-led scenario
Incidence (P0)	−0.62	−0.53	−0.86	−0.55	−0.87	−0.68
Depth (P1)	−0.87	−0.83	−1.30	−0.79	−1.31	−1.02
Severity (P2)	−0.99	−1.01	−1.56	−0.94	−1.58	−1.23

Note: 1998 food poverty line (Kw32,232 adult equivalent per month) deflated using the consumer price index. Elasticities for 1991–98 based on mean per capita consumption, while model elasticities based on real GDP.
Sources: 1991 Priority Survey, 1998 Living Conditions Monitoring Survey, and Zambia CGE and microsimulation model.

1998 household surveys (cf. Table 9.5). However, growth in the *baseline* scenario remains as effective at reducing both the depth and severity of poverty. By contrast, all poverty-growth elasticities are considerably higher under *agriculture-led* growth and lower under *industry-led* growth, suggesting that agricultural growth is substantially more pro-poor than industrial growth. The difference between the two elasticities has significant long-term implications. As mentioned earlier, the absolute number of people falling below the poverty line increases by 808,000 by 2015 under the *baseline* scenario. The sustained acceleration of GDP growth under the *industry-led* scenario reduces this increase to 263,000. By contrast, the number of poor people declines under the *agriculture-led* scenario by 584,000. This implies that even a relatively small acceleration in GDP growth driven by agriculture can lift an additional 847,000 people out of poverty during 2001–15 compared to a similar acceleration of growth driven by industry.

The results indicate that the changing sectoral structure of growth can have important implications for the rate of pro-poor growth. Therefore, increases in the aggregate growth rate may be insufficient to significantly reduce poverty if growth generates distributional changes that isolate the poor from the growth process. This suggests that the recent resurgence of industry in Zambia may not have significantly reduced poverty, despite the high overall GDP growth rate. More generally, the results suggest that agriculture plays an important role in generating pro-poor growth, even in countries like Zambia where there exist alternative growth opportunities.

Comparing the staples and food sector with export agriculture

The second part of the current debate concerns the relative importance of food crops and agricultural exports in reducing poverty. This is again examined by raising the overall GDP growth rate from 4 to 5 per cent by increasing productivity growth in each of the two sub-sectors. In the following simulations, the food sub-sector includes staples crops, such as maize, sorghum and millet, as well as agriculture-related food processing. Export agriculture on the other hand includes both traditional and non-traditional crops, such as cotton, tobacco, coffee and floriculture. The debate over the relative importance of these two sub-sectors for reducing poverty is of particular importance to Zambia, whose agricultural growth in recent years has been characterized by rapid growth in export agriculture and more modest growth in food crops. These initial conditions are captured in the *baseline* scenario, where export and staples crops grow at an average rate of 10.2 and 4.1 per cent per year respectively (cf. Table 9.6).

Agriculture's overall growth rate under the *staples-led* scenario increases from 4.6 to 7.8 per cent, while industrial growth remains almost unchanged. These results are similar to those obtained under the *agriculture-led* scenario in the previous section, since more than 90 per cent of agricultural GDP is generated by staples crops. However, despite rising agricultural productivity, rapid growth in staples crops creates greater competition for agricultural resources, especially land and labour, and this reduces the availability of these resources for other agricultural sub-sectors. Therefore, growth in export agriculture slows down from 10.2 per cent under the *baseline* scenario to 6.9 per cent under the *staples-led* scenario. Agricultural growth is therefore more evenly balanced across sub-sectors, implying that more rural households are able to participate in and benefit from increased growth in staples crops and food processing. Accordingly, rural incomes rise and poverty declines substantially, especially amongst small-scale farm households where the incidence of poverty falls to 50 per cent by 2015. Urban poverty also declines as lower food prices indirectly raise real incomes, especially for poorer urban households who typically spend a larger share of their income on food.[19]

In the *export-led* scenario, export crops must grow rapidly at 22.8 per cent per year if this sub-sector is to raise the overall GDP growth rate from 4 to 5 per cent. Such rapid growth is required because the contribution of export crops to GDP is initially very small. However, the required overall agricultural growth rate of 7.1 per cent per year is lower than under the *staples-led* scenario. This is because export agriculture has strong growth linkages to the service sector, whose growth accelerates from 3.9 per cent in the *baseline* scenario to 4.7 per cent in the *export-led* scenario. These linkages arise from the trade and transportation costs associated with moving agricultural exports from farms to urban centres and foreign markets. Therefore, while export agriculture does not raise real incomes by lowering food prices, it does indirectly create urban employment opportunities in the service sector, thereby lowering urban poverty.

Rural poverty also declines in the *export-led* scenario, although these declines are considerably smaller than in the *staples-led* scenario (cf. Table 9.6). This is because fewer small-scale farmers are engaged in export agriculture and so do not benefit as greatly from growth in this sub-sector. Accordingly, the incidence of poverty amongst small-scale farmers falls to only 56.1 per cent under export-led growth compared to 49.6 per cent under staples-led growth. Growth in export agriculture does significantly reduce poverty amongst medium-scale farmers, who typically have better access to both input and output markets and the capital necessary to cultivate export crops. However, less than 10 per cent of the rural population have farms larger than five hectares and so declining poverty amongst medium-scale farm households has little affect on overall rural poverty. Furthermore, while staples and export crops are equally effective at reducing the incidence of poverty amongst medium-scale farm households, the former is more effective at reducing the depth and severity of such poverty. This is because poorer medium-scale households are more reliant on incomes from staples crops and spend a larger share of their incomes on food.

In terms of the current debate, only staples crops have sufficient scale to foster broadbased growth and significantly reduce poverty, especially amongst rural households. In order for export agriculture to contribute significantly to aggregate growth it would have to achieve and sustain excessively high growth rates. While this sub-sector may well have greater growth potential than the staples sector, it is unrealistic to attribute such optimism, especially given past volatility in world prices for commodities such as cotton and coffee. Furthermore, even if export agriculture in Zambia is able to sustain such high growth, the sector is less effective at reducing poverty than staples crops.

The lower effectiveness of the *export-led* scenario at reducing poverty can be seen in its poverty-growth elasticity, which is substantially smaller than for staples-led growth (cf. Table 9.6). For example, a 1 per cent increase in per capita GDP under the *export-led* scenario reduces the poverty rate by 0.68 per cent, compared to 0.87 per cent under the *staples-led* scenario. Growth driven by agricultural exports also appears to be less effective at reducing poverty amongst the poorest population, as reflected in its lower poverty-growth elasticities for the depth and severity of poverty. However, while staples-led growth is most effective at generating broadbased poverty reduction, growth in export agriculture is still far more effective at reducing poverty than industrial growth. Compared to the *industry-led* scenario, export-led growth lifts an additional 384,000 people above the poverty line by 2015, thereby reversing the increase in the absolute number of poor people expected under Zambia's current growth path.

Implications for policy in Zambia and pro-poor growth in Africa

This chapter has used Zambia as a case study to address the current debate concerning the potential role of agriculture and industry in African development. Not only does Zambia have many similar characteristics to other African economies, but its recent experience demonstrates the relevance of the debate for its own development strategy. The long-standing bias against agriculture in Zambia created a distorted economic system that favoured the urban population and undermined rural development. The industrial core of the economy collapsed under structural adjustment, dramatically worsening urban unemployment and poverty. By contrast, the disconnection between rural and urban growth caused by the urban bias meant that remoter rural areas were less severely affected by the negative consequences of reforms. As such, while the incidence of rural poverty declined only slightly during the 1990s, the depth and severity of rural poverty fell substantially, partly as a result of continued agricultural growth. The differing experiences of higher-income urban households and lower-income rural households resulted in a decline in income inequality. Therefore Zambia's experiences during the 1990s demonstrated how changes in the sectoral composition of growth can have important implications for the distribution of incomes and hence the ability of growth to reduce poverty. This is particularly relevant to Zambia today. Recent growth in the country has been high, driven by a strong resurgence in mining and industrial production. However, the analysis using the dynamic CGE microsimulation model finds that industrial growth is not strongly pro-poor, thus implying that recent growth may not generate broadbased poverty reduction. Rather, it is agricultural growth, especially in staples crops, that can contribute most effectively to poverty reduction. Therefore, in terms of its own development strategy, Zambia should not rely on industrial growth alone, but should place broadbased agricultural growth at the forefront of its development objectives.

Returning to the current debate, the findings suggest that the structure of growth is important in determining the size of a country's poverty-growth elasticity. Although many African countries have potential sources of growth outside of agriculture, growth in industrial sectors is, at least in the short to medium term, unlikely to be as effective at reducing poverty as growth in agriculture. Agriculture's proponents emphasize that this sector has sufficient scale to significantly influence aggregate growth. However, agriculture's skeptics suggest that this may be indicative of Africa's failure to develop. Therefore, the analysis has looked beyond the *scale* of agriculture and industry and compared the *nature* of these sectors' growth–poverty linkages. Agricultural growth still remains more pro-poor than industrial growth because it allows for greater participation of the poor in the growth process. Furthermore, even if industry has strong growth linkages, as was the case in Zambia, the sector may still prove less effective at reducing poverty because the resulting *indirect* growth may not create employment opportunities for the poor. This is similarly true for agricultural exports, whose linkages may foster growth outside of the rural economy, but which may not necessarily benefit the poor. Therefore, while industrial growth should not be curtailed, neither can agricultural growth be bypassed. Growth in staples crops and food processing is most effective at generating rural growth linkages and raising rural incomes, especially amongst the poorest households. Broadbased agricultural growth therefore remains a necessary, but probably not sufficient, engine for pro-poor growth in Africa.

This chapter has examined how agricultural growth influences poverty, but it has not considered how such growth can be generated and sustained. Formulating agricultural growth strategies for countries like Zambia requires a better understanding of market and institutional behaviour, both of which have been inadequately addressed in the analysis. Moreover, further research is needed on the efficiency and effectiveness of public investments and on the role of the private sector. Just as changes in global conditions have questioned the role of agriculture in development thinking, so too have Africa's structural reforms over the last two decades influenced the role of the government *vis-à-vis* the private sector. While this chapter suggests that traditional thinking on the role of agriculture still applies to Africa today, it does not suggest that the government's role in facilitating agricultural growth has remained unchanged.

Notes

1. See Diao *et al.* (2005) and Hazell (2005) for a review of this debate. This section draws liberally on these sources.
2. This is a simplification of the current debate. In reality there is growth potential in both agriculture and industry, and some of the challenges facing these sectors are commonly felt. Therefore few suggest that either agriculture or industry should be the sole focus of any country's development strategy. Rather it is a question of agriculture's *relative* importance. Furthermore, it is well-recognized that agriculture plays a less important role as countries develop. Accordingly, the debate focuses on those African countries in their early stage of development.
3. Agricultural potential is calculated using the global FAO Farming Systems (Dixon *et al.*, 2004), which considers a range of factors, including natural resources, household livelihoods, market access and potential, agro-ecological conditions, and scale of production. Each country's agricultural potential is an average of the potential attributed to each farming system present in the country weighted by land coverage. Based on this measure, three-quarters of low-income SSA countries, including Zambia, have medium to high potential.
4. One-third of low-income SSA countries have sizable mineral and oil resources (UNIDO, 2004).
5. Agriculture accounts for around 20 per cent of Zambian GDP while 60 per cent of the total population live in rural areas. This is lower than the averages for low-income SSA countries, which are 33 and 67 per cent respectively (*World Development Indicators*).
6. One-third of low-income SSA countries are landlocked and contain one quarter of the total SSA population (*World Development Indicators*).
7. Governance is measured by the six World Bank governance indicators (Kaufman *et al.*, 2002), which suggest that Zambia is similar to the median low-income SSA country.
8. Zambia has the sixth lowest PPP-adjusted GDP per capita in SSA (*World Development Indicators*).
9. Zambia ranked 8th in 1991 in terms of its ratio of per capita debt to GDP (*World Development Indicators*).
10. Zambia has two official poverty lines: extreme/food and basic-needs. The former is used in this chapter and in 1998 was equal to 32,232 kwacha per adult equivalent per month, or 0.50 international dollars per day.
11. Maize production fell by one-third during 1991–95 (FAOSTAT).
12. Cassava production rose by one-third during the 1990s (FAOSTAT).
13. Most export crop production grew rapidly during the 1990s, especially cotton (102.2 %), sugar (42 %), tea (51.8 %), and coffee (291.3 %) (FAOSTAT). Tobacco has also grown rapidly since 1998.
14. Assuming a constant poverty-growth elasticity of 0.62 and the 3.7 per cent average annual growth during 1998–2001, the incidence of extreme poverty falls from 59.8 per cent in 1998 to 55.4 per cent in 2005 and 49.1 per cent by 2015. Since Zambia did not achieve the necessary growth during 1998–2005 to meet the MDG targets, the required average growth rate until 2015 has to increase from 7 per cent in 1998 to almost 10 per cent by 2005.
15. The 2003 Living Conditions Monitoring Survey has only recently become available. However, this new survey does not use the one-month recall approach to capturing expenditures (as was the case in the 1990s surveys). Therefore, the 2003

poverty measures cannot be compared with those of previous surveys and are not discussed here.

16. The targeted level of aggregate GDP growth is attained by exogenously increasing TFP growth to supplement endogenously determined labour supply and capital accumulation. The required level of TFP growth is 2 per cent per year during 2001–15. This is close to the actual TFP growth rate observed during the 1999–2001 period to which the model is calibrated (see Thurlow and Wobst, 2005).

17. This is equivalent to the World Bank's 'middle-of-the-road' projection described in Lofgren *et al.* (2002). It should be noted that the baseline scenario is a *counterfactual* against which other scenarios can be compared. It is not a growth projection and its calibration does not influence the conclusions drawn from subsequent scenarios.

18. Urban households in the model can substitute between domestic and foreign food depending on their relative prices. World food prices are held fixed in all scenarios so as to isolate the effects of expanded domestic agricultural production from those caused by changing world market conditions. Allowing world prices to decline in all scenarios would not change the findings of this study since it would equally affect the counterfactual *baseline* scenario against which all subsequent scenarios are compared.

19. The extent to which domestic production reduces urban food prices depends in part on the willingness and ability of urban consumers to shift consumption away from imported food. In these model scenarios it is assumed that there is a high degree of substitutability between domestic and foreign food (i.e., the Armington elasticity is set at three). As such, the willingness of urban consumers to shift to domestically produced food may be overstated in the *agriculture-* and *staples-led* scenarios. However, this assumption works in reverse and is applied to all scenarios. Therefore, the ability of consumers to shift from domestic to imported food may also be overstated in the *industry-* and *export-led* scenarios.

References

Adelman, I. (1984) 'Beyond Export-Led Growth', *World Development*, 12/9: 937–49.

Collier, P. (2005) 'Is Agriculture Still Relevant to Poverty Reduction in Africa?', Speech given to All Party Parliamentary Group on Overseas Development, 17 October, London, UK: House of Commons.

Diao, X., Hazell, P., Resnick, D. and Thurlow, J. (2005) 'The Role of Agriculture in Development: Implications for Africa', Washington, DC: International Food Policy Research Institute.

Dinh, H., Adugna, A. and Myers, B. (2002) 'The Impact of Cash Budgets on Poverty Reduction in Zambia', Africa Region Working Paper Series 39, Washington, DC: World Bank.

Dixon, J., Gulliver, A. and Gibbon, D. (2001) 'Farming Systems and Poverty', Food and Agriculture Organization, Washington, DC: Rome, and World Bank.

Hazell, P. (2005) 'Does Policy Research Matter? A Farewell Lecture', Presentation given at the International Food Policy Research Institute, November, Washington, DC.

Hazell, P. and Roell, A. (1983) 'Rural Growth Linkages: Household Expenditure Patterns in Malaysia and Nigeria', Washington, DC: International Food Policy Research Institute.

Hirschman, A.O. (1958) 'The Strategy of Economic Development', New Haven, CT: Yale University Press.

Johnston, D.G. and Mellor, J.W. (1961) 'The Role of Agriculture in Economic Development', *American Economic Review*, 51/ 4:566–93.

Kaufmann, D., Kraay, A. and Zoido-Lobaton, P. (2002) 'Governance Matters II: Updated Indicators for 2000/2001', Policy Research Department Working Paper, Washington, DC: World Bank.

Lewis, W.A. (1954) 'Economic Development with Unlimited Supplies of Labor', *The Manchester School of Economics and Social Studies*, 22/2:139–91.

Lofgren, H., Robinson, S. and Thurlow, J. (2002) 'Macro and Micro Effects of Recent and Potential Shocks to Copper Mining in Zambia', Trade and Macroeconomics Discussion Paper no. 99, Washington, DC: International Food Policy Research Institute.

McCulloch, N., Baulch, B. and Cherel-Robson, M. (2000) 'Poverty, Inequality and Growth in Zambia during the 1990s', Working Paper, University of Sussex: Institute for Development Studies.

Mulikita, N. (2002) 'Reform and the Crisis in Zambia's Public Administration: A Critical Appraisal', Ethiopia: Development Policy Management Forum.

Rakner, L., van de Walle, N. and Mulaisho, D. (1999) 'Zambia', Washington, DC: World Bank.

Robinson, S. and Thurlow, J. (2005) 'A Standard Recursive Dynamic Computable General Equilibrium (CGE) and Microsimulation Model: Extending the IFPRI Static Model', Washington, DC: International Food Policy Research Institute.

Saasa, O. (2003) 'Agricultural Intensification in Zambia: The Role of Policies and Policy Processes', University of Zambia: Institute of Economic and Social Research.

Thurlow, J. and Wobst, P. (2005) 'The Road to Pro-Poor Growth in Zambia: Past Lessons and Future Challenges', Development Strategies and Governance Discussion Paper no. 16, Washington, DC: International Food Policy Research Institute.

Timmer, C.P. (2002) 'Agriculture and Economic Development', in B. Gardner and G. Rausser (eds), *Handbook of Agricultural Economics*, Volume 2A, Amsterdam: North Holland: 1487–546.

United Nations Industrial Development Organization (2004) 'Industrialization, Environment and the Millennium Development Goals in Sub-Saharan Africa: The New Frontier in the Fight Against Poverty', Industrial Development Report, Vienna: United Nations Industrial Development Organization.

World Bank (2004) 'Zambia: Country Economic Memorandum', Washington, DC: World Bank.

Zulu, B., Nijhoff, J.J., Jayne, T.S. and Negassa, A. (2000) 'Is the Glass Half Empty or Half Full? An Analysis of Agricultural Production Trends in Zambia', Working Paper no. 3, Food Security Research Project, Zambia: Lusaka.

10
Romania in Transition: Growth, Jobs and Poverty

Wojciech Paczyński, Artur Radziwiłł, Agnieszka Sowa,
Irena Topińska and Mateusz Walewski[*]

Introduction

Romania is a medium-sized South-Eastern European country, belonging to the group of lower-middle-income economies. At the beginning of the 1990s, soon after the collapse of the communist regime, Romania undertook political and economic reforms intended to transform the economy 'from plan to market'. However, on the eve of the transition period a slowdown in economic growth turned into a deep-seated transitional output decline in 1989 and in the early years after the fall of communism (Figure 10.1). Between 1988 and 1992 real GDP declined by 30 per cent.[1] The rest of the 1990s was characterized by an uneven growth pattern with a short-lived early rebound followed by the recession 1997–99. Stronger and more sustainable improvements in the standard of living have been visible only in the last few years, with robust economic growth averaging above 5 per cent since 2000.

The early transition years witnessed a major rise in poverty, while on the eve of the transformation (late 1980s) a very egalitarian distribution of household incomes and consumption resulted in relatively low poverty rates, despite rather harsh economic conditions. According to the World Bank estimates, poverty headcounts increased from 4 per cent in 1989 to 20 per cent in 1993 (World Bank, 1997).[2]

[*] This chapter is based on the report 'Operationalizing Pro-Poor Growth. A Country Case Study on Romania' which was prepared by the team consisting of Radu Gheorghiu, Wojciech Paczyński, Artur Radziwiłł, Agnieszka Sowa, Manuela Stanculescu, Irena Topińska, Geomina Turlea and Mateusz Walewski as part of the Operationalizing Pro-Poor Growth work programme, a joint initiative of ADF, BMZ (GTZ, KfW Development Bank), DFID and the World Bank in 2004/2005. This earlier work benefited from advice and comments from Louise Cord and participants of the project workshops.

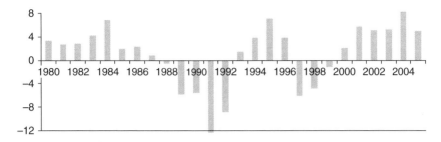

Figure 10.1 GDP growth dynamics, Romania 1980–2005 (% change)
Source: IMF, *World Economic Outlook* database, September 2005.

We conduct a detailed analysis of the impact of growth on poverty in the period between 1996 and 2002 for which data from a Household Budget Survey is available. Two distinct three-year sub-periods have been chosen: 1996–99 and 1999–2002. The first roughly coincides with the recession, while the second sub-period encompasses the rebound in economic activity that has subsequently continued to the present day. Consequently, we can investigate whether recession and recovery in Romania have had similar impacts on poverty. We also make an attempt to simulate possible scenarios of poverty reduction in the subsequent periods of 2002–05 and 2005–08, and to identify key factors of pro-poor growth.

The remainder of this chapter is organized as follows. The next section describes and analyses in detail links between growth and poverty between 1996 and 2002. This is followed by a presentation of simulation results of different poverty reduction scenarios until 2008, and a discussion of the most important obstacles to pro-poor growth in Romania. A final section concludes.

Growth and poverty, 1996–2002

According to both medium and extreme poverty measures[3] presented in Table 10.1, poverty increased during the economic recession (1996–99) and peaked in 2000, before slowly declining during the recovery period (2000–02). This refers to all three dimensions of poverty, its extent, depth and severity.

During the whole period of post-communist transition, inequality remained rather low with Gini coefficients fluctuating below 0.30 for most of the period, and Theil $T(0)$ not reaching 0.16. In contrast to the poverty level, inequality declined during the period of economic recession and increased somewhat during recovery. Therefore, in both cases it muted the impact of growth on poverty. Nevertheless the link between growth and poverty was clearly visible (Figure 10.2). Unfortunately, the growth elasticity of poverty

Table 10.1 Poverty and inequality trends, Romania 1996–2002

	Extreme poverty (%)			Medium poverty (%)			Inequality (%)	
	Head count	Poverty gap	Poverty severity	Head count	Poverty gap	Poverty severity	Gini	Theil T(0)
1996	6.3	1.22	0.37	20.1	4.79	1.70	0.308	0.158
1999	12.6	2.86	0.98	33.3	8.83	3.47	0.286	0.136
2002	11.0	2.42	0.82	29.0	7.61	2.96	0.288	0.138

Note: Weights = individuals. All poverty indices are in per cent.
Source: Based on Romanian HBSs.

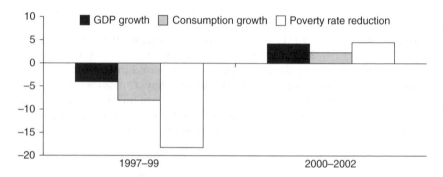

Figure 10.2 Average annual GDP, consumption and poverty dynamics, Romania 1997–2002 (% change)
Note: The series plotted are average annual changes in aggregate in GDP growth, mean equivalent consumption calculated from HBS and medium poverty rate (reversed scale).
Source: Based on Romanian HBSs and IMF, *World Economic Outlook* database.

was much higher during the recession, so that the subsequent recovery did not fully reverse the earlier poverty increases.

This picture is confirmed when we decompose poverty growth (be it positive or negative) into its constituent components corresponding to overall consumption growth and changes in inequality (Table 10.2).[4] In both periods changes in poverty were driven primarily by the growth component with much smaller impact of inequality component of opposite sign. The relative size of both components leaves no doubt that sustaining economic growth momentum is a main precondition for poverty reduction in Romania.

In order to illustrate in more detail how much the poor and the poorest have benefited from growth, Figure 10.3 represents the rates of consumption growth for population percentiles in both analysed periods, thus showing growth incidence curves (GIC).[5] The poor were hit by losses relatively less

Table 10.2 Growth-inequality decomposition of changes in poverty, two sub-periods, Romania

	Medium poverty			Extreme poverty		
	Change of headcount (%)	Growth component (%)	Inequality component (%)	Change of headcount (%)	Growth component (%)	Inequality component (%)
1996–99	0.131	0.160	−0.029	0.063	0.077	−0.014
1999–2002	−0.043	−0.050	0.007	−0.016	−0.023	0.007

Note: The average of forward and backward decompositions for each sub-period is displayed. All changes are relative to the base year (1996 and 1999, respectively).
Source: Based on Romanian HBSs.

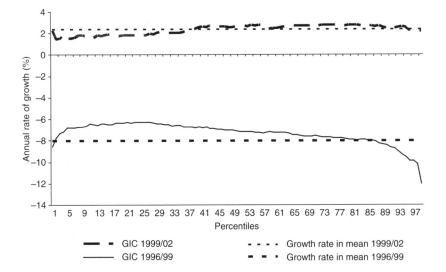

Figure 10.3 Growth incidence curves (GIC), annual growth in consumption (total population), Romania
Source: Based on Romanian HBSs.

than other groups during the recession (downward-sloping GIC), but also benefited less from the subsequent economic recovery (upward-sloping GIC). This may suggest that there are groups in the Romanian society that are somewhat cushioned from developments in the wider economy. They appear to fare relatively better during recession, but also do not fully benefit from growth. We attempt to identify these groups below.

Focusing on the question of which groups benefited most and least from growth, we start with the 2002 poverty profile.[6] Looking at the total population of poor households the following picture emerges: (i) two-thirds of the (medium) poor live in rural areas; (ii) two-fifths are members of households headed by pensioners; (iii) nearly one-quarter are members of households headed by individuals self-employed in agriculture; (iv) the vast majority have low skills, as indicated by educational attainment of household heads which can be treated as a proxy for social capital endowment (87% of heads of poor households have not completed secondary education). The population falling below the extreme poverty line fits the above characteristics even more closely; that is, the share of households living in rural areas, headed by uneducated individuals self-employed in agriculture is even higher.

To investigate the role of labour markets in pro-poor growth, we focus our attention on households headed by working-age individuals[7] and three broad high-risk factors suggested by the poverty profile: rural residence, low skills and self-employment in agriculture of the household head.[8] Poverty rates according to these criteria are shown in Table 10.3. In rural areas, extreme poverty incidence was three times higher than in urban areas. Small-scale farming, while having some role in alleviating rural poverty, is definitely not a source of economic well-being. Households headed by persons without much formal education face the highest poverty levels, while households with post-secondary and higher education of the household head were almost fully immune from poverty. Finally, households headed by persons self-employed in agriculture or unemployed appeared most vulnerable to pauperization.

The inter-group inequality in respect to these three characteristics explains a large and increasing share of total poverty variability as

Table 10.3 Poverty rates, Romania 1996–2002

	Extreme poverty (%)			Medium poverty (%)		
	1996	1999	2002	1996	1999	2002
Total	6.3	12.6	11.0	20.2	33.3	29.0
of which: Working age	6.3	12.7	11.2	19.7	32.3	28.0
Rural	10.0	20.3	19.1	29.7	47.1	42.8
Urban	3.6	7.3	5.6	12.5	21.9	17.6
Unskilled	8.9	17.6	16.7	26.7	42.9	39.1
Skilled	1.9	3.0	1.7	7.9	11.5	8.9
Non-employed	n/a	15.1	14.3	n/a	39.2	34.0
Agriculture	n/a	28.6	22.5	n/a	55.4	49.0
Non-agriculture	n/a	6.7	4.0	n/a	21.5	14.7
Non-working age	6.6	12.4	10.4	22.5	37.5	32.8

Note: Data by economic sectors for 1996 are not comparable to the figures for 1999 and 2002
Source: Based on Romanian HBSs.

Table 10.4   Inter-group inequality as per cent of total inequality, Romania 1995–2002

Criterion	1996	1999	2002
Place of residence (rural-urban)	8.7	8.4	12.0
Education of the household head	20.6	22.0	27.2
Labour market status of the household head	8.7	10.6	15.8

Note: Based on Theil mean log deviation [$T(0)$] decomposition.
Source: Based on Romanian HBSs.

demonstrated in Table 10.4. While poverty incidence remains most dependent on educational attainments, the importance of the labour-market status of the household head gains importance rapidly. This suggests that labour-market problems become the main obstacle for deeper poverty reduction in Romania.

We study inter-group as well as intra-group inequality dynamics in more detail by examining and comparing growth incidence curves for each of the groups (Figures 10A.1–10A.4 in the Appendix). Between-group inequality was increasing during the recession period despite falling measures of overall inequality such as Gini and Theil $T(0)$. Our examination confirms that while agriculture might have provided a cushion against the negative impact of economic restructuring, those self-employed in the agricultural sector have limited opportunities to enjoy the benefits of growth. Consequently, the rural population was less influenced by economic recession, but the urban population gained more from economic revival. While the poorest non-employed did not benefit from growth at all, skilled workers in industry and services benefited the most. As a result, polarization across socio-economic subpopulations increased during the growth period.

These insights about the role of labour-market dynamics are supported by data about changes in aggregate wage bills shown in Table 10.5. It seems that the industrial (and to a lesser degree the service sector) wage-bill shrinkage played an important role in the poverty increase during the economic recession, especially among urban unskilled labour. The deep reduction of employment in these sectors also resulted in a perverse employment increase in agriculture that served as the buffer sector for those losing jobs (Kollo and Vincze, 1999). Growth in agricultural employment was not accompanied by output increases or investment rebound, and therefore also negatively affected those previously working in the sector.

Table 10.5 also explains why skilled groups benefited the most from growth during the period of economic recovery. The increasing wage bill and ongoing employment decreases in industry indicate that wage increases have acted as a reward for increasing productivity. Part of the unskilled urban labour force most probably managed to find jobs in the booming service sector, which also led to a slight improvement in the poverty headcount of

Table 10.5 Average annual growth rates, Romania 1996–2001

	1996–99	1999–2001	1996–99	1999–2001
	Output		Employment	
Agriculture	−3.0	1.2	1.4	0.4
Industry	−6.5	6.9	−9.4	−0.7
Services	−4.2	3.9	−3.4	2.8
	Wage bill		Average wage	
Agriculture	−8.0	1.7	−9.3	1.2
Industry	−18.9	4.1	−10.5	4.9
Services	−7.5	9.8	−4.2	6.8

Sources: Based on HBS 1996–2002 data and *Statistical Yearbook for Romania*, 2002.

this group. On the other hand, the rural unskilled labour force was unable to benefit from economic growth as it was largely stuck in weakly growing and unproductive subsistence agriculture.

Growth and poverty: simulation results 2002–08

The basic message that emerges from the backward-looking analysis reported in the previous section is the importance of productive job-creation, especially for those without skills in rural areas. In order to better understand the link between economic growth, employment and poverty, we have simulated poverty dynamics for two 3-year periods (2002–05 and 2005–08) using a simplified version of the Poverty Analysis Macroeconomic Simulator (PAMS), originally proposed by Pereira da Silva *et al.* (2002). We continue to focus on three essential household characteristics: place of residence, education and labour-market status.

PAMS is a relatively simple model comprising three main elements: a macroeconomic module used to project sectoral patterns of GDP growth, a labour market module breaking down labour categories by selected characteristics, and a poverty module using the labour model results for each labour category to simulate the income and consumption paths for each individual across deciles within each group (Pereira da Silva *et al.*, 2002).

In the labour-market module we distinguish between as many as 21 labour household groups (classified by the status of household head). These groups reflect, firstly, binary classification (rural/urban and skilled/unskilled) and secondly, occupational categories (agriculture/industry/market services/non-market services/non-employed). The last, 21st group, comprises households headed by individuals who are non-working and not in the 15–64 age group. Individuals belonging to different groups are assumed to have different characteristics resulting in the divergence in their chances in the labour market. It is assumed that wages of the unskilled workers are rigid downwards as these workers command wages close to their reservation wages determining their participation in the labour market. Firms find it relatively easy to substitute other factors of production for unskilled labour. As a result, the employment rate among unskilled labourers is volatile. On the other hand, wages of skilled workers are more flexible and adjust rapidly to keep the employment rate relatively constant.

In addition to the wage income, the poverty module accounts for non-wage sources of household income. In our specification, the total amount of social transfers per household (comprising all social assistance transfers as well as pensions, etc.) is dependent on the wage bill in the economy and on the implicit payroll tax rate. The impact of higher redistribution and/or better targeting of social transfers can therefore be analysed. Adding the total household income separately for each of 21 household categories (that is, for representative households in each category) allows one to calculate consumption per adult equivalent (under assumptions of an unchanged relationship between total income and total consumption). By assuming an unchanged consumption distribution by decile within each labour category it is then possible to calculate poverty indices within groups. Knowing the size of each labour category allows calculating poverty rates for several more aggregated groups.

One of the important limitations of the model is that there is no endo-genous mechanism driving labour-force movements between sectors. Nevertheless, it is possible to analyse the poverty impact of various exogenous assumptions concerning inter-sectoral labour mobility as discussed below.

In the baseline scenario an average 3.7 per cent annual GDP growth was assumed, consistent with various estimates of growth potential (for example IMF, 2003) and in line with the past experience of Romania. With other parameters set at realistic values and in the context of prudent macroeconomic policies, the model predicts an overall reduction in the poverty rate in 2003–08 by nearly one-third (Table 10.6). However, a modest reduction in poverty incidence among vulnerable groups: (unskilled and residents of rural areas) is not satisfactory – poverty remains at around 32 per cent in both cases. This result is explained by the fact that those working in agriculture continue to face substantial poverty risk, while there are limited opportunities for transition to other sectors of economy, so that the share of employed in agriculture is not reduced.

In the next step, we investigate scenarios that could potentially lead to a deeper reduction in poverty, especially among groups particularly vulnerable to poverty incidence, as of 2002. This analysis provides some directions for policies aimed at poverty eradication and, importantly, reveals some important trade-offs in designing these policies. Figure 10.4 compares the likely poverty outcomes of different policy scenarios. It presents

250

Table 10.6 Size and poverty rates in selected groups under the baseline scenario, Romania 2002–08

	Share in total population (%)			Medium poverty rate (%)		
	2002	2005	2008	2002	2005	2008
Total	100.0	100.0	100.0	29.0	21.8	20.5
of which: Working age	81.1	81.1	81.1	28.0	21.7	20.0
Rural	36.2	36.0	35.9	42.8	34.3	32.2
Urban	45.0	45.1	45.2	17.6	12.7	11.4
Unskilled	52.0	50.2	48.6	39.1	33.3	31.5
Skilled	29.2	30.9	32.5	8.9	3.8	3.8
Non-empl.	19.8	16.3	12.5	34.0	25.5	20.6
Agriculture	25.3	25.9	26.5	49.0	39.6	39.0
Non-agr.	34.8	38.8	42.0	14.7	11.0	10.2
Non-working age	18.9	18.9	18.9	32.8	21.9	21.9

Note: Baseline scenario is defined by the following parameters: average annual aggregate, urban and urban GDP growth of 3.7 per cent; by sectors: agriculture 0.4 per cent, industry 3.6 per cent, market services 4.8 per cent, non-market services 3.2 per cent. Constant unskilled real wages over the whole period (unless labour shortages are present in which case growth rate in the sector is 3 per cent). Average annual skills upgrading: 1 per cent of the unskilled population. Average annual net migration from rural to urban areas: 0.1 per cent of rural population. Implicit payroll tax rate: 36 per cent.
Source: Calculations using PAMS model for Romania.

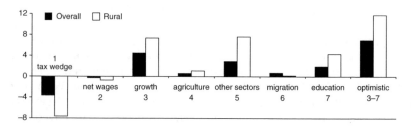

Figure 10.4 Additional reduction in poverty rates in 2008 as compared to the baseline scenario, Romania (percentage points)
Notes: Positive values indicate lower 2008 poverty rate (compared to baseline). All scenarios defined relative to baseline:
1 Implicit tax wedge increases from 36 per cent to 42 per cent after 2004.
2 Net wage among unskilled grows by 2 per cent annually
3 Aggregate GDP growth increased from 3.7 per cent to 5.6 per cent with the same structure as baseline
4 Agriculture growth is 2.3 per cent annually, aggregate GDP growth as in baseline, i.e. 3.7 per cent
5 Non-agriculture growth is 7.1 per cent annually, aggregate GDP growth as in baseline, 3.7 per cent
6 Average annual net migration from rural to urban areas: 1 per cent of the rural population.
7 Average annual skills upgrading: 2 per cent of the unskilled population.
3–7 Optimistic: combination of scenarios 3–7 (overall growth 5.6 per cent).
Source: Calculations using PAMS model for Romania.

percentage point changes in poverty rates relative to the baseline scenario, as of 2008.

The first scenario for poverty eradication involves increased redistribution. Our results confirm that an increase in the tax wedge imposes additional distortions in the labour market. As the implicit tax rate increases (from 36% to 42% of the wage bill in our example), many unskilled workers lose opportunities for employment at net wages above their reservation wages. The overall impact of higher direct income support at the cost of reduced employment is ambiguous, and under our calibration of labour-market elasticities is negative (that is, poverty by 2008 would be expected to be higher than in the baseline case). This result implies, at the very least, that there are important risks related to increased redistribution and all policy actions should be carefully evaluated taking into account the trade-off between enhanced assistance and higher wage costs.

A similar trade-off is inherent in the second scenario analysed in our model, characterized by a trend towards faster growth in real wages of unskilled workers. In policy terms, such a trend might be due to choices made in the restructuring of state-owned enterprises, labour union pressures, employment protection, policies that reduce incentives to work (including availability and level of social benefits), as well as public perceptions and the low esteem of low-wage jobs. While the combined effect of higher wages and lower employment among the unskilled is generally ambiguous, our results suggest that even a moderate rise in unskilled real wages (an annual increase of 2 per cent instead of 0 per cent in the baseline scenario) can minimally hinder reduction of poverty rates. Further experiments show that a more substantial surge in unskilled wages might lead to a significant worsening in poverty rates. Policies protecting unskilled jobs and promoting faster wage growth might well be counterproductive. Given the prospect of integrating the Romanian economy into the single European market, it would appear that holding real wages in check would be a necessary condition for pro-poor growth. This is also confirmed by the experiences of other countries. In the words of Blanchard (2002): 'In an economy . . . open in trade, capital, and most importantly in labour markets, wage explosions can kill; on the other hand, wage moderation can do miracles.'

Successful fostering of faster aggregate economic growth (5.6 % annually) with the same structure as in the baseline scenario is the third analysed case and, unsurprisingly, it brings unambiguous poverty eradication benefits. But the sectoral and regional patterns of economic growth prove also very important – it turns out that development of a non-agricultural rural economy is key for poverty dynamics. Under the fourth scenario, the annual aggregate growth rate is again at the baseline 3.7 per cent; but the growth rate in the agriculture sector is increased from 0.5 per cent to 2.3 per cent at the expense of other sectors of the economy. It is clear that the gains are rather limited even in the case of rural poverty – agriculture does not generate jobs that are productive enough to guarantee an escape from poverty. In the fifth scenario, we analyse what happens if much faster growth takes place in non-agriculture sectors of the rural economy as a result of more aggressive policies for rural diversification. We assume 7.1 per cent growth in rural non-agriculture output compared to 4.0 per cent in the baseline scenario,[9] while aggregate growth is still set at the baseline 3.7 per cent. In our model, such a policy proves extremely effective in rural and overall poverty reduction.

As poverty is concentrated among the unskilled in rural areas, it seems reasonable to look at the impact on poverty of measures that can affect skills and where people live and seek work. Potential determinants of migration flows or commuting to work from place of residence are many and can be affected by numerous state policies (such as promotion of the development of transportation infrastructure, legal issues in the real estate market, etc.). However, migrations are long-term processes and even the very substantial increase in the rural–urban migration rate – from 0.1 per cent observed over the last few years (that is assumed in the baseline case) up to 1 per cent annually in the sixth scenario – has a limited impact on poverty trends to 2008.

We suspect that skills-upgrading might be a more important determinant of poverty trends. Skill upgrading itself can be affected by policies determining effectiveness and availability of education for youth and adults from various backgrounds (in particular the rural population). In the seventh scenario, improvement in skills is assumed to be twice as fast as in the baseline scenario. The impact on rural poverty appears surprisingly small – it turns out that increasing the pool of skilled workers in rural areas does not automatically translate into higher standards of living unless accompanied by the emergence of non-agriculture sectors. This result may be due to the short time horizon of the analysis and simplicity of the model – the lack of a dynamic response of economic structure to changing skills pattern.

To conclude our results we present an optimistic eighth scenario, in which the emergence of the non-agricultural sector in an environment of strong 5.6 per cent annual GDP growth is concomitant with increasing productivity in agriculture, fast skill accumulation and increased migration. This scenario is therefore the combination of key characteristics of scenarios 3–7. It is instructive to look at a comparison with the third scenario, where the overall economic growth rate was the same. It turns out that a combination of other factors, as specified in the last optimistic scenario, allows for a further lowering of the rural poverty rate by 4.4 percentage points and overall rate by 2.5 percentage points relative to the third scenario. This confirms the importance of the structure of growth for poverty reduction.

Main policy challenges

Economic growth is a necessary, although – as evident from the jobless growth experience of several countries – not a sufficient condition for employment creation, and particularly for employment creation for low-skilled workers. There are structural problems in the Romanian economy that need to be addressed in order to realize the poverty reduction potential of geographically balanced job-creating growth, as outlined above. They are discussed briefly in the following.

The first and most immediate challenge is the reform of the labour market. Specifically, the minimum wage should be maintained at sufficiently low levels, while in 2003 the share of workers paid the minimum wage was as high as 30 per cent of total employment (NIS, 2004). Excessively generous unemployment benefits and restrictive labour regulation need to be avoided. The tax wedge of 45.2 per cent for low-wage earners is very high even by European standards and further increases will most likely lead to employment reductions. Any increases in social spending that might improve the poverty outcomes of non-active groups of the population should be therefore cautiously weighed against their possible employment impact. Also, taking into account the important role of income tax in the total tax wedge for the unskilled, any lowering of the effective rates for this group could be considered a potentially attractive policy option. For employers, Labour Code regulations play a role in shaping their willingness to hire workers. In a potentially volatile economic environment, what matters is not only the ease of hiring but also the ease of firing workers (OECD, 1998). Respective regulations that were in operation in Romania were not conductive to job-creation, and Romania was characterized by one of the strictest labour regulations among all EU and EU candidate countries (Figure 10.5). Only very recently (2006) have plans for liberalization of the Labour Code been presented.

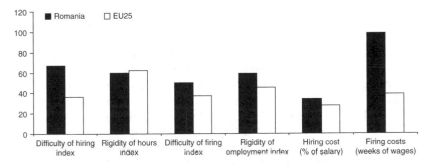

Figure 10.5 Strictness of regulations on hiring and firing workers, Romania
Source: World Bank, *Doing Business*, 2006.

Job-creation, and particularly job-creation for the unskilled, is conditioned by the fast development of small and medium-sized enterprises. Barriers to this development include corruption, excessive bureaucracy and volatility of the legal system related to the legacy of communism and the erratic transition process.[10] For instance, according to the Transparency International 2005 *Corruption Perceptions Index*, Romania was ranked 85–88 out of the 159 countries surveyed, largely unchanged from previous editions. Unequal competition from highly subsidized state-owned enterprises has also limited the development of a competitive enterprise sector. In 2002, for instance, tax arrears amounted to nearly one-third of total state-owned enterprises' assets (World Bank, 2004). Our analysis did not attempt to model complex trade-offs between the speed of restructuring and privatization and ensuing unemployment. It is nevertheless clear that slow progress in restructuring of the large state-owned sector implies substantial fiscal costs and impedes the functioning of other branches of the economy, thus risking hindering growth potential over the medium to long term.

Since the agriculture sector has become a poverty trap, economic growth can only be truly pro-poor if it creates opportunities for productive employment for the rural population, both working in and outside of agriculture. Productivity improvements in agriculture should build on achievements, but also on the correction of imperfections of the 1991 land reform. Currently, 4.17 million households own about 10.3 million hectares of agricultural land, and the average area of the family farm is only 2.47 hectares. Without land concentration, agricultural workers in Romania will not be able to engage in modern mechanized farming or gain access to large scale markets and credits (Tesliuc, 2000). Hence, increasing farming productivity cannot happen without massive flows of abundant labour from agriculture into non-agricultural activities. This would require the development of the land market, improving administrative conditions for the development of rural SME's and, last but not least, serious investment in underdeveloped and/or run-down rural infrastructure, including health and education facilities.

An effective, high-quality and widely and uniformly accessible educational system is another prerequisite for increasing employability and preventing poverty. Quality of access to education has been, unfortunately, declining during the transition period and differs considerably between urban and rural areas. Quality of education also varies considerably. Only 72 per cent of rural teachers are qualified, compared to 88 per cent of those working in urban areas, and rural school buildings are often dilapidated and lack sufficient equipment. The skills mismatch can also be a problem affecting the functioning of the labour market. Romania is characterized by the lowest share of tertiary graduates in the labour force among all EU and EU candidate countries (9.1 % compared to above 21 % in the EU25 in 2003, as indicated by the World Bank *World Development Indicators* database). Additionally, lifelong learning is virtually non-existent in Romania. Eurostat data shows that the percentage of people who participate in trainings increased from 1.1 per cent in 2001 to only 1.6 per cent in 2004. In the EU15, respective figures were 8.4 per cent and 10.1 per cent, and among eight Central and East European new EU member states 4.8 per cent and 7.7 per cent.Part of these problems is due to low public expenditures on education (World Bank, 2004), however, boosting funding to education should be accompanied by reform measures to improve the quality of education and, in particular, to correct the mismatch between skills that are taught and those that are needed in the labour market.

Conclusions

The simple model-based simulations confirmed the results of our backward-looking analysis that sustaining economic growth momentum is a main precondition for any efficient poverty-reduction strategy. Nevertheless, even fast growth concentrated in urban areas does not solve the problem automatically, with rural job-creation in non-agriculture sectors emerging as a key element of the strategy. Productivity improvements in agriculture are important; although it is difficult to expect large poverty reductions from this process alone. Educational and training systems also impact poverty trends positively, but only if coupled with concomitant generation of productive jobs. While this impact would not materialize in the short term, its longer-term importance cannot be overestimated.

The findings discussed above appear intuitive but direct interpretation of poverty outcomes from a simplified version of the Poverty Analysis Macroeconomic Simulator requires caution. The simplicity of the model and in particular lack of endogenous mechanisms facilitating flows of workers between predefined socio-economic groups may make it impossible to represent some of the underlying processes. Moreover, model assumptions were derived from the analysis of the 1996–2002 period, while Romania subsequently entered its pre-accession path to the EU which may have affected some mechanisms relevant for the growth–employment–poverty nexus. This in particular refers to availability of EU pre-accession and post-accession funds.

Several directions for further research can be indicated, and Romania appears to be well-suited to serve as an excellent laboratory for an in-depth investigation of various linkages between growth, employment and poverty. One important question pertains to labour-supply responses (in terms of skill upgrading, geographical mobility, intra- and inter-sectoral shifts, etc.) to changing patterns of labour demand and factors facilitating or inhibiting flexibility and adjustment speed of labour supply. From the perspective of poverty-reduction objectives, the behaviour of low-skilled workers linked to declining sectors of an economy is particularly important. Another set of key questions relates to incentives for employment for those inactive or unemployed relative to incentives to rely on various social transfers and poverty outcomes of these alternatives. Better understanding of these issues could be embedded in further development and refinement of the model presented in this chapter to transform it into a more reliable tool for poverty-growth analysis.

Appendix: growth-incidence curves and poverty profiles

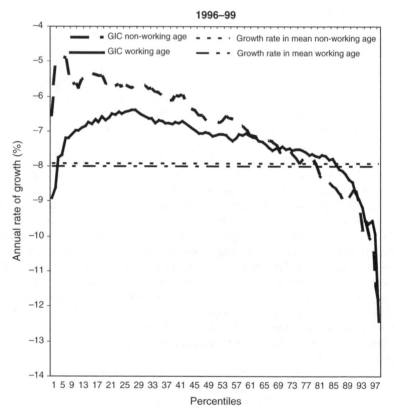

Figure 10A.1   Growth incidence curves (GIC): annual growth in consumption for working and non-working-age groups, Romania
Source: Based on Romanian HBSs.

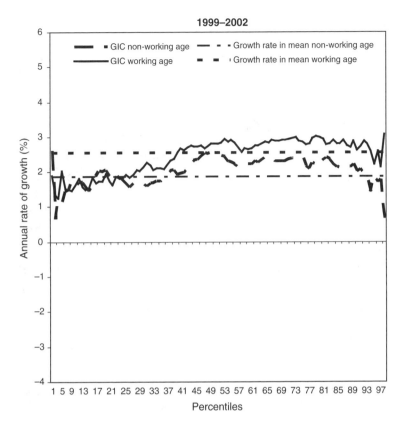

Figure 10A.1 (Continued)

258

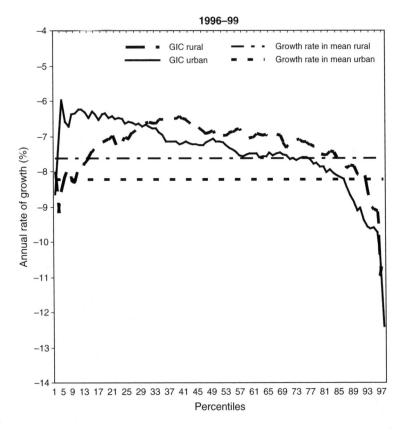

Figure 10A.2 Growth incidence curves (GIC): annual growth in consumption by place of residence (working-age population only), Romania
Source: Based on Romanian HBSs.

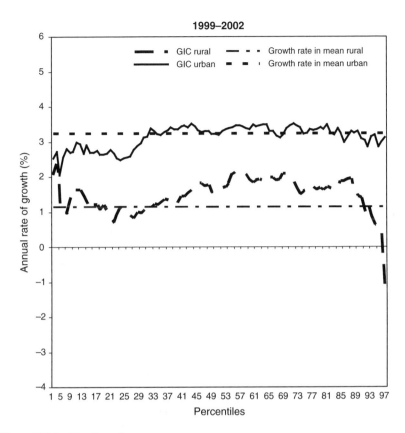

Figure 10A.2 (Continued)

260

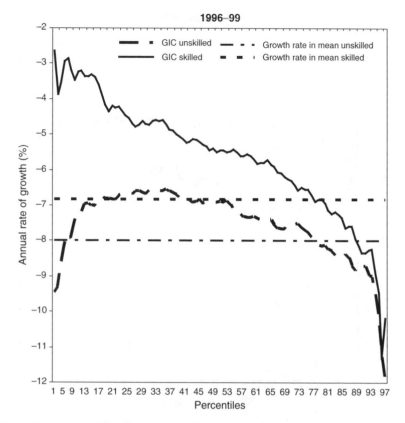

Figure 10A.3 Growth incidence curves (GIC): annual growth in consumption by level of education (working-age population only), Romania

Source: Based on Romanian HBSs.

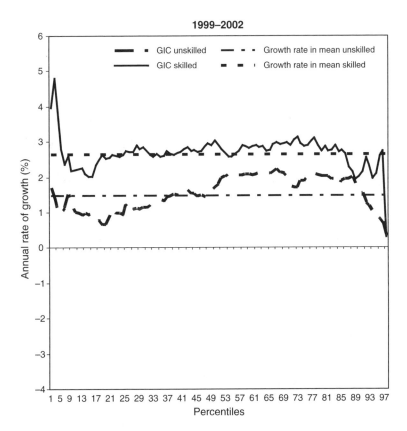

Figure 10A.3 (Continued)

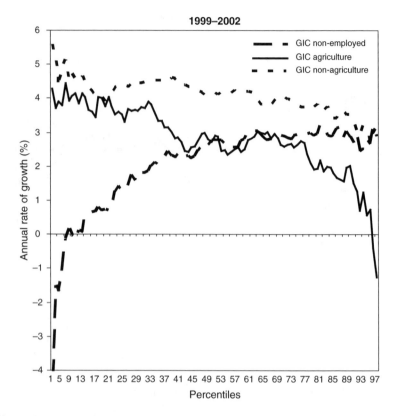

Figure 10A.4 Growth incidence curves (GIC): annual growth in consumption by labour-market status (working-age population only), Romania

Note: This decomposition is not available for the 1996–1999 period.

Source: Based on Romanian HBSs.

Table 10A.1 Poverty profile, Romania 2002

Categorization	Composition of the population (%)			Headcount (%)		Watts index (%)	
	Overall	Below extreme poverty line	Below medium poverty line	Extreme poverty	Medium poverty	Extreme poverty	Medium poverty
By sex of the household head							
Male	82.4	79.2	79.4	10.58	27.94	2.77	9.43
Female	17.6	20.9	20.6	13.05	33.87	4.18	12.18
By age of the household head							
16–24	1.0	1.3	0.9	14.68	26.08	4.89	12.13
25–34	15.1	12.4	11.5	9.02	22.18	2.38	7.79
35–44	20.8	21.1	20.2	11.17	28.25	2.95	9.74
45–64	43.2	46.6	44.7	11.85	30.00	3.49	10.78
65+	19.9	18.8	22.6	10.39	32.83	2.48	9.73
By number of children							
No children	51.0	35.4	42.3	7.64	24.04	1.94	7.31
1	26.6	23.7	24.6	9.81	26.91	2.54	8.85
2–4	20.8	32.6	29.0	17.22	40.47	4.27	14.35
5 or more	1.6	8.5	4.0	57.36	70.93	28.46	52.27
By ethnic group of the household head							
Romanian	90.3	82.5	87.4	10.05	28.07	2.51	9.04
Hungarian	5.9	4.4	4.7	8.24	22.76	2.07	7.11
Roma	2.5	12.6	6.8	55.52	79.60	24.75	50.03
Other	1.3	0.6	1.1	5.23	24.07	0.91	6.45
By place of residence							
Urban	54.4	26.8	33.2	5.42	17.69	1.54	5.42
Rural	45.6	73.3	66.7	17.71	42.48	4.79	15.29
By region							
North-East	17.2	30.7	25.3	19.60	42.57	6.21	17.20
South-East	13.1	14.6	14.7	12.25	32.45	3.29	11.14
South	15.5	16.9	17.7	11.99	33.24	2.80	10.62

Table 10A.1 (Continued)

Categorization	Composition of the population (%)			Headcount (%)		Watts index (%)	
	Overall	Below extreme poverty line	Below medium poverty line	Extreme poverty	Medium poverty	Extreme poverty	Medium poverty
South-West	10.7	11.3	12.1	11.58	32.60	2.74	10.35
West	9.0	5.9	6.9	7.18	22.30	1.98	7.06
North-West	12.6	9.4	10.1	8.21	23.10	2.33	7.59
Centre	11.8	9.2	9.5	8.61	23.47	2.34	7.76
Bucharest	10.0	2.2	3.7	2.43	10.63	0.42	2.31
By education of the household head							
No formal schooling	2.8	10.3	6.6	40.01	67.03	13.50	33.12
Primary (grades 1–4)	15.0	28.5	26.1	20.94	50.62	6.60	19.14
Middle (grades 5–8)	20.8	31.7	29.1	16.79	40.62	4.36	14.34
Vocational	26.7	21.9	25.5	9.03	27.70	2.06	8.20
Secondary	20.3	6.8	10.6	3.69	15.08	0.90	4.04
Post-secondary	6.0	0.7	1.6	1.31	7.93	0.20	1.59
University	8.5	0.1	0.4	0.19	1.51	0.04	0.27
By economic activity of the household head							
Employee	36.9	9.0	16.4	2.70	12.94	0.50	2.96
Employer &self-employed	4.7	5.7	5.0	13.31	31.04	4.12	11.93
Self-employed in agriculture	11.6	32.7	24.0	30.91	59.77	8.97	25.45
Unemployed	6.3	14.0	11.0	24.34	50.18	6.64	20.12
Pensioner	38.8	33.4	40.3	9.47	30.12	2.25	8.88
Other	1.7	5.3	3.2	34.99	56.11	18.26	35.19
By the size of land owned, 2000							
No land owned	53.5	42.8	42.3	11.14	28.46	3.43	10.28
up to 1 ha	20.9	31.2	28.6	20.78	49.02	5.67	18.09
1–4.99 ha	22.9	24.1	26.9	14.64	42.13	3.26	13.07
5+ ha	2.7	1.9	2.2	10.06	30.20	1.49	8.62

Source: Authors' calculations based on Romanian HBSs.

Notes

1. All GDP growth figures in the text refer to aggregate GDP rather than GDP per capita. The difference between the two is not important as the population was relatively stable over the analysed period.
2. The poverty line used in that study was set at the level of the first consumption quintile of 1993, and kept constant in real terms for the whole period under investigation. This is different from the poverty line used here which are described in note 3.
3. Poverty measures are constructed by comparing household equivalent consumption against poverty lines established in relation to median consumption of the base year (1996) and kept constant in real terms in the following years. Thus, the level of the extreme poverty line is set at 45 per cent of the median equivalent 1996 consumption (1,064,211 ROL per month) and the level of medium poverty at 65 per cent of this median (1,537,193 ROL per month). This approach ensures comparability with previous poverty analysis (World Bank, 2003).
4. See Datt and Ravallion (1992) for the methodology.
5. See Ravallion and Chen (2003) for concept and methodology.
6. The full poverty profile is shown in Table 10A.1 in the Appendix.
7. We do not discuss the impact of pension reforms on poverty here. However, reduction of poverty among households headed by pensioners depends fundamentally on reversing the negative trends in dependency ratios and thus higher employment rates among individuals of working age.
8. Other key risk factors included ethnic group, number of children, and sex of the household head – Roma households, those headed by women, and households with many children were more affected by poverty.
9. Such a non-agricultural rural growth rate does not appear excessive if a very low starting point is taken into account. This scenario implies rather moderate overall rural GDP growth of 4.3 per cent.
10. Compare a survey conducted among SME owners and managers (OECD and EBRD, 2004).

References

Blanchard, O. (2002) 'Comments on "Catching Up with the Leaders: The Irish Hare"', *Brookings Papers on Economic Activity*, no. 1.
Datt, G. and Ravallion, M. (1992) 'Growth and Redistribution Components of Changes in Poverty: A Decomposition with Application to Brazil and India', *Journal of Development Economics*, 38: 275–95.
International Monetary Fund (2003) 'Romania: Selected Issues and Statistical Appendix', *Country Report*, no. 12. New York: IMF.
Kollo, J. and Vincze, M. (1993) 'Self-Employment and Unemployment: Lessons from Regional Data in Hungary and Romania', *Romanian Economic Research Observer*, no. 5, Bucharest: Romanian Academy, National Institute of Economic Research, Centre for Economic Information and Documentation.
National Institute of Statistics (2004) *Statistical Yearbook of Romania*. Bucharest: NIS.
Organization for Economic Cooperation and Development (1998) *Employment Outlook*. Paris: OECD.
OECD and EBRD (2004) 'Romania Enterprise Policy Performance Assessment', Bucharest: Romanian Centre for Economic Policies .
Pereira da Silva, L., Essama-Nssah, B. and Samaké, I. (2002) 'A Poverty Analysis Macroeconomic Simulator (PAMS): Linking Household Surveys with Macro-Models', World Bank Working Paper Series no. 2888.

Ravallion, M. and Chen, S. (2003) 'Measuring Pro-Poor Growth', *Economics Letters*, 78(1): 93–9.

Teşliuc, E. (2000) 'Agriculture Policy: Achievements and Challenges', in C. Ruhl and D. Dăianu (eds), *Economic Transition in Romania: Past, Present and Future*, pp. 91–142, World Bank and Romanian Centre for Economic Policies, Arta Grafica, Bucharest.

Transparency International (2005) *Corruption Perceptions Index*, available at www.transparency.org

World Bank (1997) 'Romania: Poverty and Social Policy', Report no. 16462-RO.

World Bank (2003) 'Romania: Poverty Assessment', Report no. 26169-RO.

World Bank (2004) 'Romania. Restructuring for EU Integration – The Policy Agenda. Country Economic Memorandum', Report no. 29123-RO.

World Bank (2006) *'Doing Business*, dataset available at http://rru.worldbank.org/ DoingBusiness.

World Bank (2005) *World Development Indicators*, dataset available at http://devdata. worldbank.org/data-query.

Index